FILM AND LITERATURE
A COMPARATIVE APPROACH
TO ADAPTATION

FILM AND LITERATURE
A COMPARATIVE APPROACH TO ADAPTATION

Edited by
Wendell Aycock
and
Michael Schoenecke

TEXAS TECH UNIVERSITY PRESS
1988

STUDIES IN COMPARATIVE LITERATURE NO. 19

Library of Congress Cataloging-in-Publication Data

Film and literature : a comparative approach to adaptation / edited by Wendell Aycock and Michael Schoenecke.
    p. cm.—(Studies in comparative literature ; no. 19)
  ISBN 0-89672-159-0 (alk. paper). ISBN 0-89672-169-8 (pbk. : alk. paper)
    1. Motion pictures and literature. 2. Film adaptations—History and criticism. 3. Literature, Comparative. I. Aycock, Wendell M. II. Schoenecke, Michael K. (Michael Keith), 1949-   .   III. Series: Studies in comparative literature (Lubbock, Tex.) ; no. 19.
PN1995.3.F5 1988
791.43—dc19   88-24965
                                               CIP

Texas Tech University Press
Lubbock, Texas 79409-1037 U.S.A.

STUDIES IN COMPARATIVE LITERATURE
TEXAS TECH UNIVERSITY PRESS

*Out of print

PREFACE

The purpose of Studies in Comparative Literature is to explore literatures of various cultures and linguistic groups in comparison with one another and to compare literature with other disciplines or fields of study. First published in 1968, volumes of the series derive from annual symposia founded by Wolodymyr T. Zyla under the auspices of the Interdepartmental Committee on Comparative Literature at Texas Tech. In subsequent years, the series flourished, and volumes have been devoted to the study of authors (e.g., Kafka, Camus, Shakespeare), genres (e.g., the short story, science fiction), and movements and themes (e.g., surrealism, mythology).

In this volume, focusing on notable literary works and superior films adapted therefrom, both literary scholars and film experts explore the way in which classic films evolve from works of literature. The comparisons comprised herein analyze not only the basic nature of the novel or drama that inspired the film but also the film's striking and original images as they trace the important links between the original and adapted works.

Wendell Aycock
Series Editor

CONTENTS

INTRODUCTION

Within the last twenty years, there has been a burgeoning of film studies in the universities of the United States. Film courses and departments of film have developed on many campuses, and one of their legitimate and intriguing topics of study is the adaptation of literary classics to film. The following studies, written by scholars and film experts, explore various comparisons of literature and films. These comparisons have been, in fact, a subject of debate since movies came into being. In 1971, for example, the critic Stephen Bush maintained that the introduction of literary classics was the mission of the motion picture. Bush, of course, was wrong, but filmmakers have continued nonetheless to see plays, novels, and even short stories as sources for their movies.

The chapters in this volume are divided into three general sections. The first two chapters express the views of two widely recognized experts in the field of film adaptation. Both Horton Foote and Samuel Marx have had much experience in the world of filmmaking. The next section is made up of chapters that discuss the film adaptations of various American literary works. The final section concerns literary works from other countries and foreign films.

The first chapter in the volume is written by Academy Award winner Horton Foote, who is widely acknowledged as an accomplished screenwriter. His work on *Trip to Bountiful, 1918,* and *Tender Mercies* illustrates his knowledge of his craft. Because he has adapted works by such American writers as William Faulkner and Flannery O'Connor, he is well aware of the problems involved in film adaptation. In "Writing for Film," he says that adapting another writer's work to the screen is "the most difficult and painful process imaginable" because the screenwriter is "under constant tension not to violate" the other writer's vision. Because the screenwriter is involved in the process of construction, the screenwriter has to "approach consciously what must have been an unconscious process for the original writer." Therefore, he says, imagination and creativity are necessary if the screenwriter is going to be able to create a film with its own rhythm, its own life.

The other chapter in the first section is by Samuel Marx, whose experiences working for producers and as a producer in

Hollywood during the 1930s and 1940s help to make him the
interesting raconteur that he is. His "A Mythical Kingdom: The
Hollywood Film Industry in the 1930s and 1940s" centers on the
early Hollywood methods of making movies. According to Marx,
1930s filmmakers like Samuel Goldwyn and Harry Cohen
possessed a tremendous sense of showmanship; as a result, their
movie decisions were instinctive: "They didn't know much about
making movies; they had a feeling for what the audience
wanted—entertainment, enjoyment, attraction to the stars."

The four chapters in the second section all concern film
adaptations of American literary works. Robert Murray Davis, in
"'The whole world...Willie Stark's: Novel and Film of *All the
King's Men*," points out not only the failures in the attempt to
adapt this literary classic, but also some of the reasons for the
failures. He says that "characters, action, and motivation are
consistently simplified, even melodramatized." He also observes,
however, that "Rossen's film was perhaps too close to the battle
against fascism to take a more detached view of a charismatic
political leader." In *"One Flew Over the Cuckoo's Nest*: A Tale
of Two Decades," Thomas J. Slater points out that "Milos
Forman remains true to the spirit of Kesey's novel by keeping his
basic message but renovating the story to make it relevant to a
mid-seventies audience."

Joanna E. Rapf explores the difficulties of changing a play
into a movie in *"Bus Stop* as Self-Reflexive Parody: George
Axelrod on Its Adaptation." Her essay, based upon her personal
interview with Axelrod, reveals interesting details about how the
movie was made. Another chapter concerned with the adaptation
of a play into film is "The Author Behind the Author: George
Cukor and the Adaptation of *The Philadephia Story*," by Gary L.
Green. After describing the contributions that Cukor made by
adapting theater for film, Green says that the "'essence' of film
for Cukor is in the word, the common denominator between
theater and film and between the screenwriter/adapter and
director."

The final section of this volume involves foreign filmmakers'
adaptations of literary works from other countries. Comprising by
far the largest section of the volume, some of these nine chapters
share common links and form topical or thematic subdivisions.

The works of Harriet Margolis, Peggy Kidney, and Richard J.
Golsan all discuss novels and movies that pertain to World War
II, and, in some ways, all of these works involve the topic of

collaboration or the ambience of Nazi Europe. Margolis's "'Nur Schauspieler': Spectacular Politics, *Mephisto*, and *Good*" examines the film that won the 1981 Academy Award for Best Foreign Film. The chapter concerns the problem of the artist as collaborator. Peggy Kidney's "Bertolucci's Adaptation of *The Conformist*: A Study of the Function of the Flashbacks in the Narrative Strategy of the Film" also concerns a work that involves the matter of collaboration, but her emphasis falls more nearly on the filmmaker's structural technique. The problems of life during the occupation in World War II appear again in Richard Golsan's examination of *Lacombe, Lucien* and Modiano's fiction in "Collaboration, Alienation, and the Crisis of Identity in the Film and Fiction of Patrick Modiano."

Two other chapters that specifically concern French adaptations are Lynn Hoggard's "Writing with the Ink of Light: Jean Cocteau's *Beauty and the Beast*," which treats a single adaptation, and Ghislaine Géloin's "The Plight of Film Adaptation in France: Toward Dialogic Process in the *Auteur* Film," which deals generally with the matter of adaptation in recent French cinema.

The next two chapters both discuss *The Third Man*. Edward A. Kearns, in "Greene's Fictional Treatment: An Experiment in Storytelling," begins his comparison of novel and film by explaining that "the novel is Calloway's story," but "the film...is the story of Holly Martins." Paul W. Rea's "Individual and Societal Encounters with Darkness and the Shadow in *The Third Man*" explores the film as a *film noir* that "challenges Cold War orthodoxies" and "explodes...Cold War assumptions."

The volume concludes with chapters about film adapations of two works of the popular Brazilian author Jorge Amado. "*Dona Flor and Her Two Husbands*: A Tale of Sensuality, Sustenance, and Spirits," by Enrique Grönlund and Moylan C. Mills, and "Mythical Patterns in Jorge Amado's Novel *Gabriela—Clove and Cinammon* and Bruno Barreto's Film *Gabriela*," by John Martin and Donna L. Van Bodegraven, both discuss the novels as interpreted in films produced by Bruno Barreto and featuring such stars as Sonya Braga and Marcello Mastroianni.

Although hardly exhausitve, this survey of comparative aspects of film adaptation embraces a variety of ideas and insights that illustrates the intriguing and complex nature of the process. The chapters in this book should prove both stimulating and useful to devotees of the movies as well as to students and teachers of film studies and of Comparative Literature.

WRITING FOR FILM

Horton Foote

We all know there was a time when films were silent, no sound, no talking. I thought that's how movies were meant to be. Some people still feel that way. My good friend, that great actress, Lillian Gish, although she has made her peace with the talkies, will find a way to tell you that she still has some moments of doubt about the transition, asserting that the silent pictures were creating a universal language that everyone understood all over the world (in China, Japan, Russia, Europe, everywhere). You didn't need to know Russian or Japanese or English to understand the films of Chaplin or Griffith. But the talkies, when they came along, reinstated as it were the Tower of Babel. Suddenly to understand American films, for instance, you needed to know English, or to understand French films, French.

I remember well the first talking picture that I saw. I'm not sure whether it was all talking, for in those early days, they were part talking or part singing, at first, and then there were the all talkies. Anyway, I rode with my parents sixty miles to Houston to see Al Jolson in *The Singing Fool.* I remember that my father cried all the way through it and said afterwards that there ought to be a law against making people cry like that. It wasn't long after that that the talkies arrived in my home town of Wharton at the Queen Theatre, and forever after the silent films disappeared from my experience.

I wasn't very interested in the writing of films, silent or talking, in those days, but in the actors because that was the goal I had set for myself, to become an actor. But it didn't turn out that way, and, through a series of circumstances, I wound up in New York City and began writing plays. The writing of plays led to the writing of early television plays, and that in turn led me to writing films.

It was my second assignment in Hollywood that I think of importance here. I was hired by Warner Brothers to adapt a short novel by Erskine Caldwell. I'd had four plays done on Broadway by then and ten plays on television, and had already done one film working closely with a director-producer. But this was the first time I was entirely on my own writing a film at a studio.

I arrived on the Warner lot, punched the required time clock as I would on my arrival and departure each day, and was led to a two-story building with a number of offices, all empty except for the one assigned to me and one occupied by Marion Hargrove, who was working on "Maverick," a TV series.

My secretary told me the first day how it used to be when the offices were all filled with writers. She pointed out where Christopher Isherwood worked, and Faulkner, and she said that she hoped they would be full again one day with writers working on screenplays for theatrical distribution. They never were.

I worked for six weeks and saw no one the whole time except my secretary and Marion Hargrove. I had no idea who was to be the producer, the actors, or the director. My secretary, who was my information on all studio politics, inferred that the film might never have any of these, and she began to list the films written here on this lot that had never been produced at all.

I met other writers then, Hollywood writers we called them back east, and they would tell me stories of the horrors of the old studio system: how as many as five writers would be assigned to one project, how a producer would have complete control over a writer's work. But there are many such stories about the terrible things that happened to Hollywood writers.

I finished my draft then and went home. I heard soon after that that it had been given to a producer who had brought in another writer and then another producer and another writer. A year passed and my phone rang, and it was still another producer at Warners who said he had been assigned the film now and, after going over all the scripts, had decided mine was the best. He said that he had, based on mine, a final version, which he would like to send to me and that he would like to put me back on salary to do some final polishing. I thanked him and said I would be most happy to read this version, which I did, but it had nothing to do with my original script. And how he felt it did, I'll never know. So I thanked him politely for thinking of me and said I hadn't the time, and I thought, "Well that will be the end of my Hollywood career."

I didn't know it at the time, but it was certainly the end of a way of working, for it was the end of the old studio way. Writers are no longer hired *en masse*, put into offices, and assigned projects to write. That's not to say that producers no longer interfere with writers or directors in Hollywood, for they do, but it is done on a more one-to-one basis, as it were.

A year later, Alan Pakula called and asked me to read a novel he had recently purchased called *To Kill A Mockingbird*. Robert Mulligan was to direct the film. I had worked with him before in television, and had known Alan for a number of years. Alan told me that Harper Lee did not want to dramatize the novel and that I was the choice of all of them to do it. I read it and liked it, and I consented to the task.

It was an experience that's changed my notion of the writer and his relation to films forever—or rather, made me understand the possibilities for creative work for the writer of films. The director and producer treated this writer with as much respect and dignity as was ever given to a writer in the theater.

Since *To Kill A Mockingbird*, most of the theatrical films that I have done have been adaptations of my stage plays or the short stories or novels of other writers. I've written directly for the screen only once, and that was *Tender Mercies*.

Adapting my own plays presents certain problems, certainly, but adapting the work of other writers is in some ways for me the most difficult and painful process imaginable. And I do anything I can to avoid it. You see, when you're dealing with your own work, you're inhabiting a familiar world, and you can move around with some confidence and freedom. But when you try to get inside the world of another writer, you're under constant tension not to violate this person's vision.

I remember after agreeing to dramatize *To Kill A Mockingbird* feeling very depressed. I read it over and over searching for a way to begin my share of the work. Then I happened to read a review by R. P. Blackmuir called, I believe, "Scout In The Wilderness," comparing the book in a very imaginative and profound way to *Huckleberry Finn*, a great favorite of mine, and suddenly I began to feel at home in the material.

Then Alan Pakula asked me to consider changing the time span of the screenplay to one year rather than using the three year time span of the novel. And somehow this restriction that he placed on the work became very helpful, making me rethink the original structure in a creative way.

To be really successful adapting one must like the original work. I don't have to always understand it, but I have to like it and be willing to try to understand it and go through the painful process of entering someone else's creative world. And each time, I find that entrance into that world is different. I have dramatized three works of Faulkner, including "Barn Burning" for the

American Short Story Series and "The Old Man" and "Tomorrow" for *Playhouse 90*. I have also done Flannery O'Connor's "The Displaced Person" for the *American Short Story Series*, and Truman Capote's *The Grass Harp*, which has not yet been produced.

Each of these works required a different approach in order for me to be able to enter the writer's world. In "The Displaced Person," it was the characters that intrigued me most and proved wonderfully comic companions in my stay in the O'Connor country. What often eluded me here was the mystic, visionary aspects of the story. Qualities that almost defy dramatization.

So with "Barn Burning," I knew the people in the story like the back of my hand. I'd seen their prototypes in my father's store in Wharton and the streets of my town when I was a boy. I was able to flesh out some minor characters and invent additional scenes that I felt were necessary in the screenplay, and all went well until I reached the end of the story.

Those of you that know the story will remember that Snopes is a barn burner and that his son, Colonel Sartoris Snopes, informs his last victim, Major DeSpain, of what is to happen, and then runs away. All that is vivid and immediate and was for me usable as the dramatist. And then Faulkner, in the last two paragraphs, compresses time in a way a dramatist never can, so that it all became inner and subjective.

The first of the two paragraphs starts, "At midnight he sat on the crest of a hill." And in the second paragraph it continues, "He knew it was almost dawn, the night almost over. He could tell that from the whippoorwills." In those two paragraphs between midnight and near dawn, the boy is alone with his thoughts, his guilts, his continuing inner defense of his father, his emotions, and finally his wordless decision to go on alone.

I worked and worked upon these last two paragraphs. What I finally came up with was acceptable, in my opinion, but in no way matched the original ending.

In making screenplays of my own plays, the task was easier. The danger is in the freedom of being able to move around indoors and outdoors without the financial or technical limitations of the theater, to get drunk, as it were, with this new freedom and end up with a travelogue, losing all sense of the dramatic purpose behind the play.

In *1918* I was benefited by a remark made by Herbert Berghof, who produced the play in his theater in New York City. He said this play is about imagined death and real death. And it was by this phase that I measured everything that I chose to use in the screenplay.

1918 is a part of a cycle of nine plays I have written, many already produced in the theater, and there are plans to film them. *1918* is the seventh in this series of plays and the sixth is *On Valentine's Day*, which is to be released early in March.

The play *On Valentine's Day* takes place in a living room. There is one set, the bedroom of a young husband and wife. Various people come to their home, and we hear stories of various activities in the town.

When I was writing the screenplay, the challenge was to use the great variety of scenes that a film can afford without overwhelming the thrust of the story, which is the growth of the young couple. Maintaining the proper balance between the outer world and the world in the house needed constant watching, even through the editing process.

The Trip To Bountiful was a very special problem. It was written thirty-five years ago and first produced on television with Lillian Gish, and then later on Broadway, again with Lillian Gish. The first production on television was done in the days of live television, which meant that the action was continuous and once started could not stop because it was performed live and unedited. Budgets were small then and four sets a luxury, so the writers had to be very selective in their choice of sets.

Through the years, there have been many offers to make a film of *The Trip To Bountiful*, but they wanted to change the location from Texas to New England, modernize the story, or cast it with actors I didn't like. Peter Masterson, the director, was spending the summer working at Robert Redford's Sundance Institute. He said he was talking one day to Redford about doing a feature film and Redford said, "Direct something you really like."

Peter had remembered seeing *Bountiful* in an off-Broadway revival many years before and had been very moved by it. I was in Dallas at the time, editing *1918*, when he called and asked permission to do the film. And we agreed at once that Geraldine Page was right for the mother.

The stage play and television play takes place in five sets. The restriction of those mediums never allowed us to show the trip itself, and that is the task I gave myself in writing the screenplay—how to make the trip as interesting and meaningful as its start and its conclusion.

Because this session is about adapting work to the screen, I will only dwell briefly on *Tender Mercies*.

In the late sixties and early seventies I had spent a great deal of time working on the nine plays. I had financed this writing period myself, and I needed to earn some money. My agent suggested that I write a film. She said that if I would outline an idea, she would arrange for me to meet with someone from a studio and would try to get that studio to finance the writing of the film. I have never felt comfortable talking about work before it is written, but I decided to try it one time. I met with a studio representative to tell him the idea, and he was responsive. He asked my agent to fly out to the coast to arrange a contract. She did, and the day she arrived he was fired by the studio. I took this as an omen of some kind, so instead of seeking another executive to tell my story to, I decided to write it first.

When it was finished, I read it to Robert Duvall, and he agreed to appear in it. I thought we would have studios knocking at our doors for an immediate production, but we didn't. There was rejection after rejection after rejection—change this, change that. This is when one has to be steadfast and say, always politely, "no thank you, this is how we want to do it." At the end of a very long year, everything changed. One day, a producer called and said his company wanted to do it. And they did.

Now I wish to discuss, at some length, how I approached adapting Faulkner's "Tomorrow" first for television, then for the stage, and, finally, for the screen.

"Tomorrow" takes place in Mississippi early in the twentieth century. Jackson Fentry, who has spent most of his life on a cotton farm, leaves one fall to work in a sawmill. He lives alone in the sawmill, and, one winter day, a pregnant woman, ill and tired, comes there. He takes her in. She lives on there until her baby is born. He falls in love with her, and, although she has a husband, she agrees to marry him just after her baby is born. She dies soon after, but, before she dies, she gets him to promise to raise the baby as his own. He raises the baby, a boy, and the child becomes his life. One day the woman's brother appears and takes the baby. Fentry is heartbroken and leaves the area for a number of years. When he returns, he hears of a troublesome and vicious young man in the neighborhood and surmises that it is the boy he had been given to raise. He goes to town to look at him. They meet, and the grown boy does not recognize him. Later, the boy is killed, and Fentry is chosen to serve on the jury trying the man who killed him. Fentry refuses to acquit the man who killed the boy, and the jury is hung.

Faulkner's story, through relatively short, is not told in this straightforward manner. When Herbert Brodkin sent me the short story "Tomorrow," I hadn't remembered reading it before, although I had read most of the other stories in the collection *Knight's Gambit*. My chief concern was whether there would be enough material for a ninety-minute television play. As is the way with television and particularly television at that time, they were most anxious to have a quick decision from me, and my first inclination was to say that I really didn't feel I could undertake it. However, I found myself all afternoon postponing this decision and thinking more and more about certain elements of the story. I remember being very intrigued by the character of Fentry, and the way that Faulkner undertook to tell his story. It is told from three points of view—four really, if you count Gavin Stevens, who is mostly a listener, but at times expresses a point of view and some facts. Each of the narrators is important to the story because each one has knowledge of certain events that the others can't possibly know, and there is an erratic time sequence.

I've explained something about the nature of adaptation in an interview I gave after I dramatized a Flannery O'Connor story. The interviewer asked if there was anything about the day-to-day working when you're attempting an adaptation that is different from when you're working on an original script. I answered:

> Yes, when you are working on something of your own, it's like going into an unchartered world, and part of the secret is to find form, the structure. When you are restructuring a story in dramatic form, you are involved in the process of construction, but there are so many things that you assimilate differently. When you're working on something of your own, you call upon a lot of unconscious things that you have been storing up and thinking about. Well, here a great deal more is conscious, and you have to approach consciously what must have been an unconscious process for the original writer. But there are times, for instance, when I was dramatizing Faulkner's story, "Tomorrow," the character of the woman became alive to me even though Faulkner gives only a few paragraphs to her. He told me enough about her so that my imagination began to work, and she became somebody I knew.

These are the paragraphs I was referring to that first made me really want to enter the world of Jackson Fentry:

> "Then one afternoon in February—there had been a mild spell and I reckon I was restless—I rode out there [the Quick boy is talking.] The first thing I seen was her, and it was the first time I had ever done that—a woman, young, and maybe when she was in her normal health she might

have been pretty, too; I don't know. Because she wasn't just thin, she was gaunted. She was sick, more than just starved-looking, even if she was still on her feet, and it wasn't just because she was going to have that baby in a considerable less than another month. And I said, 'Who is that?' and he looked at me and says, 'That's my wife,' and I says, 'Since when? You never had no wife last fall. And that child ain't a month off.' And he says, 'Do you want us to leave?' And I says, 'What do I want you to leave for?' I'm going to tell you this from what I know now, what I found out after them two brothers showed up here three years later with their court paper, not from what he ever told me, because he never told nobody nothing . . . I don't know where he found her. I don't know if he found her somewhere, or if she just walked into the mill one day or one night and he looked up and seen her, and it was like the fellow says—nobody knows where or when love or lighting either is going to strike, except that it ain't going to strike there twice, because it don't have to . . . and I don't believe she was scared or ashamed to go back home just because her brothers and father tried to keep her from marrying the husband, in the first place. I believe it was just some more of the same kind of black-complected and not extra-intelligent and pretty durn ruthless blood pride that them brothers themselves was waving around here about an hour that day.

"Anyway, there she was, and I reckon she knowed her time was going to be short, and him saying to her, 'Let's get married,' and her saying, 'I can't marry you. I already got a husband.' And her time come and she was down then, on that shuck mattress, and him feeding her with the spoon, likely, and I reckon she knowed she wouldn't get up from it, and he got the midwife, and the baby was born, and likely her and the midwife both knowed by then she would never get up from that mattress and maybe they even convinced him at last, or maybe she knowed it wouldn't make no difference nohow and said yes, and he taken the mule pap let him keep at the mill and rid seven miles to Preacher Whitfield's and brung Whitfield back about daylight, and Whitfield married them and she died, and him and Whitfield buried her. And that night he come to the house and told pap he was quitting, and left the mule, and I went out to the mill a few days later and he was gone."

And I dramatized their meeting this way:

(ISHAM goes out the door. FENTRY has finished the little food he prepared for himself. He scrapes the dish outside the door and then starts outside to wash the dishes, when he hears a noise. It is the low moan of someone in pain. He stands listening for a moment; then sound comes again. He steps outside the door and calls.)

FENTRY: Isham, Isham.

(There is no answer to his call. The sound comes again and he walks toward it. He goes over to a stack of lumber inside an open shed. Lying against the logs is a young woman, black-haired, poorly dressed, thin, gaunt, almost emaciated, her clothes patched and worn and no protection at all against the cold. If she were not so ill and starved-looking, she might be pretty. Even so, there is pride and dignity in her face. He goes over to her and gently rolls her over on her back. It is then that we see she is pregnant. He sees how cold her thin arms and legs are and he takes his coat off and puts it over her. It is difficult to tell at first whether she is alive or dead, and he stands for a moment looking at the careworn, hurt face. He feels her pulse and knows then that she is living. He watches her for a moment longer and then, shaking her gently, he tries to rouse her.

FENTRY: Lady. Lady.

(He gets no response. He goes to the well, gets a dipper of water, comes back with the water, and pats her face gently with it. She opens her eyes slowly.)

SARAH: Where am I?

FENTRY: You're at Ben Quick's sawmill over at Frenchman's Bend.

(He looks down at the thin, emaciated face.) I'm Jackson Fentry. I'm the watchman out here in the winter time when the mill is shut down. I heard you when I came out the door of the boiler room. You sounded to me like you was in pain. Are you in pain?

(The woman shakes her head weakly, "No." She shivers and he puts his coat more securely around her.)

FENTRY: How long have you been here?

SARAH: I don't know. I remember walking down the road back yonder. I don't remember passing the sawmill. I knowed I was feeling dizzy, and I said to myself, I hope I ain't going to faint, but I guess I did. Though when I did, and how I got here, I don't exactly remember.

(She rests her head back on the logs.) What day is it?

FENTRY: Christmas Eve.

SARAH: Is it morning or the afternoon?

FENTRY: It's the late morning.

SARAH: Then I haven't been here too long. It was early in the morning on Christmas Eve when I started this way. (She tries to get up.)

FENTRY: Let me help you.

SARAH: Thank you. I think I'd better be getting on now. (He helps her up, but she is still very weak and has to lean against the pile of logs and against Fentry.) I'm sorry, I guess I will have to rest a while longer. I haven't quite gotten my strength back.

FENTRY: Let me help you in here so you can rest by the fire. It's so raw and cold out here.

SARAH: Thank you. It has been a cold winter, hasn't it?

FENTRY: Yes'm.

SARAH: There was ice this morning early when I left the house. I seen it in the ditches as I passes.

FENTRY: Yes'm.

SARAH: I said to myself, Jack Frost has been here.

FENTRY: He sure had. (She is grasping for breath and holds onto him. They pause for a moment.)

SARAH: How far we got to go?

FENTRY: Just in this door here. Can you make it?

SARAH: Yes sir. I can make that. (They start on again slowly. They reach the doorway. She rests again by the doorway for a moment.) Thank you. You say it's warm in here?

FENTRY: Oh, yes, ma'am. (He helps her inside the door and to the chair. She sits slowly down and rests her head against the back as if this little exertion was made at great cost.) You set here, Mrs. —

SARAH: Thank you. (She looks around) It is nice and warm in here. I love a good fire in the stove.

FENTRY: I could get it warmer. I was letting it die out because I was about to leave for my Papa's farm for Christmas. (He goes to the stove and starts to feed the wood.)

Now I know a lot about cotton fields; I know nothing about sawmills. In any case, I began somehow in the most obsessive, vivid kind of way to want to discover, for myself as a writer, what went on between Jackson Fentry and his black-complected woman.

It's interesting that both actresses, Kim Stanley and Olga Bellin, who have played Sarah, are blonde, but they did understand the fierce pride of the woman, "black-complected pride" Faulkner calls it. I called this woman Sarah although Faulkner never names *her*, and I had her married to a man named Eubanks. And so that night I sat down and began to dramatize what I felt was the story of Jackson Fentry and Sarah Eubanks. I worked on it that night and finished it early the next morning. And from that time until this, I have never changed it. It seemed to me moving, but I realized that what I had written was monstrously out of proportion to the rest of the story. I wanted to retain this, and I wanted to see it used, so I began to construct the rest of the play around the story of these two people. In looking back over the original copy of the story that I worked with, I find that I have marked these paragraphs.

The first one reads:

> And the story itself was old and unoriginal enough: The country girl of seventeen, her imagination fired by the swagger and the powers of the daring and the glib tongue; the father who tried to reason with her and got as far as parents usually do in such cases; then the interdictions, the forbidden door, the inevitable elopement at midnight, and at four o'clock the next morning Bookwright waked Will Varner, the justice of the peace and the chief police officer of the district, and handed Varner his pistol and said, "I have come to surrender. I killed Thorpe two hours ago." And a neighbor named Quick, who was first on the scene, found the half-drawn pistol in Thorpe's hand; and a week after the brief account was printed in the Memphis papers, a woman appeared in Frenchmen's Bend who claimed to be Thorpe's wife, and with the wedding license to prove it, trying to claim what money or property he might have left.

Now surely if one had the imagination, a whole play could be done on the basis of that one paragraph. It is curious that I have marked it because in every attempt that I have made to dramatize "Tomorrow," I have always in some measure tried to use effectively the element of the story that has to do with Buck Thorpe as a grown man and, in all candor, I don't think I've ever found a way to integrate it into any version.

The next paragraphs marked are these:

"I went close enough," Pruit said. "I would get close enough to the field to
hear him cussing at the nigger for not moving fast enough and to watch the
nigger trying to keep up with him, and to think what a good thing it was
Jackson hadn't got two niggers to work the place while he was gone, because
if that old man—and he was close to sixty by then—had had to spend one
full day sitting in a chair in the shade with nothing in his hands to chop or
hoe with, he would have died before sundown. So Jackson left. He walked.
They didn't have but one mule. They ain't never had but one mule.

"He came that first Christmas," Mrs. Pruit said.

"That's right," Pruitt said. "He walked them thirty miles home and spent
Christmas Day and walked them other thirty miles back to the sawmill."

"Whose sawmill?" Uncle Gavin said.

"Quick's," Pruitt said. "Old Man Ben Quick's. It was the second Christmas
he ever come home. Then, about the beginning of March, about when the
river bottom at Frenchman's Bend would be starting to dry out where you
could skid logs through it and you would have thought he would be settled
down good to his third year of sawmilling, he come home to stay. He didn't
walk this time. He come in a hired buggy. Because he had the goat and the
baby.

And then later Pruitt says:

"In the next summer, him and the boy disappeared."

"Disappeared?" Uncle Gavin said.

"That right. They were just gone one morning. I didn't know when. And
one day I couldn't stand it no longer, I went up there and the house was
empty, and I went on to the field where the old man was plowing, and at
first I thought the spreader between his plow handles had broke and he had
tied a sapling across the handles, until he sees me and snatched the sapling
off, and it was that shotgun, and I reckon what he said to me was about what
he said to you this morning when you stopped there. Next year he had the
nigger helping him again. Then, about five years later, Jackson come back I
don't know when. He was just there one morning. And the nigger was gone
again, and him and his pa worked the place like they used to. And one day I
couldn't stand it no longer, I went up there and I stood at the fence where he
was plowing, until after a while the land he was breaking brought him up to
the fence, and still he had never looked at me, he plowed right by me, not ten
feet away, still without looking at me, and he turned and come back, and I
said, 'Did he die, Jackson?' and then he looked at me. 'The boy,' I said. And
he said, 'What boy?'

"They invited us to stay for dinner.

"Uncle Gavin thanked him. 'We brought a sack with us,' he said. 'And it's
thirty miles to Varner's store, and twenty-two from there to Jefferson. And
our roads ain't used to automobiles yet.' "

I am not really sure now why I marked those paragraphs when
first attempting to dramatize "Tomorrow," but I am very moved
now when I read this description of the father. I think that I
wanted to try and retain in the character this wonderful sense that
Faulkner can give us of a man and his need to work, his total

absorption into whatever he has been given to do and his ability to live in solitude under the most primitive and unlikely conditons. That the man can also express pride, loyalty, integrity, and many most admirable virtues, and that Faulkner always finds a way to give us these qualities in a very unsentimental way. I think I was successful in retaining these qualities in the television and stage versions. In the latter paragraph, I suspect I was interested in the relationship of the neighbors to the story—how they had to know what was going on and what means they had to use to find out what was going on. I've always been haunted by the question that Pruitt asked Fentry after he had returned and the boy had been taken from him: "That boy?" he asks. And Fentry's answer: "What boy?"

One of the obvious problems in dramatizing this story is the matter of time. In "The Old Man," although the story was also told out of sequence, time was very clearly defined from the beginning of the flood to the end of the flood. In "Tomorrow," time, although it is approached in various ways, and not in sequence, covers a period of roughly twenty years or more. This span presents enormous technical difficulties, first of all, in the demands it makes on the actor to play convincingly a character who ages twenty years even though Jackson Fentry would always seem to have very specific characteristics that were almost timeless; in other words, one would imagine that as a young man, he already seemed old, and that as an older man, he did not change much. Still, there was a question of the characters around him aging naturally as one would in the span of twenty years. At first this time scheme was a great worry to me, but then I decided that this was not really my problem and that what I had to address myself to was dramatizing, as best I could, the story Faulkner had given me; I had to let the director and the producer take care of solving the casting problems for my play. I decided therefore to begin with the search of the lawyer, Gavin Stevens. Why had a Mississippi dirt farmer named Jackson Fentry hung his jury? Instead of three characters telling the story of Fentry to Stevens, I decided to confine it to the Pruitts. It was apparent that, given the character of Fentry, Stevens would never go directly to him, and I felt that my structure would be served best by one point of view or narrator. And so, these choices—the choice of where to begin the story, the choice of dramatizing very fully the relationship of Sarah Eubanks and Jackson Fentry, the choice of the Pruitts as narrator, the choice of trying to accommodate in some way Faulkner's time structure—all dictated the form that finally began to evolve as the first adapted version of "Tomorrow."

There was always in this version, for me, a worrisome problem. The more completely I dramatized the relationship between Fentry and Sarah, the less room it left for the dramatizing of other elements of the story. I finished the first version of the story—my dramatization of it—very quickly in four or five days. Brodkin read it and immediately called to say that he liked it and wanted to do it. It was scheduled for six weeks from the time of acceptance; there was casting to be done, but I had the time then to think about any further changes or improvements I wanted to make. Most of my thinking, as I remember, was spent in wondering what happened to Fentry from the time he left the cotton farm after the boy he adopted had been taken away from him until the time when he returned, and I made a very logical sequence of events for myself, but I was unable to use any of it in the play.

Another problem that I felt I was never able fully to solve satisfactorily for myself, in any version, was how to use the return of the grown Buck Thorpe, and how to dramatize properly the telling of Fentry about him and what happened when Fentry decided to see for himself the spectacle of the evolution of Buck Thorpe.

In all versions, in the television and the theater, and on the screen, we attempted this meeting. I think it was most effective in the theater. There was something immediate and quite wonderful about the meeting of the two in the scene that occurred in the play version. In the screen version, the scene was shot but eventually cut out, which I understand was very difficult for Bob Duvall, because he felt so strongly that in some ways it was his best work, and the producer and director told me that they did indeed agree that it was.

After I finished my work on the television play, I had a meeting with Robert Mulligan, who was to direct it. He liked what I had done, but he felt that it lacked theatrical excitement, which is a term that I've heard often in my life. His first suggestion to give it theatrical excitement was to somehow start with the trial and try to build the story from there. I had thought earlier of starting the play with the trial, but, given the ninety minutes (or seventy minutes really) allotted for playing time, it had seemed to me uneconomical. Anyway, I tried again for four or five days, but felt it was no improvement over my beginning, so it was agreed to return to what I had already written.

I started the play on the front porch of the Pruitts' farmhouse. Ed Pruitt and his mother are there and they see Thornton Douglas's car come up the road. (I had to change Gavin Stevens to Thornton Douglas for legal reasons).

> MRS. PRUITT: Whose car is that coming up the road?
> PRUITT: I think it's Lawyer Douglas's son's car.
> MRS. PRUITT: What's he doing around here this time of morning. (The car stops.)
> PRUITT: Looks to me like he's coming to see us.
> MRS. PRUITT: What's he want with us?
> PRUITT: He probably is going to ask us some questions about Jackson Fentry.
> MRS. PRUITT: Don't you tell him nothing, Pruitt.
> PRUITT: Yes'm. (Thornton Douglas, thirty, and his nephew, Charles, fourteen, come up to the porch.)
> THORNTON: Howdy.
> PRUITT: Howdy, Thornton.
> THORNTON: How are you, Mrs. Pruitt?
> MRS. PRUITT: Pretty well.
> THORNTON: You're looking very well.
> MRS. PRUITT: Thank you, I can't complain.
> THORNTON: This is my nephew, Charles. He's my partner, aren't you, boy?
> CHARLES: Yes, sir.
> THORNTON: He likes to ride out in the coutnry with me.
> MRS. PRUITT: Hello, son.
> THORNTON: I don't know if you folks know it or not, but I'm a lawyer now.
> PRUITT: Yes, sir. We heard.

And then Douglas begins to tell them why he's here. In this speech, he uses a great deal of the material Faulkner gives him when making his jury summation. And the Pruitts change their mind and decide to tell him what he wants to know about Jackson Fentry, beginning their story on the night Fentry tells them that he is going away to work in a sawmill and asks them to look in on his father while he's gone. And I followed the action directly until the end of the story, using Pruitt as a voice-over narrator to make certain scene transitions or give us the facts we needed to know.

This version was produced on *Playhouse 90*, March 7, 1960, and repeated again July 18, 1961.

Some years later, Herbert Berghof called me about doing the play in his small off-Broadway theater on Bank Street in New York. He said his production would be based on the idea of compressed time. I didn't quite understand what he meant then (I talked to him about it again a few days ago and I'm still not sure I understand), but I have great respect for his directorial talents and agreed to let him do it. He wanted to use my play basically as it was done on television with the exceptions of using Thornton Douglas rather than Pruitt as our narrator, and starting the play with Douglas's speech to the jury, or part of it, and having him address the audience as if they were the jury. He was casting Robert Duvall in the role of Fentry and Olga Bellin as Sarah.

I was living in New Hampshire then and only came to a run-through in the last week. I was very impressed with the work of the directors and the actors. It was his production that Paul Roebling and Gilbert Pearlman saw. A few weeks later, they called to ask me about doing it as a film and if I would care to do the screenplay. They wanted to use Robert Duvall and Olga Bellin in the two parts.

In our first discussions, they both said that the presence of Sarah Eubanks, which was so felt in the first part of the story as I dramatized it, should somehow be kept in the second part. So I took that as a kind of task for myself. Then, of course, there's always the notion of having enormous visual and physical freedom with the camera, which was not allowed me in theater or television. They wanted to do it on location in Mississippi and wanted to make it as authentic as possible. They said they would do everything they could to maintain that authenticity.

The screenplay we went into rehearsal with had a great deal of material in the second half of the film trying to keep the memory of Sarah alive, but most of it was cut in the rehearsals before the filming began. There were additions: we started the film in the courthouse and the trial; we used the jury, had Douglas address the jury, witnessed Fentry hang the jury, and from there went out into the country with Douglas as he began his search for why Fentry had done this. We took Fentry and Sarah outside the cabin as much as possible, dramatizing the moment when he shows Sarah where he hopes to build her house. We added a scene between Sarah and Fentry when it is raining and she speculates about walking on water; another after Sarah dies, with Fentry's trip home with the baby and a goat; and many new scenes between Fentry and the boy.

A film has its own rhythm, its own life. Joseph Anthony, the director, has a wonderful sense of detail, the kind of detail that makes the life on screen believable; the details were valuable and interesting, but they took a great deal of time. The first cut of the film was extremely long; Roebling, Pearlman, and Anthony worked many hours with Reva Schlesinger, the cutter. All the Pruitt scenes were cut; most of Papa Fentry's scenes were cut. What was retained (there had been some cuts here in rehearsals) were the scenes between Fentry and Sarah. There were substitutions: the boy playing Jackson Longstreet was not a trained actor and was very shy. Duvall spend many hours with him on the set and off winning his confidence. When it came to the actual shooting of the scenes, however, he would become stiff and self-conscious when he had to say the dialogue. So Duvall—and he is a master at this—simply improvised the scenes with him using whatever the boy said spontaneously.

I have thought each time when finishing the dramatizing of another's work that the next time I will know more and it will get easier. I hope each time I know more, but it never gets easier. Each work presents its own problem.

There is only one rule I'm sure of. Do something you really admire.

A MYTHICAL KINGDOM:
THE HOLLYWOOD FILM INDUSTRY
IN THE 1930s AND 1940s

Samuel Marx

I really went to Hollywood to be a writer—and for about fifty years people have diverted me from writing. I got into the story department at MGM under Irving Thalberg who was, to my mind, the movies' greatest producer, and I stayed there with him until he died. At that time I went over to Sam Goldwyn. I sometimes say, "I spent ten years one year with Sam Goldwyn." And then I went to Columbia Pictures with a man named Harry Cohn who was head of that studio.

In a later chapter, Bob Davis writes about *All the King's Men*; that film was made at Columbia by Harry Cohn. Irving Thalberg was the head of MGM, which was the great major studio of its time. Samuel Goldwyn was an independent producer, very independent, and Harry Cohn was head of a smaller studio, but one that turned out reasonably interesting films. At least once a year there was a great hit, usually superintended by Harry Cohn even if Frank Capra was the principal director.

In those ten years of the 1930s the system was to make a lot movies—not one at a time. To make all of those movies, they had to have a collection of writers. And I must say that, looking back at all the great writers of the 30s, I think all of them trooped into my office at some time. I don't want this to be an autobiography, but I did bring Scott Fitzgerald to Hollywood at that point, as well as William Faulkner. I tried to get Thomas Wolfe, but he turned me down. I tried to get Ernest Hemingway, and he turned me down. But I did get to know them all, and I'm going to relate a few funny stories because, basically, I feel that it was a fun time.

Shortly after I was put in the job as story editor I received a letter from a man. We had just announced a picture laid in a mythical kingdom—it may have been *Scaramouche* or *Prisoner of Zenda*—one of those—and the letter said that he was applying for a job as a technical advisor. He wanted particularly to be technical advisor on any movie dealing with a mythical kingdom because, as he said, "I've lived all my life in one." Now that I

21

look back, I feel that I was living in a mythical kingdom—with very unreal but very real characters populating it.

I have great respect for and considerable interest in Horton Foote's assessment of Hollywood writing as he's known it. Having been there before him, I knew a rather different system. Mr. Foote was at Warner Brothers. I was never at Warner Brothers. He mentions that writers there had to punch a time clock. Well, at MGM, at Goldwyn, and at Columbia, you did not punch a time clock, and so he saw a somewhat different system than I did. And I'm very respectful of his work. I've seen most of it; I've loved most of it, and I think it's an honor to know him. I have to say that he had the unique advantage of working with his own material. Now back in the earlier days, it almost never happened that way. Because we had a great staff of scenario writers, we tried to keep them up to tops at all times. We would buy books, plays. It may astound you that the story department at MGM then covered 20,000 stories a year, and I swear that's true. Approximately 400 a week passed my desk. I did not try to read all the books and plays. I read synopses. We had readers who would break down the books and plays, but we made pictures from newspaper items, from original stories, from any area. A writer might even come in and suggest an idea.

We had a great gallery of stars. Everybody knew that we were looking for movies. Whether it was for Greta Garbo, Spencer Tracey (well, Spencer Tracey came later), Wallace Beery, Marie Dressler, Joan Crawford, or Jean Harlow—or for any of the stars who were passing through in those early days and were under contract—I had to try to find the stories. In many cases, I succeeded, and quite a few times, I guess I should say, I did not.

The thing that impresses me about Horton Foote in his discussion of his adaptations is that he mentioned that he had been an actor; I think that as an actor he'd had the opportunity to realize how he must dramatize stories for films. Many writers did not always understand that.

There are quite a few anecdotes about the early days in Hollywood. There was a great educator, George Pierce Baker, who had been the head of the Harvard and the Yale schools of playwrighting. He came to the studio one day because he wanted to meet Thalberg, but Thalberg wasn't there. Thalberg was totally in command of that studio. He had associates who worked as producers or, as they called them, supervisors, but basically everything passed through Thalberg's mind and received his okay and his blessing. It was marvelous to have a man like Thalberg. He respected writers, wanted the best, made fabulously fine films, as least as far as I am concerned, and I think he was among the greatest. When Professor Baker came to lunch at the commissary, he had wanted to meet Thalberg who was not available, and I was a poor substitute. He spent most of the lunch asking me about Thalberg's methods. He had just previewed a film called *Billy the Kid*, directed by King Vidor and written by a very fine playwright scenarist named Lawrence Stallings. The picture was a bomb at the preview. The preview was what we called a sneak preview. We went out to, I think, San Bernardino about 60 miles away from the sophisticates of Hollywood to find an average audience. The picture died in that preview. As I explained to Professor Baker, we had our usual little sidewalk conference, and Thalberg said, "The trouble with this picture is that all the motivations are wrong." Motioning to Stallings and Vidor, he added, "What we're going to do tomorrow is get together: we're going to write a whole new first reel and we're going to get everybody including Billy the Kid, Pat Garrett, and the man who was employing Billy the Kid—everybody is going to get new motivations for this movie."

Professor Baker jumped out of his chair and said, "You can't do that." I replied that he might as well sit down because it had been done and Thalberg had done it. And the picture went out and was a big smash. Well, I won't say it was the greatest, but it was a good hit.

Another thing I saw Thalberg do had to do with the end of a movie. We had made a picture with Wallace Beery called *The Champ*, in which Beery, playing his usual kind of slob, a broken-down roustabout boxer, has a little boy that he has custody of (this picture, by the way, was also directed by King Vidor), and at the preview the picture died. Thalberg was in Europe. When he came back, he was told that the picture was a sick picture, that it was in trouble, so he went to look at it. It had been written by Frances Marion, who was a fine scenario writer. She had a marvelous faculty for creating stories for the screen and putting them on paper. In this story, Beery, to impress his son (who is played by Jackie Cooper, the famous child star), goes into the ring totally unprepared for the fight and dies. He actually clasps his heart and drops dead. When Thalberg came back from Europe and screened it alone in a projection room, he had no need of an audience reaction. He came out and said,

"You've got to put it back for about 15 minutes of retakes. We're going to have Beery win the fight and then he can drop dead." He did, and the picture won academy awards for Beery and writer Frances Marion, as well as nominations for Best Picture and for Best Director in 1931-32. It was a very simple solution for the story, but nobody in the studio noticed it, even those who went to the preview. It explains my regard for Thalberg, which is very high. I could go on about him, but I will say only that, in relation to the producers, in relation to writing and writers at that time, of those three producers that I was involved with and worked for (Thalberg, Goldwyn, and Cohn), only Thalberg was not illiterate. I have many anecdotes to prove I'm right about that.

Playwright Robert Emmett Sherwood wrote *The Best Years of Our Lives*, which had been a very great Goldwyn hit as well as a great picture. Goldwyn said, "Let's make another picture. Do you have any ideas?" Sherwood said, "Yes, I'll give you a book to read." He went out looking for the book, and the best he could find was a children's copy. It was *The Wizard of Oz*. He brought back this enormous coffee-table book, richly illustrated, with big letters, and gave it to Goldwyn. About three weeks later as Sherwood was getting ready to go back to New York, totally impatient, he asked, "Have you read the book?" And Goldwyn said, "Well, I'm reading it; it's fascinating." Sherwood said, "How far have you gotten?" He'd gotten to about page four in three weeks.

Herman Mankiewicz, who wrote the screen play for *Citizen Kane* and *Pride of the Yankees*, was a celebrated Hollywood writer, but he also had a penchant for liquor and gambling, and he was always in trouble. Half the time, he couldn't deliver a script in time because he might have been drunk or escaping his bookies so as not to get caught without any money. For a while, it was tough for Mankiewicz to get a job. Some of his friends at Columbia wanted to help, and we found him an assignment. It required getting Harry Cohn's permission. Cohn was one of the Hollywood producers who liked to gamble himself, but really didn't want Mankiewicz to, and we sort of ganged up on him and got him to say okay. Then his friends at the studio went to Mankiewicz and said, "Now for God's sake, stay out of Harry Cohn's path; don't go near him." At Columbia Pictures, there was a small executive dining room with a table about eight feet long, and about twelve chairs around it. And Harry Cohn sat at

the head. "Above all," we said to Mankiewicz, "don't ever go in
the executive dining room," for he would be confronted by Cohn.
Any time anybody told Herman Mankiewicz what he must not
do, it was a signal: do it. So sure enough, Mankiewicz showed up
one day in the dining room. Cohn was not there; we were hoping
he would not show up that day. Herman, I think, left a lot of his
writing on dining room tables. He was a great raconteur, and he
began talking about a new picture that he had seen, an Ernst
Lubitsch picture called *Bluebeard's Eighth Wife*, which was not
yet out to the public. Herman liked it very much, but then he
was a great admirer of Lubitsch. Almost at that moment, Harry
Cohn bounced in, sat down at the table, usurped all conversa-
tion, and immediately mentioned that he had seen one of the
worst movies of the year the night before. What should it be but
Bluebeard's Eighth Wife? We all looked at Herman and the man
next to him nudged him and said, "Don't say what you're
thinking." But it was too late. You couldn't tell Herman
Mankiewicz not to say something. So he spoke up, "Mr. Cohn,
how would you know that a picture that's not yet out to the
public is such a terrible picture?" Cohn said, "I have many ways
to know. It's going to open next week at New York's Rivoli
Theatre, but it won't do any business at all. It won't do
anything." Mankiewicz said, "I'd be ready to bet that the picture
will do great business at the Rivoli Theatre. It will probably turn
away 50,000 people over the weekend." Cohn jumped in on that
and said that the Rivoli didn't hold 50,000 people. Mankiewicz
said, "Mr. Cohn, you can turn away a million people from the
Yankee stadium, you can turn away five million people from the
Sistine Chapel—it doesn't matter how many they hold. I think
it's a great picture; how do you know it's not?" Cohn said,
"Because when I looked at it in my projection room, I was very
antsy in my seat. I kept moving around. If it was a good picture,
I'd have been sitting still. I was just terribly restless looking at
this movie—it's a sure flop." Thereupon Mankiewicz said, "What
you're telling us is you have a monitor ass which is wired to
another 150 million asses and that's why you know this picture is
a flop." I might add that Mr. Mankiewicz was fired that
afternoon.

Those three men—Thalberg, Goldwyn, and Cohn—really were
born showmen, and showmanship is a very important key word
or buzz word. I don't think that you can teach showmanship—
you may learn it, but generally it is an instinct. It didn't

necessarily matter too much how much they had known about making movies. They had a feeling for what they felt the audience should see. And probably inborn in them was the feeling for entertainment, enjoyment, attraction—all of those figured in the movies that we were making at that time. And all of those resulted in superb movies based on great plays, great books, and general ideas. As a sort of tribute to Thalberg, I should say that he was born in Brooklyn and only went through high school. He had bad health as a child; he was in bed a great deal, and he read a great deal, which was a marvelous help— something that neither Goldwyn or Cohn did. But like Goldwyn and Cohn, he, too, had a sense of showmanship. He died in 1936 of a heart ailment. He never took a credit on any film. He once said, "Credit you give yourself isn't worth having."

In the last year or so of his life, Thalberg personally produced *Camille* with Greta Garbo, probably her best picture; *Mutiny on the Bounty*, the Clark Gable-Charles Laughton version, which is a good one; *A Night at the Opera*, with the Marx Brothers, undoubtedly their best movie; *The Good Earth*, the best movie of all Pearl Buck's books. He did *The Barretts of Wimpole Street*; he did *Romeo and Juliet* with his wife Norma Shearer. I know that Juliet played by a 30-year-old actress who is already a wife and mother is not exactly the Juliet that Shakespeare conceived. But Thalberg was wildly in love with his wife, and Shakespeare also said that "love looks on hurricanes and is never shaken," so I guess you can miscast someone you love in a Shakespearean play.

Most of Shakespeare, when it's adapted to the movies, is not always precisely movie material, but, in the serious renditions of it, I mean *Romeo and Juliet*, we did try very hard to be faithful to Shakespeare. Professor William Strunk of Cornell, considered then the most eminent authority on Shakespeare, came to the studio as a technical advisor, and it is interesting that Strunk, who, I think, knew a great deal about Shakespeare (much more than many other experts), used to say that the system of making movies that he saw in Hollywood was to a great extent what he thought Shakespeare would have liked. He saw Shakespeare as an entrepreneur, a man who owned shares in the Globe Theatre and who, like all theater owners, had to have a play to put on or had an empty theater. So to find those plays, Shakespeare would sit around the Mermaid tavern with his pals and ask who's got an idea for a show for next month. That was Struck's idea, and it was very much the way we were trying to make fifty pictures a year at MGM, which, by the way, we never got to make, but we tried.

Concerning Shakespeare on film, which may be of interest to some students of the adaptation, it strikes me that in the musicals of Shakespeare, the writers take the greatest liberties, yet make the best Shakespearean movies. *Kiss Me Kate* had music by Cole Porter and was adapted by Sam and Bella Spewack from *The Taming of the Shrew*. When that same play was done straight, or fairly straight, with Elizabeth Taylor and Richard Burton, it wasn't as good. Then, of course, there was that marvelous picture *West Side Story*, which is generally known to be a modern version of *Romeo and Juliet*. I think that taking Shakespeare and adapting him for the screen requires a certain amount of liberty, which nobody gives because there is such reverence for Shakespeare's text. Even in the Norma Shearer-Irving Thalberg *Romeo and Juliet*, Strunk's knowledge was used wherever a scene was changed. Strunk was able to help so that every line of dialogue was actually out of *Romeo and Juliet*, even if used in a slightly different context.

I stayed as a story editor willingly enough for Thalberg in the six and one-half years I was there; when he died, I got pushed into producing. I really and truly didn't want to—I wanted to write. Louis B. Mayer, who took over the studio, said, "I'll make you a boss of writers," and the next thing I knew I was presumably a producer. I did do a couple of pictures, one of which was the first Hardy family picture.

Then I moved over to Sam Goldwyn. Goldwyn said, "You can be a writer and a producer for me, but you always helped MGM find fifty stories a year; now why don't you help me find the four that I want. It will only take you a month and we'll be off and running." Well, one month later, we hadn't found any, and a year later, we'd only found two. That was the difficulty of working with Sam Goldwyn.

There are a lot of stories about Goldwyn and the funny, so-called Goldwynisms. I was asked a couple of years ago by his son, Samuel Goldwyn, Jr., if I would work on a biography of his father. He explained that they had every memorandum that ever passed through the office; they had every letter that had been received or copies of those that went out, and I could have all of this research at my fingertips. We were getting along fine; I was really quite tempted until Mr. Goldwyn said to me, "No Goldwynisms; my father never said any of those; you can't use those in the book." And I said, "Well, Sam, I once brought Edna Ferber in to meet your father, and Mr. Goldwyn said to her, 'What are you doing now? What are you writing?' And she said, "My autobiography." And he said, 'What's it about?'"

He's really very famous; some men tried to get him into a deal, and he said, "Include me out," a great Goldwynism that he did say. He did say, "A verbal contract isn't worth the paper it's written on." He did say, "In two words, impossible." There are some Goldwynisms that I will admit I don't believe that he said—they're funny, but they don't have the ring of reality to me. One is that he looked at a sundial and said, "What will they think of next?" And another one is that, when one of his employees had a child and it was going to be named Bob, he said, "Oh, every Tom, Dick, and Harry is named Bob." They are pretty funny, but I, as an expert, feel I can put a finger on those that are real and those that are not.

He was leaving for a vacation in Hawaii, and his staff, which consisted of about only eight men or so, was called to his office. We all stood very gravely around the outer fringe of the office while he gave us a pep talk to work hard while he was away. Then he walked around and shook every hand and said, "Bon voyage," and it wasn't until we got outside that someone said, "Why is he saying that to us? He's the one going away."

Two incidents dealing with productions that were being made when I was there bear relating. Goldwyn was making *Hurricane*, and the director was a rough character, indomitable, the best kind of director, the kind of man who always knew what he wanted and was going to get it at all costs. He was John Ford, and Goldwyn was afraid of him. With great trepidation, Goldwyn asked the staff to return one night to look at the film that had then been shot. Goldwyn had an instinct. He could look at film and know whether he was getting what was needed. In the case of *Hurricane* (and I think he was probably right), he felt that there weren't enough closeups of his two leading players. Now the question was how was he going to get the word to Ford, of whom he was so frightened that he didn't even want to tell him he'd seen the film. But nevertheless he called me the next morning and said, "I've decided it's very important. I've got to talk to Jack Ford. Come with me." I was then built kind of like a body guard, which is why I guess he selected me, and we went to the stage where they had built a little grass shack. It was supposed to be on an island in the Pacific for this story. We had no sooner opened the door to the stage when we heard a voice, "What are you doing here?" It was John Ford, and Goldwyn stopped cold. And then the voice said, "You, Mr. Goldwyn, what are you doing here?" So he said, "Jack," in a high-pitched voice that I won't imitate; "Jack, I'd like to talk with you." So John Ford came over, and Goldwyn said very gingerly, "I've been thinking about the movie (he didn't want to tell him he saw it), and I wonder if you are making enough closeups of Jon Hall and Dorothy Lamour." Ford said, "Mr. Goldwyn, I'm making the picture; I'm making it the way I want it. If I want closeups of them, I can do them." And he hit Goldwyn straight in the belly and Goldwyn backed up. Ford went right after him, "Or I can make them from here up," and he hit him in the chest. And then he put his fist in Goldwyn's face and said, "Or I can..." Goldwyn signaled me, and we walked out. We went about a city block down the studio streets in silence. Then Goldwyn said, "Well, anyway, I put it in his mind," which showed me how Mr. Goldwyn always had to have the last word.

The second incident also involves a Goldwyn last-word story—I didn't like him that much, but I like the stories. He was making a picture called *They Shall Have Music*, with Jascha Heifitz, and it was being directed by Norman Taurog. Again Goldwyn looked at the rushes, and not liking what he saw, called the director from the set and said, "I don't understand these shots you're making." Taurog said, "What is it you don't understand, Mr. Goldwyn? I believe a six-year-old would understand what's up there." It seems that the picture was using a boys' choir that day and that the assistant director, having noticed that his director had been summoned around noon time, decided to take advantage of the opportunity and break the company for lunch. So he released everybody, and the little boys' choir was walking past the projection room just as Taurog said a six-year-old could understand it. Goldwyn jumped out of his seat, ran out of the stage, into the street, ran up to every little boy, and asked him how old he was. Finally, he came back dragging a six-year-old. He screened the rushes for him, and when he got through he said, "Did you understand what you saw there?" The little boy said, "Yes," and told him precisely what was there. Then Goldwyn turned to the director and said, "So, I'm making pictures for six-year-olds now, huh?"

I should also mention Charlie McArthur and Ben Hecht. Charlie McArthur was Ben Hecht's collaborator when they did that great play *The Front Page.* I have a copy inscribed to me: "These epic sparks, these words elect, to Sammy Marx from Benny Hecht." Right under it is another autograph: "One charm of Hecht's collaboration is the way he hogs the dedication," signed Charlie McArthur. Their particular characters are actually evident there.

Charlie McArthur once said, "Irving Thalberg goes on the premise that a writer doesn't write the story that he intended to write; that's why he [Thalberg] changes everything." And that's part of what little I may touch on concerning adaptation, because both McArthur and Hecht came to Hollywood, worked very long, worked on some great films, although not always in collaboration, and I believe that, in many ways, the writers who came to Hollywood liked the system of making movies and were very willing to work under it. It was a very great time of camaraderie; it was a great time of pleasure. I had a lot of fun there, which is why I still look back and laugh at it and say it was a mythical kingdom. It revolves around those types of people. We did have writers who were violently opposed to it, but who were still willing to show up at the paymaster's window every Saturday. I didn't hear her say it, but it's reported that Dorothy Parker leaned out of the window of the writers' building at MGM and screamed at some tourists, "Get me out of here; I'm as sane as any of you." There were writers who complained about the system. A very fine playwright, S. N. Behrman, is quoted as saying, "It's slave labor, they murder your material." He went on with that for quite awhile and then said, "But what do you get for it? A lousy fortune."

Many writers were willing to take that kind of money and liked getting it. There were many writers who even appreciated being in Hollywood. I did, too. I know that Jerome Kern, the composer, was hearing a complaint one time and said, "Look, we're going to Los Angeles; there are boats that go out of here, there are trains, there are roads. You can get an automobile, a bus, a bicycle, you've got shoes. If you don't like it here, find a way and go." That, in many ways, was the way I felt about some of the people who didn't like the system. We made pictures for the masses, which, to my way of thinking, is the way they should be made. One of the writers that I was instrumental in bringing to Hollywood (he had a terrible time there) was Scott Fitzgerald. When he came out, we were about to make a picture called *Red-*

Headed Woman. It was a *Saturday Evening Post* story by Katherine Brush, and we were going to adapt it for Jean Harlow. Scott was already far along in his career and was one of the writers I most admired when I was growing up. I was very taken with him and I know Thalberg was too. But Thalberg called me toward the end of the assignment. Fitzgerald had been there about six weeks or two months and was going back to Baltimore. He had finished his writing, and Thalberg said, "I have really bad news—I'm not going to use Fitzgerald's script. He could not seem to get my idea to adapt this story so people will laugh *with* the girl, not *at* her. In Fitzgerald's script you laugh at her all the way—it's like laughing at a Charlie Chaplin or Buster Keaton comedy." Thalberg wanted something far more subtle. He wanted the audience to have a certain understanding of her motivation. In this case, it was a girl from the wrong side of the tracks in a small town who slowly worked her way up through bedrooms. (The picture created censor boards everywhere). But the general idea of the girl was that she was acquiring a great deal of success through her sexual activity. In fact, in the last shot of her, she's driving away from Longchamps race track in Paris, surrounded by bearded millionaire Frenchmen. She had reached the top at that time. Well, Scott Fitzgerald couldn't get the idea that you should see the movie through the viewpoint of the girl and that you should laugh and enjoy her antics with her. I had the sad task of giving him transportation home, and I wished him well. He was coming to the studio because he wanted to say goodbye to some people he knew, so we entered into a conspiracy. No one was to tell him that we were not using his script. That was because Scott, as we all knew, had a proclivity for drinking. We were going to try to protect him until he got back to Baltimore. Unfortunately, really unfortunately, a Romanian director named Marcel De Sanc ruined the plan. As Scott was at the gate of the studio, actually walking out, De Sanc said, "They've pulled a trick on you; they're not going to use your script." Fitzgerald went on a monumental drunk for about three weeks.

I relate this incident mainly because I want to say that I've carefully watched the Scott Fitzgerald movies. His *The Last Tycoon* was made into a movie from a book that he was working on when he died. And there's no question that the character of Monroe Stair in that book is fashioned after Irving Thalberg. The picture was not a success. Robert De Niro played Stair. *The Last*

Tycoon was written for the screen by a British playwright, Pinter, who is very successful in his own way. I claim that he was totally wrong for that assignment. If I had been in charge of MGM writers, he would not have gotten it. I had walked out of the play, *The Caretaker*, by Pinter because I felt it was all pauses. I didn't think a movie should have more pause than action, and that's the way Pinter wrote the screenplay for *The Last Tycoon*. The same was true to some extent with *The Great Gatsby*. I had seen, when I was in New York, a play based on *The Great Gatsby*, and, after all these years, I still remember the curtain line. Gatsby, a gangster who was trying to lift himself up in Long Island society, gets shot and killed in the end. As his friends from Long Island society walked out of the room, they looked back at the body on the floor, and a girl said, "He was the best of the whole damn lot of us." That was the curtain line. It was a very impressive, dramatic line.

When the movie was made of *The Great Gatsby*, Robert Redford played the lead. Francis Coppola, who is a very accomplished director and a very fine writer, wrote the screen play, but he elected to be totally faithful to Fitzgerald's book and that line that I just quoted, I'm reasonably sure, was not in the movie. What I do know is that while his body is lying on the floor, Coppola's voice comes in as a voice-over; he reads a very esoteric lecture about gangsters and Long Island society, and the picture slowly fades out. The picture was a failure. I say that primarily because I actually advocate that people who are going to adapt books not be quite so respectful. I do not see why they need to be that respectful of material that was written for the mind of the reader, not for movie producers who want to appeal to the eyes and ears of a movie audience. Because of the change in audience, other changes must be made. Movies are made a great deal differently today than they were in my day. They are not always made for the masses. They make them for special audiences, and I'm not sure what happens to those pictures when the special audience decides not to come. If they don't come, the movie draws nobody. With the all-round universal, human-interest story, you may one day get a movie that everyone on earth will want to see. I think that this kind of movie would be very desirable.

THE WHOLE WORLD . . . WILLIE STARK:
NOVEL AND FILM OF *ALL THE KING'S MEN*

Robert Murray Davis

At a point when Jack Burden, the narrator of Robert Penn
Warren's *All the King's Men*, is beginning to move beyond
idealist and mechanist philosophies into an acceptance of the
interdependent moral responsibility of all men, he admits that
people who condemn his working for political boss Willie Stark
"aren't right and they aren't wrong. If it were absolutely either
way, you wouldn't have to think about it, you could just shut
your eyes and let them have it in the gut" (Warren 1968, p. 403).
In the novel, Warren expends considerable technical and stylistic
expertise to show that you *have* to think about it, that you
cannot ever know, that you have to act anyway, and that Willie
Stark may have been a great if complex and often confused man
operating in a web of political necessities and moral ambiguities
that he cannot be quite blamed for not resolving. Such doubts
and ambiguities apparently did not plague Robert Rossen in his
film version, released in 1949: characters, action, and motivation
are consistently simplified, even melodramatized, and the political and moral contexts are so severely curtailed that Willie
becomes a stock protofascist villain who is to be identified and
rejected rather than analyzed and comprehended.

It is easy to sympathize with Rossen as he grappled with the
novel. Judged by the standards of Hollywood in 1949 and even
today, Warren's Pulitzer Prize novel seems insanely complicated.
It begins *in medias res*, at the height of Willie Stark's power as
governor and political boss of an unnamed Southern state, and
uses the events of the next two years to frame episodes that span
twenty-three years of the characters' lives. By means of inserted
documents, it also presents material from seventy years past that
has thematic but no plot value. Furthermore, as the reader learns
late in the novel, Jack Burden narrates the story from the vantage
point of 1939, about two years and a whole moral universe
removed from the novel's major events. The style as well as the
structure is convoluted, leisurely, and designed to promote
questioning and reflection rather than suspense, and though Jack
has by the end of the novel married his childhood sweetheart and

33

come to terms with his past so that he can deal with the future, that future seems, in intention if not in rendering, to be left open, problematic.

Rossen certainly worked hard enough on the script, making "ten complete drafts of his adaptation before he began work" (Brenton 1950, 33). In fact, Rossen may have had too great a reverence for the text. Feeling that "he couldn't improve on a Pulitzer Prize novel . . . he commenced shooting the film from the book." The resulting footage was cut and premiered unsuccessfully, and Robert Parrish came in to re-edit. Even that was unsuccessful. Then Rossen, Parrish, and their associates "decided to take each scene in *All the King's Men*, roll it on on the synchronizer, find the center, or climax of the scene, roll it back a hundred feet, cut—then roll forward from the center a hundred feet and cut, arbitrarily." The result, with three minutes reinserted, was "acutally like an exciting 106-minute montage," cut, as Parrish said, like modern pictures "where dramatic effect is more important than conventional continuity" (Rossen 1972, pp. 106-108).

Rossen and Parrish could work this way because the movie has a straightforward chronological structure rather than the involuted, recursive, structure of the novel. The movie's time span is difficult to determine, but it seems to cover not more than eight years and possibly less. Of course, the movie sacrifices— inevitably—all of the virtually unfilmable historical material that is essential to Jack's moral growth. And though the movie preserves Jack as voice-over narrator and moral viewpoint, it is, to a far greater degree than the novel, the story of the rise and fall of Willie Stark.

In the novel, Willie is first shown at the height of his power as a charismatic and cynical populist political boss (all the contradictions implied are fully apparent to Warren and his narrator). This position and these attitudes are followed and to some degree qualified by the presentation of Willie's early career as an honest, dogged defender of democratic procedure, his unwitting employment by corrupt political interests, his awakening to political realities, and his subsequent election and emergence as "The Boss." Thereafter, even when Willie's career is not subordinated to Jack's excursions into the past, Warren is more interested in what he *is* rather than what he *does*. And Willie is enigmatic, perhaps even to himself, in his growing complexity of tone and his increasingly quizzical responses to others as he does what needs to be done to maintain his power. He can maintain that humans are inherently corrupt, but he does not lose his sense of humor, and he retains, or perhaps regains, something like his original purity of purpose when, having defeated an attempt to impeach him, he promises his followers a hospital that will embody the best of his aspirations. He invests some of that idealism in Adam Stanton, brother of the woman whom he and Jack love, and when Adam fatally shoots him to avenge the family honor, he can assert in forgiveness, "He was all right. The Doc" and in apologia, "It might have been all different" (400). After he dies, Jack is left to assess the meaning of his experience of Willie and others, and, although it is not entirely clear what Jack has learned from Willie, Jack is able to come to terms with his past, marry Anne, and face the future.

The Willie Stark of the film is far more like Humpty Dumpty than the novel's character: he rises, is corrupted or reveals his corruption, and falls. He can't be put back together; there is nothing to understand; and he is to be repudiated rather than remembered. Although Rossen tried to remain faithful to the setting (while leaching out the novel's specifically Southern flavor) and kept many of the novel's scenes and Willie's dogged determination, the film is, as Guy Brenton says, "a work of propaganda . . . a deliberate exposure of the abuses which American democracy can suffer at the hands of an amoral egoist" (Brenton 1950, 36). At first quite subtly and then more and more blatantly, Rossen establishes Willie's greed and egomania. For example, when in the novel Willie first tells Burden about his campaign for county treasurer, Warren emphasizes the process by which Willie is being eased out of the courthouse, and he is supported in his determination by Lucy, with a girlish face and "soft, soothing contours and large deep-brown eyes, the kind that makes you think of telling secrets in the gloaming over a garden gate when the lilacs are in bloom along the picket fence of the old homestead" (Warren 1968, p. 59). In the film, however, Rossen emphasizes not the content of Willie's lines but the voracity with which he gnaws at a drumstick (an image repeated later in the movie). Lucy is not soft but stereotypically schoolmarmish, angular and stern as she insists that Willie respond to her moral dictates. In both novel and film, Willie loses the election; the schoolhouse is built with shabby materials; children die as a result, and Willie is publicly vindicated as a champion of truth and justice. Much of the movie's scene derives

almost directly from the novel, but the conclusions—and their
implications about Willie's response and inner motivation—are
quite different. After Willie is acclaimed as an honest man, the
people crowd around him, and the novel continues, "Pretty soon
there was scarcely a dry eye in the crowd. Willie's weren't dry
either" (Warren 1968, p. 65). In the scenario, the script reads,
"On Willie's face is the realization that something important has
happened to him" (Rossen 1972, p. 23), but the actor's face looks
smug. There is a cynical overtone to the novel, but the cynicism
is that of the narrator, not the characters, and the sense of
Willie's essential innocence is preserved.

Rossen underlines this interpretation of Willie's egotism in the
shots which show the effect of Willie's first popular triumph:
Willie reading headlines carrying his name and pasting them in a
scrapbook, looking up at Lucy and saying "How about that,
Lucy, that's me." The direction, played quite straight, continues,
"She looks at him, unsmiling" (Rossen 1972, p. 24).

The scenes depicting Willie's first gubernatorial campaign are
among the most successful in the movie, in part because Rossen
stays close to the novel's portrait of Willie as bemused populist
jolted into an anger that galvanizes the crowd of hicks who have
been apathetic to speeches full of ideals and statistics. Rossen
does add the brilliant and justly famous shot of the befuddled
candidate sitting in a swing and waving away a solemn little girl
waiting her turn, and he makes Jack and Sadie gush like
groupies at Willie's outburst to his fellow hicks in which he first
reveals his power over the crowd. But he compresses the
aftermath and uses 1940s film shorthand to show that Willie's
new political knowledge has corrupted him by showing him with
a coat draped over his shoulders like a Central European gigolo,
a drink in his practiced hand, telling Jack, with a slit-eyed, close-
up leer, that he has learned how to win.

What he learns and how he wins are not dramatized in the
movie but conveyed in a series of brief shots: checks fluttering
through his hands, one signed by Jack's corrupt stepfather
McEvoy, illustrating McEvoy's earlier dictum that everyone can
be bought; larger and larger posters with slogans and photos of
Willie; and shots of Tiny Duffy, the quintessential poolroom
politician, as Willie's aide. In the novel, Burden is more aware of
political realities: partisans of a discredited politician turn to
Willie because they have nowhere else to go; Willie keeps Duffy
around because "'he reminds me of something. . . . I don't ever

want to forget'" (Warren 1968, p. 97; in the script, Rossen 1972, p. 44, "something I never want to forget"), but Burden speculates, as the film does not, that Willie keeps him around because "Duffy was nothing but what one self of Willie Stark did to the other self because of a blind, inward necessity" (Warren 1968, p. 98). In other words, Warren is able to provide both context and analysis.

In the movie, Rossen provides a very limited context by which to judge rather than to understand Willie. Duffy and the other political figures—Pillsbury, Sugar-Boy, Sadie—define Willie by reflection, not contrast or conflict, and the ambiguity and sharp, cynical, folk-tinged humor of the novel disappear into the stereotypical politician with fascist overtones. Rossen shows us Willie's private army, his hugh photos dominating the crowds who surge at his direction, his speech from the balcony of the capitol proclaiming his humility, a scene in which he implies that he will abandon Jack and Sadie, his most faithful followers. And, late in the film, a newsreel screened for Willie recapitulates many earlier scenes and concludes with the question, "Willie Stark: messiah or dictator?" (Rossen 1972, p. 85) to which Willie acquiesces while implying that he will soon have enough power to control the national media's portrayal of him. This depiction of Willie as a tyrant is far cruder than anything in the novel, but it is clearly the point—not even a real question—to which the movie has been building. Of course, the novel never quite resolves the question of whether Willie is for the people or for himself. But in the novel, Willie's sense of humor, sardonic view of human frailties, ability to laugh at himself, and complex affection for Jack make him seem something more than a self-absorbed tyrant.

The movie conflates and radically revises two incidents to show that Willie has become, or has revealed himself to be, utterly corrupt. In the novel, Tom Stark, Willie's son, has a car wreck in which a girl is injured, but her father is paid off with state contracts. She recovers; there are no consequences, and the incident is used primarily to show Tom's wildness. Later in the novel, Tom is named in a paternity case, and Willie's attempts to extricate himself from the political consequences ultimately, and ironically, lead to his death. Although Willie's attitudes towards these incidents are revealing, he is essentially a bystander rather than an agent, and the fact that he must react to as well as control events is an important aspect of Warren's characterization.

In Rossen's revision, Willie is moved to the center of the stage. In the movie, a girl is fatally injured in Tom's car wreck and her father, spare and righteous, comes to confront Tom and Willie in the plush drawing room of the governor's mansion. The scene, which has no counterpart in the novel, is used to brand Willie with the iconography of screen villainy. He is clad in a monogrammed dressing gown and a knotted scarf, signs of terminal decadence in American films of the thirties and forties. Moreover, he is not only drunk but slopping whiskey into his glass from a decanter (another sign of weakness) as he tries to extricate Tom, now sober, upright, and supported by his proud, stern mother, from the consequences of drunken driving. The scene ends with a high angle shot of the drunken Willie sprawled on the stairs, calling feebly after Lucy as Jack wishes aloud that Anne could witness his sodden state. (In the novel, Willie does get drunk, and he does make a deal on the contract of the new hospital, but he drinks out of frustration because the hospital has come to symbolize the idealism with which he began and to which he hopes to return.)

The real point of the confrontation between the foppish Willie and the rural, righteous Hale—the center, perhaps, of the two hundred feet allowed for it—is the speech in which Hale refuses Willie's crude attempt at a pay-off:

> You're pretty good at talking. I remember when you first started talking. A place called Upton. You did a lot of talking then and the things you said made sense, to me and a lot of other people. I believed in you . . . I followed you . . . and I fought for you. Well, the words are still good. But you're not. And I don't believe you ever were. (Rossen 1972, pp. 74-75)

This sentiment is echoed by Willie's pappy—in the last of his five monosyllabic lines in the whole movie—after the radio report that Hale's body has been discovered: "No good, Willie. No good" (Rossen 1972, p. 89).

For the rest of the movie, Willie's every action and expression heavily enforces this judgment. In both novel and movie, Jack discovers at Willie's behest evidence of the past wrongdoing of the Judge (in the novel named Irwin and Jack's natural father, in the movie named Stanton and made the uncle of Adam and Anne as well as Willie's attorney general) and gives it to Anne to help her persuade Adam to become director of Willie's new hospital by changing his picture of the idealized world he inhabits. In both novel and film, the Judge commits suicide rather than capitulate to Willie's demands or live with the stain on his honor; however, the texture, tone, and direction of the scenes in which Jack confronts the Judge are quite different. In both versions, Jack wants the Judge to have the chance to prove that the evidence—which he has not given Willie—is not valid and goes to Burden's Landing to confront him. The Judge admits that the charges are true, refuses to capitulate to Willie's demands, and in the novel implies that he could stop Jack (by telling Jack that he is his father). In the movie, Jack has only time to beg the Judge to release his votes when Willie arrives, knowing all the facts, and frees Jack from the onus of threatening the old man.

In the movie, Willie is at the center of the scene. Although much of the dialogue is taken directly from the novel, the tone differs considerably because Willie, not Jack, is the speaker. In the novel, the Judge has to be prompted to remember taking a bribe thirty years ago and then says:

> "You know, sometimes—for a long time at a stretch—it's like it hadn't happened. Not to me. Maybe to somebody else, but not to me. Then I remember, and when I first remember, and when I first remember I say, No, it could not have happened to me."
> Then he looked at me, straight in the eye. "But it did," he said.
> "Yes," I said, "it did." (Warren 1968, p. 346)

In the movie, the affection and pain between the two men are dispelled by Willie's presence and by Jack's demands to know how Willie found out, and the Judge's strength does not come through in Raymond Greenleaf's portrayal of an aging and not very forceful man. In dialogue parallel to that just quoted, the Judge says to Jack:

> It's all so long ago it's hard for me to realize it ever happened.
> Willie, Yeah, But it did.
> Judge. Yes, it did. But it's difficult for me to realize it. (Rossen 1972, p. 95)

The novel's Judge is more reflective and direct than that of the movie, where the line "But it did" is given to Willie to underline his brutality and undercut the Judge's self-knowledge and resolution. Because Anne gives Willie the information, Rossen implies that Burden's Landing is too weak to stand against the brutal or seductive power of Willie Stark.

Rossen emphasizes Willie's terrifying power most strongly, however, in the climactic impeachment scene in which Willie manipulates the crowd to intimidate the Senate and emerges in triumph as the modern Caesar. Here the imagery of fascism is strongest: the huge photos of Willie, the leather-clad state policemen, the loudspeakers and stage-managed hysteria, Willie's appearance in silhouette and then as dominant figure at the top of the capitol steps. Here Willie is using power for the sake of power. In the novel, where Willie never quite loses sight of what power will enable him to do for the people, Warren makes the impeachment only an incident in Willie's career, and in fact Warren presents the scene (and shows that the crowd is irrelevant to the historical process) a hundred pages before he gives us the content of the speech (Warren 1968, p. 152, p. 260). Rather than making Willie a Caesar, Warren emphasizes in both passages that Willie "seemed lonely and lost against the mass of stone which reared behind him" (Warren 1968, p. 260). As in the scene with the Judge, Rossen uses many of Warren's words to produce a very different effect. In the novel, long after the threat of impeachment is over, Jack relates Willie's speech in which he promises to build a hospital and roads and provide relief from crushing taxes so that "'you shall not be deprived of hope'" and goes on to promise that in fulfilling "'your will and your right'" he will break anyone who opposes him. He concludes with the three one-paragraph sentences: "Your will is my strength . . . Your need is my justice . . . That is all" (Warren 1968, pp. 261, 262).

These statements echo in far more sophisticated and positive fashion the speech at Upton which was the beginning of Willie's political career, and it is clear that he believes them, however cynically he might express himself elsewhere.

In the movie, Willie's promises are shifted to his inauguration speech; at the impeachment, he simply asserts his power. Moreover, in this scene, Willie is not alone but, as he often is, flanked by the embodiments of his political corruption, and he "grabs hold of the mike" rather than standing in silence and immediately declaims:

> They tried to ruin me. But they are ruined. They tried to ruin me because they did not like what I have done. Do you like what I have done?
>
> Remember, it's not I who have won, but you. Your will is my strength, and your need is my justice, and I shall live in your right and your will. And if any man tries to stop me from fulfilling that right and that will, I'll break him. I'll break him with my bare hands. For I have the strength of many. (Rossen 1972, p. 103)

The order is at least as important as the content of the speech. In the novel, Willie not only appeals more effectively for the passion and strength of those behind him and emphasizes the concrete rights of the people but also concludes with principles that, however populist and in the context of the novel aconstitutional, are far from venal. The rest of the novel shows him trying to live up to those principles, and as he dies—anticlimactically, in a hospital bed—he pleads with Jack, "'It might have been all different. . . . You got to believe that. . . . And it might even been different yet. . . . If it hadn't happened, it might—have been different—even yet'" (Warren 1968, p. 400). Jack does believe, finally, as Lucy has to believe, because he has learned to live in hope as well as in responsibility.

In the movie, Willie ends his speech in complacency, welcomes Jack back into the fold, and turns to greet Adam, who shoots him and is shot by Sugar-Boy and three policemen with tommy guns (Sugar-Boy's pistol and that of a state policeman are sufficient in the novel). Anne turns away from her brother's body in desperation, but Jack hurriedly convinces her that

> We've got to go on living . . . So that Adam's death has meaning, so that it wasn't wasted. Anne, our life has to give his death meaning. Don't you see that? Look at those people . . . They still believe in him. And we've got to make them see Willie the way Adam saw him, or there's no meaning in anything . . . anything. (Rossen 1972, p. 104)

He is called to hear Willie's dying words, "It could have been the whole world, Willie Stark. The whole world . . . Willie Stark. Why did he do it to me . . . Willie Stark? Why?" (105)

Rossen would, I suspect, like for the audience to believe that Adam did it because of the purity of his ideals, to repudiate the idea that Willie Stark could own him or any Stanton, and because, as Jack says, "Your brother is an old-fashioned man. He believes in his sister's honor" (99). The first motive is stated after the fact, when Jack and Rossen try to make Adam into a political martyr; the last is the only one established in advance. And the belief that the people can see the truth and then act on it is, even in the movie's terms, nothing but a pious hope.

It is merely pious because, unlike Warren, Rossen has not been able to create a real context for Willie. In emphasizing Willie's mindless and unexamined will to power, Rossen has reduced the complexity of the other characters' motivation and response and made them mere pawns. Thus in both novel and movie, the only alternatives to the world of Willie Stark are embodied in Burden's Landing and in Lucy Stark. The Burden's Landing of the novel represents to Jack both security and alienation, pain and pleasure, rendered all the more convincingly because past and present are juxtaposed and interwoven and because Jack is ambivalent about all the major figures from that past. He is both attracted and repelled by his financially powerful and seductive

mother and both embarrassed by Judge Irwin's childishness and
impressed by his ability to stand up to Willie. When he discovers
that the Judge is his father, he is relieved to exchange a good,
weak father for a bad, strong father. And when his mother reveals
that she has been capable of love, Jack is able to accept her and
the new version of the past that she has given him—no longer a
burden but a heritage—and can therefore face the future.

In the movie, Burden's Landing is presented less as an
alternative to the modern world than, as a refuge from it,
"separated from the mainland by a body of water. For the first
time [after meeting Willie] I wondered if it wasn't separated by
more than that" (Rossen 1972, pp. 13-14). Adam and Anne
Stanton have never left its shelter—as they do in the movie, in
which the Judge is converted into their uncle and made into a
rather feeble object of reverence. Jack has no father, and therefore
no patrimony. His mother is turned into a pathetic lush
dominated by her autocratic and ultraconservative second husband. Unlike her counterpart in the novel, she cannot be
converted into a positive force because she has been symbolically
neutered.

Lucy Stark, in the novel elevated, without the irony earlier
used to describe her, into a kind of 'United States Madonna"
(Warren 1968, p. 334), is literally neutered. Tom is made into a
neighbor's child whom Willie and Lucy have adopted because
Lucy cannot have children. On one level, this renders not only
her person but her values sterile, and produces an uncompromis-
ing and unlovely justice. On another, more subtle and perhaps
unconscious level, she is the stern mother to Willie, contrast and
counterpart to Jack's weak mother. The movie's Anne Stanton is
made into the flabby heir of Jack's mother, even to the point of
avoiding conflict by suggesting that they all have a drink and
meeting all crises with a side-ways whip of the head that is
certainly flexible if not spineless. In the novel, Anne became
Willie's mistress in part because Jack's discoveries about the
Judge's peculations and her father's condoning of them destroyed
the restraints that would have kept her pure. In the movie, Anne
gushes over Willie on first meeting him and becomes his mistress
before she knows anything about the Judge. Furthermore, she
betrays the Judge to Willie and is therefore indirectly responsible
for the deaths of both men.

Because the movie has no fathers and no mothers, it has to
dispense with the children as well. Tom is adopted; there is no

paternity suit and therefore no baby to survive him and bear Willie's name and become, as he does in the novel, the focus of Lucy's love, the symbol of her faith that Willie was a great man and of her hope in the future that helps to sustain Jack in the novel's final pages. In these pages, Jack realizes also that "each of us is the son of a million fathers" (Warren 1968, p. 436) and reveals he has come to accept his putative father and his spiritual ancestor, Cass Mastern, whose story he can now understand. But in the movie, Jack is fatherless and motherless; Willie is on one level the bad child rejected by the stern mother. Burden's Landing, in the figure of Adam, has avenged itself on Willie for his destruction of its illusion of separateness from the corrupt world, but it cannot provide an alternative to Willie or a worthy leader of the good but gullible masses who follow Willie. In a sense that Rossen probably did not intend, the whole world of the movie has become Willie Stark.

Judging from the film's popular success and from the awards it received, the audiences of 1950 were willing to accept a fastpaced melodrama with conventional symbols—a kind of updated and politicized "Little Caesar"—was a serious investigation of politics and character. Although early highbrow critics were less enthusiastic (see Tyler), Rossen was clearly right, on one level, to depend on the principle that if you do something fast enough, you can get away with almost anything.

Of course, continuity, or at least the interdependency of cause and effect, is central to Warren's novel. Small wonder, then, that Warren should say, while testifying to his friendship with Rossen, that "'The movie . . . does not 'mean' what I think my book meant. It is Bob's movie.'" In fact, during the editing process—though Warren does not say which of the three editings was involved—Rossen consulted Warren about the "several different endings" that had been shot and

> asked me which I liked best. I said the second, or third, or whatever it was, but added that none of the endings had a meaning like my novel—this said in the friendliest way. And Bob replied: "Son, when you are dealing with American movies you can forget, when you get to the end, anything like what you call irony—then it's cops and robbers, cowboys and Indians." (Casty 1966-67, p. 9)

Perhaps we should not judge too severely words reported at second hand and long after the fact. Warren was not himself immune to melodrama in *All the King's Men*, and Rossen was by no means a hack. But he suffered under the burden of trying to adapt another man's plot while lacking the technical resources and perhaps the desire to represent his vision. Warren's novel was possibly too good and certainly too complicated not to suffer in any film adaptation; Rossen's film was perhaps too close to the battle against fascism to take a more detached view of a charismatic political leader. And of course, Warren was interested in something else—the moral development of Jack Burden and his recovery of a personal past. Rossen may have had other interests, but they were left in the cutting room with the hour or more of discarded film. What remained—apart from a number of exciting sequences and some remarkable framing of characters, and perhaps these are enough to redeem the picture—was a confused and very Hollywood melodrama.

Works Cited

Brenton, Guy. 1950. "Two Adaptations." *Sequence* 12:33-36.

Casty, Alan. 1966-67. "The Films of Robert Rossen." *Film Quarterly* 20:3-12.

Rossen, Robert. 1972. *Three Screenplays: All the King's Men, The Hustler, Lilith.* Edited by Steven Rossen. Garden City: Anchor.

Tyler, Parker. 1950. "Movie Letter: Novel into Film: *All the King's Men.*" *Kenyon Review* 12:369-376.

Warren, Robert Penn. 1946. *All the King's Men.* Reprint. New York: Bantam, 1968.

ONE FLEW OVER THE CUCKOO'S NEST:
A TALE OF TWO DECADES

Thomas J. Slater

When adapting Ken Kesey's *One Flew Over the Cuckoo's Nest* for the screen, Milos Forman faced one very significant problem: the novel's narrator is a paranoid-schizophrenic who sees things that nobody else can. Seen through the eyes of the six-foot-eight American Indian named Chief Bromden, *Cuckoo's Nest's* main setting of a mental ward at the Oregon State Hospital becomes a surrealistic world controlled by hidden wires and fog machines that help the head nurse and her staff to work their will on the patients. Although the Chief's vision is comic and absurd, it also reveals the reality of the world and the events that take place. As he accurately notes, "It's the truth, even if it didn't happen" (Kesey 1962, p. 13).

Forman also faced the problem of making Kesey's liberal early-sixties' theme of fighting conformity relevant to the mid-seventies. Forman had to make the story contemporary without losing its essence. He was successful mainly because he gave the novel's unusual narrative perspective to his camera and transformed Kesey's mythic characters and surrealist setting into human beings in a unique but recognizable world.

To many readers, the novel's apparent hero is Randle Patrick McMurphy, a big, boastful Irishman who lies his way into the Oregon State Hospital to escape the drudgery of a prison work farm. Once there, he leads the patients in a fight against the hospital staff's attempt to impose mind control. The narrator, Chief Bromden, sees McMurphy as a hero because he merely laughs at the whole situation on the mental ward instead of living in fear.[1] Through his swaggering, boastful nature and his defiance of conventions despite the consequences, McMurphy eventually helps instill the other men on the ward with the confidence to face life again. He creates a virtual metamorphosis in his fellow patients, which leads the Chief to present him in mythic terms.[2]

For example, the Chief's depiction of McMurphy as a Christ figure is blatantly obvious. McMurphy comes into the ward, gathers his followers about him, instructs them in how to live,

45

and then sacrifices himself for them even though he has done nothing wrong. He dies merely because he is a threat to the status quo. The Chief leaves no doubt about his analogy when he includes a description of the electroshock therapy table as looking like a cross (Kesey 1962, p. 64) and of himself as wanting to touch McMurphy merely because "he's who he is" (Kesey 1962, p. 188). A fishing trip that McMurphy organizes is also directly out of the Christ story. McMurphy leads his twelve followers out to sea and goes down into the hold, but when chaos breaks out on board, he is forced to come back up and calm everything down (Kesey 1962, pp. 191-218). The Chief completes the analogy by saying that the last time any of them saw him conscious "he let himself cry out" (Kesey 1962, p. 267).

Despite this convincing portrait, McMurphy is not really the man that the Chief presents him to be. Throughout the novel, Kesey subtly undercuts the Chief's biased presentation of McMurphy as a mythic figure. At midpoint in the story, McMurphy learns that Nurse Ratched (the ward's controller and novel's villain) has the power to keep him in the hospital as long as she wants. He first responds by fully cooperating with her so that he can gain his release (Kesey 1962, pp. 148-49). But then he changes his mind and spends the rest of the novel doing exactly what he wants, consciously antagonizing Big Nurse (Ratched's nickname). The Chief never explains why McMurphy becomes rebellious again, but he does reveal several factors operating on his hero's mind at that point in the novel. McMurphy feels responsible for the suicide of fellow patient Charlie Cheswick (Kesey 1962, p. 151), and he also discovers that the other men are in the hopsital only because they do not have the courage to be on the outside (Kesey 1962, p. 168). McMurphy therefore realizes that conformity and fear are interrelated, feeding on each other and producing the kind of hollow men that Nurse Ratched desires.

Thus, when McMurphy once more defies Nurse Ratched, he is acting under strong feelings of guilt and doubt. Just when Nurse Ratched believes that she is in full control of the ward, McMurphy deliberately smashes her office window, an act that the Chief relates in mythic terms as a calculated act of self-sacrifice (Kesey 1962, pp. 171-172). Most likely, McMurphy is attempting to redeem himself and preserve his self-identity. The Chief notes that Nurse Ratched felt she had gained a "final victory" (Kesey 1962, p. 172). McMurphy is mainly fearful of losing his own soul, and he is not basically concerned with saving others.

Nurse Ratched is also a larger than life character in the novel. The Chief pictures her as a machine who sits at the center of a system (which he calls "The Combine") that operates both outside and inside the ward to keep people contentedly going about their business without complaint. The Chief sees her battle with McMurphy as a struggle between two large conceptions of what America is, and his hero's one chance of victory is to get Nurse Ratched to recognize her own humanity.

At the end of the novel, Kesey undercuts the mythic stature of both McMurphy and Ratched when fellow-patient Dale Harding denies that McMurphy is a Christ-figure while at the same time denying Big Nurse a chance to regain her power. She feels that if she can make an example of McMurphy, the ward will return to its former routine. Taking over the words of Christ, she tells Harding that McMurphy is going to return: "I would not say so if I was not positive. He will be back" (Kesey 1962, p. 268). Harding responds, "Lady, I think you're so full of bullshit" (Kesey 1962, pp. 268-269). By finally dispelling the notion of McMurphy as Christ, Kesey makes it clear that the novel's true hero is the Chief himself. Throughout the novel, the Chief undergoes a complete spiritual transformation and is ready at the end to continue struggling against society's oppressiveness, but not by adopting McMurphy's recklessness. He represents a middle path between these two extremes and exemplifies Kesey's message of individual responsibility. The Chief's story represents the end of one phase of his battle and the beginning of another.[3]

Milos Forman remains true to the spirit of Kesey's novel by keeping his basic message but renovating the story to make it relevant to the mid-seventies. In the film, Forman's camera appropriately takes over the narrative perspective of both the Chief and Ken Kesey. Like the Chief in the novel, the camera presents McMurphy as a mythic figure while, at the same time, undercutting that notion. In the end, the viewer must realize his own responsibility for going beyond the philosophies of both McMurphy and Nurse Ratched. Once again, the Chief provides the final example to be followed.

In contrast to the book, the movie establishes the Chief as the only character that McMurphy sets free because he is the only one who has gained the courage to act on his own. Forman gives the story a contemporary meaning by showing it as a struggle for power among McMurphy, Ratched, and Harding. On its surface, Forman's film appears to have a conservative message because the hero is battling an oppressive social system dominated by a woman and a homosexual (Dale Harding), but his film is neither sexist nor anti-gay. His depiction of all three characters as failing to achieve or maintain power because of their very lust for it presents his true theme. Forman shows that people who strive for power are susceptible to their own human weaknesses, a fact that everyone needs to realize. In the end, each individual must work towards his or her own freedom or remain entrapped by the whims of those in power.

Forman begins by translating the Chief's characterization of McMurphy as a mythic hero onto the screen. The opening shot shows the red light of daybreak glowing out over a dark mountain. The music starts with the sound of an American Indian drumbeat, which is joined by a gentle folk guitar and a mournful harmonica that also has a mocking tone to it, like something has passed but does not really merit deep sympathy. Emerging from the deep shadows of the mountain are the headlights of the police car bringing McMurphy from the prison camp to the hospital.

In this one shot, Forman creates McMurphy as a mythic figure. McMurphy represents the freedom and elemental forces associated with the American wilderness. The mountain becomes an important symbol of manhood. When the Chief is ready to leave the hospital at the end of the film, he tells the comatose McMurphy that he is "big as a damn mountain." The native and folk music associates McMurphy with the basic instincts of Americans who are closely related to the land and do not have much power, people such as American Indians, farmers, and mountain people. The harmonica sounds like a lament, but McMurphy is not a character who would mourn anything and so the slightly mocking tone is appropriate. When the Chief makes his escape at the end, the harmonica tune becomes a brief, joyously orchestrated crescendo before lapsing again into a gentle murmur. The music thus emphasizes Forman's theme that the human spirit can, at times, overcome despair and burst forth in triumph.

For the second shot of the film, Forman pans from a window inside the hospital ward across the bed of one of the patients and on through the room. The shot is from the viewpoint of a patient who could have been watching the car coming and then turned to look back across the room. Scattered patches of red light coming from the window break the darkness of the ward, like sunlight seen from under water. Forman maintains the association of the red light with freedom and the idea of the men being kept like fish in an aquarium throughout the entire film. The ward's red exit signs constantly beckon the men towards a different world, one whose uncertainty makes them reluctant to leave their safe confines, despite the abuse they suffer.[4]

Forman's starting the shot from the barrier formed between the two worlds by the wall and the opposite movement of the camera from the opening shot further support his quick division of the world in the film between the outside and the inside. This division does not exist in the novel, where the Combine operates everywhere. In the film, McMurphy enables the men to experience freedom and dignity by taking them away from the hospital by involving them in sports such as basketball and fishing. McMurphy starts simply, within the ward. When he arrives, four of the men, Charlie Cheswick (Sidney Lassick), Billy Bibbit (Brad Dourif), Harding (William Redfield), and Martini (Danny DeVito) are playing cards.[5] McMurphy gathers his first follower by flashing his own deck of pornographic playing cards at Martini and luring him away. This action demonstrates that McMurphy is presenting the men an alternative reality more appealing to them than anything they have experienced before. Forman, however, has already begun to undercut McMurphy. When the police first take the handcuffs off him, McMurphy begins jumping around and screeching like a monkey. The action is funny, but it also shows that an uncontrolled nature is not completely desirable. Society has good reasons for taming the forces with which McMurphy is associated. But, in the mental hospital, it has gone too far. The film, therefore, like the novel, must demonstrate that a middle path between the extremes of McMurphy and Ratched does exist.

McMurphy is also a Christ-figure in the film, but Forman suggests the idea much more subtly than the Chief does in the novel. He shows McMurphy on the ward for the first time exercising with the other men before the daily therapy session. Forman shoots him from behind as McMurphy stands briefly with his arms stretched out in the crucifix position. The camera angle is significant because it emphasizes that McMurphy is not conscious of others seeing him as a Christ-figure. In the film, he never shows any intention of playing the hero. He makes all of his challenges to Nurse Ratched when he has no knowledge of her power to keep him institutionalized indefinitely. He acts openly only because he does not understand the risk he is taking.

For example, during the scene in which McMurphy tries teaching the Chief (Will Sampson) how to play basketball, Forman demonstrates the enormity of his spirit in comparison with the other men. McMurphy climbs onto the shoulders of another patient, Bancini. When Bancini begins to run around, McMurphy starts screaming, "Hit me, Chief! I'm open." His voice fills the soundtrack, giving the impression that he is now the dominant force at the hospital, but Forman's camera is on Nurse Ratched, watching from an omnipotent position inside the hospital. She maintains the power and McMurphy's optimism is false. Once again, Forman uses the perspective of another patient, this time one who is standing on the sidelines, whose simple vision both supports and undercuts McMurphy's lofty stature.

In the fishing trip sequence, Forman undercuts McMurphy through a combination of the camera's point of view and an alteration in the narrative structure. In this scene, Forman strongly emphasizes the idea that the men are taking on new identities. McMurphy manages to confiscate a rental boat by telling the harbor manager that the men are doctors from the mental hospital. Forman captures the men in individual shots as McMurphy introduces them, and they all look suddenly sophisticated.[6] McMurphy gets the men started fishing and then goes below deck with his girlfriend. Martini immediately leads the men up front to try to peek in the windows. Chaos erupts when Cheswick turns around, sees no one on deck, and leaves the steering wheel. The boat starts going crazy, McMurphy comes up on deck, and Taber (Christopher Lloyd) hooks a fish. All of the men struggle together to bring it in while Harding and Cheswick fight over the steering wheel. Forman pulls up to a high shot to show the boat going in a circle, thus communicating one of the problems with McMurphy's influence. Though the men are feeling free, McMurphy is actually leading them in circles. They are merely bouncing from Nurse Ratched's control into his.

In this shot, Forman copies the Chief's narrative perspective in the book exactly. The difference is that the Chief interprets what he sees in purely optimistic terms, whereas Forman's shot captures the full complexity of the situation. Although he is a part of the group, the Chief also imagines himself high above the men and sees their laughter crashing in waves on shores all over the world (Kesey 1962, p. 212). In the film, the Chief is not even on the boat, a fact relevant not only to Forman's change of narrator, but also to his alteration of the story to emphasize his own distinct themes. In the novel, the fishing trip and the basketball game between the patients and the aides both take place after McMurphy has already learned about Nurse Ratched's power over him. Forman places both events before McMurphy's discovery of this fact. Thus, McMurphy is not taking a conscious risk in the film; he is acting out of a pure desire to prove himself to the men and have some pleasure, feeding his own ego and libido at the same time. Kesey makes the trip a major step in McMurphy's aid to the Chief's transformation, but Forman replaces the theme of spiritual growth with an examination of individuals in a struggle for power. The three characters who seek it, McMurphy, Ratched, and Harding, all fail, leaving each of the men ultimately responsible for facing the world on his own.

By showing that he never consciously plays a hero's role, Forman undercuts McMurphy's mythic image thoroughly. In the novel, when McMurphy smashes the glass in Nurse Ratched's office window, the Chief describes him as carefully contemplating his action beforehand. In the film, McMurphy acts out of anger while surrounded by chaos. Taber has been carried away screaming after being burned by a cigarette that became lodged in his pant cuff, and Cheswick is hollering to get his confiscated cigarettes back. McMurphy first tries to silence him, but then goes in frustration to smash the window.

Similarly, at the end of the novel, McMurphy simply chooses not to leave the ward, and the Chief once again allows for the possibility that McMurphy's act is a heroic gesture. Forman shows McMurphy as unable to leave; when the aides arrive in the morning, he is still passed out on the floor from the previous night's party. Forman's shot of him lying there summarizes his conception of the character. The empty liquor bottle next to him, its former contents a source of both liberation and entrapment, is a reflection of McMurphy himself. Without self-control, the spirits of both have been wasted.

When McMurphy finally attacks Nurse Ratched, he is again acting impulsively. Shortly before, he is about to escape when Billy Bibbit's body is discovered. McMurphy's girlfriends call from outside the open window, but he cannot keep himself from returning to the scene. Nurse Ratched attempts to reassert the old order, and McMurphy, realizing that he is losing his power, attacks. Even if his action is interpreted as a sacrifice, his own lack of conscious behavior has created the entire situation in the first place. Ultimately, McMurphy has no one but himself to blame for his suffering.

Jack Nicholson deserves much credit for creating McMurphy as a powerfully ambiguous character, both appealing and repulsive.[7] When he acts like a baboon upon entering the hospital, Nicholson indicates that McMurphy is a character who lives on his own level of existence. This factor is the source of both his power and his downfall; he fascinates everyone, but no one can figure him out. All the patients think he is crazy for acting as boldly as he does, but follow him as if he were sane. All the doctors, and Nurse Ratched, believe he is sane, but treat him as if he were crazy. Meanwhile, the audience must question who is really mentally ill, the patients or the staff. Nicholson illustrates the power in McMurphy's own brand of insanity in one key scene.

McMurphy's attempt to lift a shower control panel seems idiotic at first. He begins by taking some deep breaths, working himself into a frenzy, and uttering some gibberish as if he were speaking in tongues. As he strains to lift the panel, every vein in his arms and neck seems to pop up. He is clearly entering his own distinct reality. When he fails and challenges the other patients for not even trying, he gains the admiration of his fellow patients. By contrast, Forman questions McMurphy's sanity most at a time that appears to be his peak. At the end of the party he creates on the ward, the night before he is supposed to leave, McMurphy sits down to wait while Billy Bibbit goes to make love to the prostitute, Candy (Maria Small). The ward is in chaos, and the men are all drunk. It is McMurphy's moment of triumph. He gazes around with a self-satisfied smirk on his face. The camera holds him in a long close-up, forcing the viewer to stop to consider the image deeply. McMurphy's destructiveness does not make him an admirable figure to follow.

If McMurphy's ideal world is one of complete disarray, Nurse Ratched's is one of total order. Forman reveals this aspect of her personality in his first shot of her entering the ward. She wears a black cape and hat that forms a perfect color balance between herself and the three black aides, who all wear starched white uniforms. Later, Forman uses red light, which indicated a new day dawning for the men in the opening shot of the film, to represent the entrance to what Nurse Ratched considers to be freedom. Significantly, the hallway of the ward is lined with jail cells filled with men probably considered to be hopeless cases. The dominant empty whiteness represents the blank future toward which the hospital methods are leading the men. In one shot, a bright rectangular white light shines at the end of the hall, an image of the future. In contrast with McMurphy, Nurse Ratched promises a future devoid of life and color; however, Forman never makes Nurse Ratched into a mythic figure. Instead, she is a very human character whose evil is greater than she realizes. She is as unconscious of her destructiveness as McMurphy is of his positive aspects.

The combination of Forman's camera and Louise Fletcher's performance truly defines Nurse Ratched as a person whose initially good intentions have been transformed into oppressiveness.[8] Because she is not a character of mythic proportions, Nurse Ratched is never called Big Nurse in the film. She is even referred to by her first name, Mildred.

Forman presents Nurse Ratched as a character who genuinely believes that she has the patients' best interests at heart, and Louise Fletcher offers no hint that the situation might be otherwise. The most obvious example of her nonmaliciousness occurs at the staff meeting when the doctors are trying to decide what they will do with McMurphy. When Nurse Ratched calmly states that they should not pass on their problem by sending him back to the prison farm, the camera is unable to capture a note of malice. Her statement that she thinks they can help him is made away from the camera and is dramatically ambiguous.

In this scene, Forman's camera once again correlates exactly with the Chief's perspective in the novel, and the film is again more complex because Nurse Ratched is seen as a human being. The Chief's view of her is clearly dehumanizing. He imagines her taking a sip of coffee and setting the cup smoldering from the heat of her lips (136). The novel then requires the reader to discern between the Chief's point of view and reality. Nevertheless, Bromden clearly presents Nurse Ratched as a mechanistic villain. In the film, Nurse Ratched does not blatantly overrule the other doctors' diagnosis as she does in the book. Instead, they ask for her opinion as a skilled professional. The viewer must ponder what is wrong about her judgment, which seems perfectly logical. The distinction between Nurse Ratched as the villain and McMurphy as the hero becomes significantly blurred.

Paradoxically, even though Forman's Nurse Ratched is more human, she is also more evil. In the novel, the Chief describes her as only the Combine's representative (Kesey 1962, p. 165). In the film, there is no Combine. Nurse Ratched is the sole barrier between the men and the outside world, a fact that Forman strongly emphasizes when she returns to the ward in the morning after the party. She and the aides stand opposite the patients, forming a human wall between the men and the red exit sign beckoning them towards the outside.

Forman's presentation of Nurse Ratched as the evil oppresser left him vulnerable to being accused of sexism, as Ken Kesey had been earlier.[9] Kesey escapes the charge by virtue of the fact that not endowing Nurse Ratched with masculine qualities would completely ruin his novel's comic structure.[10] But, superficially, Forman seems to go even further in his antifemale imagery. Except for Nurse Ratched's young impressionable aide, the other women in the film are either sexual treats and builders of male egos or castraters. The prostitute whom McMurphy takes along on the fishing trip and later brings onto the ward for the party represents the woman as treat. McMurphy first introduces her to the others by saying, "Boys, this here is Candy." Candy's function is obviously to help turn boys into men, and she succeeds with Billy Bibbit. When McMurphy is about to leave the hospital at the end of the party, he stays only because Billy wants a quick "date" with Candy. Through Billy, the other men also gain maturity. They eagerly wheel him up to the room where Candy awaits. McMurphy affirms the act's communal nature when he tells Billy, "I've got twenty-five dollars that says you burn this woman *down!*" Eliminated from the film are references to the Chief's mother as the cause of his father's drinking and to Billy's mother as the cause of his shyness. Forman thus avoids any attacks on motherhood. He also removes from the story the young, intelligent, and humanitarian head nurse of another ward who completely opposes Nurse Ratched's methods.

Discarding the Chief as narrator necessitates these changes. The camera can only present what it sees, and no dialogue informs the audience about the patients' backgrounds. Using the camera as narrator also accounts partially for Forman's creation of Dale Harding as a more negative character than he is in the book. In both works, Harding is a weak-spirited homosexual, but Kesey explains that his personal problems originated from social factors when he was very young. He is intelligent, and McMurphy has no trouble accepting him.

Forman makes him a negative figure because he challenges McMurphy for power, counseling conformity to Nurse Ratched's wishes. Every time McMurphy attempts something new, refusing to take his medicine, trying to get the World Series on television, stealing the hospital bus, or organizing the patients' basketball team, Harding either opposes him or goes along very reluctantly. Harding is in a leadership position, running the patients' games and speaking like an intellectual at the first group therapy session, but he is intimidated by Nurse Ratched, and all his talk is meaningless. He is weak because he is more committed to holding empty power than to resolving his personal problems and becoming a real leader. Harding frustrates the other patients, particularly Taber, because he wants to keep their respect without taking any chances.

After McMurphy's attempt to lift the control panel, Harding realizes that he has lost his leadership position. In the next scene, he reluctantly joins the vote to watch the World Series on television. But Harding never gives up his desire for power. When McMurphy receives his lobotomy, Harding immediately attempts to take his place and destroy the masculine image that the men are trying to hold on to. But the men will not let him, even though he alone acknowledges that McMurphy has finally been defeated for good. Harding is not McMurphy either as a card dealer or as a leader. In the end, he is still trapped inside his personal weaknesses by his desire for power. In the final shot of him, Harding is standing behind an iron gate, a picture representing his state of mind, as the Chief runs off into the night.

McMurphy continually challenges Harding's masculinity and insults him throughout the film. On the fishing boat, when he is introducing all the other men to the dock manager as doctors, he introduces Harding as mister. McMurphy is also constantly asserting his own sexual prowess, such as when he returns from electroshock therapy and tells the men, "Next woman who takes me on is going to light up like a pinball machine and pay off in silver dollars." McMurphy is thus a sexual hero as well as a spiritual one, and Forman is thereby able to satisfy his audience's contrasting desires for rebellion and reassurance. Through his revolt against bureaucratic control and association with freedom, McMurphy is a sixties' hero; but through his reassertion of a traditional social hierarchy, he is definitely one for the seventies.

Yet, the film does by no means condemn homosexuals. During the party sequence, when McMurphy seems to be firmly in

charge, Forman does show homosexuality as acceptable.
McMurphy calls Harding by his first name, Dale. Forman
presents Fredrickson (Vincent Schiavelli) and Sefelt (William
Duell), who are together throughout the film, as clearly
homosexual. They dance together during the night, and aides
push their beds apart the next morning. Scanlon also demonstrates deviant sexuality at the party by putting on a dress and
nurse's cap. McMurphy never objects to Fredrickson, Sefelt, or
Scanlon because they never challenge him. Scanlon has only one
line in the whole film. Harding's offensiveness, therefore, is
clearly because of his desire for power, and in this respect he is
no different from either Nurse Ratched or McMurphy.

   In *One Flew Over the Cuckoo's Nest*, Milos Forman manages
to capture many important popular attitudes of the immediate
post-Watergate era. His presentation of three characters who each
fail in their struggle for power because of personal weaknesses
matches the public's dominant beliefs about the fall of Richard
Nixon. People did not tend to blame the political system for
Watergate, but they did generally distrust social institutions.
Cuckoo's Nest reflects this attitude, and Forman's emphasis on
individual responsibility fit the "Me" decade's concern with
personal development perfectly.[11]

   Forman's presentation of the outside world supports his theme
of each person being responsible for working towards his or her
own freedom. Forman's camera again parallels the Chief's
narration in the novel by revealing more about the world than
most of the other characters seem to realize. Unlike those in the
novel, however, Forman's references are very brief and require
more interpretation from the viewer.

   When the men go out on their fishing trip, they see mostly
deserted streets. The few people who are around are as lifeless as
the chronics on the ward. One couple has pulled a pair of folding
chairs up to a television set playing in a department store
window. They turn their backs on life in order to enjoy the
culture presented to them. Forman thus presents television as
another dictator of the social order.

   When the men arrive at a trailer park to get McMurphy's
girlfriend, an old man stares blankly at the camera. Upon their
return from their fishing trip, a number of people line the dock,
staring at the men just as blankly. These are people, young and
old, who have been worn down, who go places to observe life
rather than experience it themselves. When they are no longer

able to do that, they just sit and stare. The vision that Forman thus presents of America in October of 1963 is not one filled with the optimism of the Kennedy Administration's Camelot, but of stifled individuals for whom being on the outside is no guarantee of freedom. Forman captures the social conformity that Kesey was attacking in his writing, and he does not pretend that McMurphy's victory would make much difference in it.

As indicated in the film's opening, McMurphy represents the unbridled freedom of the American wilderness. His opponent, Nurse Ratched, represents a highly structured and institutionalized social system, one that is concerned with men only as physical beings who need to perform as required without complaining. When the Chief throws the water control panel through a window at the end, he produces the unity of body and spirit for which McMurphy was striving. Hearing the crash, Taber wakes up and gives a triumphant yell; but he and the other men still remain inside the ward. Each of them, like each viewer, must take the first steps towards freedom on his own and be prepared to keep fighting to preserve it. *One Flew Over the Cuckoo's Nest* expresses many of Milos Forman's long-held beliefs about power and feelings of compassion for the people who lack it.[12] By capturing the spirit of Ken Kesey's novel while also giving its meaning a contemporary significance, Forman gained a popular audience and established himself as a prominent film adaptor of contemporary American works.

NOTES

1. Ronald Wallace explains the comic structure of Kesey's novel, arguing, "What McMurphy learns in the course of the novel is how to control and direct his laughter, how to use it as an effective counter to repression and sterlity. What he really learns, and nearly masters, is the typical pose of the comic spirit" (97).

2. Donald Palumbo traces the metamorphosis McMurphy produces in the other patients.

3. Wallace concludes,
The final result of the Chief's new knowledge is the novel itself. Bromden learns to perceive his life as a comic fiction and to transform that fiction into art. Laughing at himself and his society, he writes a novel that makes the reader laugh, thus perpetuating his own comic vision. Form and content merge as Bromden writes a book in praise of laughter that itself induces laughter. (112)

4. Stanley Kauffmann gives Forman particular credit for his control in these opening shots and also heaps praise on Nicholson.

5. Casting the patients was crucial to Forman: "Since [they] have few lines to say, [the] audience must remember each simply by their look" (Burke, "The Director's Approach," 15).

6. Michael Wood finds Forman's theme of individual responsibility clearly expressed in the scene of the men boarding the boat (4).

7. Pauline Kael provides significant insights into Jack Nicholson's careful handling of the McMurphy role, showing how Nicholson created ambiguity while avoiding the temptation to flaunt his shrewdness.

8. Aljean Harmetz explains the importance of Louise Fletcher's contributions.

9. Robert Forrey delivers the charges of racism and sexism.

10. Ronald Wallace gives a significant defence of Kesey.

11. Social and political analysts verify Forman's assessment of the struggle for power and social institutions as matching public attitudes at mid-decade. For analysis of public opinions about Nixon and social institutions, see Muzzio (161) and Carroll (235).

12. Josef Skvorecky quotes Forman as saying,
I think all that which is noble, and which has remained in art and literature since ancient times . . . and which is also significant for strong contemporary works of art, has always concerned itself with injuries and injustices perpetrated against the individual. There, at the bottom of all those great works, are the injustices, which no social order will eliminate. Namely, that one is clever and the other is stupid, one is able and the other is incompetent, one is beautiful while the other is ugly, another might be honest, and yet another dishonest, and all of them are in some way ambitious. And it indeed does not matter that we are arriving at eternal themes. (84)

WORKS CITED

Buckley, Tom. 1981. "The Forman Formula." *New York Times Sunday Magazine* 1 March: 28,31,42-43,50-53.

Burke, Tom. 1976. "The Director's Approach—Two Wives." *New York Times* 28 March 2:15.

Carroll, Peter N. 1982. *It Seemed Like Nothing Happened: The Tragedy and Promise of America in the 1970s.* New York: Holt, Rinehart, and Winston.

Forrey, Robert. 1975. "Ken Kesey's Psychopathic Savior: A Rejoinder." *Modern Fiction Studies* 21.2:222-30.

Harmetz, Aljean. 1975. "The Nurse Who Rules The 'Cuckoo's Nest.'" *New York Times* 30 Nov. 2:13.

Kael, Pauline. 1975. "The Bull Goose Loony." *New Yorker* 1 Dec.: 131-36.

Kauffmann, Stanley. 1975. "Jack High." *The New Republic* 13 Dec.: 22-23.

Kesey, Ken. 1962. *One Flew Over the Cuckoo's Nest.* New York: New American Library.

Muzzio, Douglas. 1982. *Watergate Games: Strategies, Choices, Outcomes.* New York: New York University Press.

Palumbo, Donald. 1983. "Kesey's and Forman's *One Flew Over the Cuckoo's Nest*' The Metamorphosis of Metamorphosis as Novel Becomes Film." *CEA Critic* 45.2:25-32.

Skvorecky, Josef. 1971. *All the Bright Young Men and Women: A Personal History of the Czech Cinema.* Toronto: Peter Martin Associates, Ltd.

Wallace, Ronald. 1979. *The Last Laugh: Form and Affirmation in the Contemporary American Comic Novel.* Columbia: University of Missouri Press.

Wood, Michael. 1976. "No. But I Read the Book." *New York Review of Books* 5 Feb.: 3-4.

BUS STOP AS SELF-REFLEXIVE PARODY: GEORGE AXELROD ON ITS ADAPTATION

Joanna E. Rapf

George Axelrod, who describes himself as a typical New Yorker (he was born there in 1922), lives in an elegant home nestled high in the hills above Los Angeles. He bought the house, looking out over a city that is sometimes visible through the smog, from fellow comic writer Mel Brooks. And as with Mel Brooks, Axelrod's focus as an artist comes from a view of the world that says "most things are funny."[1] Yet his vision is a dark one: "I love black jokes." André Breton, in his landmark work *Anthologie de l'humour noir* (1939), has written that *"l'ennemi mortel de la sentimentalité"* is that amoral outlook on life which he called *"l'humour noir"* (Breton 1966, pp. 21-22). One of Axelrod's favorite techniques is to pull the rug out from under a sentimental moment with a dash of off-color humor. For Richard Corliss, "all of Axelrod's scripts read like suicide notes, for which the morning-after hangover—and not the night-before revelry— has provided the inspiration" (Corliss 1975, pp. 91-92). Axelrod's 1971 novel *Where Am I Now—When I Need Me?*, patterned loosely after events in his own life, begins with its main character, Harvey Bernstein, a "failed poet, failed novelist, failed husband, failed father, and failed drunk," writing a suicide note.

Corliss places Axelrod among his "Authors-Auteurs," a group of writers whose work, when examined as a whole, bears their distinctive stamp—for better or for worse. With Axelrod, who has done almost all adaptations, and many from his own plays—*The Seven Year Itch* (1955), *Will Success Spoil Rock Hunter?* (1957), *Goodbye Charlie* (1964)—and from his own stories—*Phffft* (1954), *How To Murder Your Wife* (1965), *The Secret Life Of An American Wife* (1968)—it is easy to find recurring themes and a consistent comic thrust. Corliss sees the Axelrod world as one "of wish-fulfillment and want-frustrations" (Corliss 1975, p. 91). *Bus Stop*, particularly as Axelrod renders it, is structured around this basic conflict of ideal *versus* real, a conflict between Bo's wishful dream of his perfect "angel," Cherie's of a perfect love rooted in mutual respect, and the reality that frustrates them. One of Axelrod's mocking fingers always seems to be pointing at

59

American society, and in particular, what he sees as American vulgarity. But the other four fingers, "point back accusingly at himself," (Corliss 1975, p. 92). He admits that American vulgarity is his favorite theme. "We're dying of it. It's the great disease. You turn on the goddamned television, you look out your window . . . I'm not a moralist—that wouldn't be right—but I'm against stupidity, I'm against brainwashing and that television set."

Corliss suggests that this obsession with American vulgarity, like that of Tashlin, Sturges, and occasionally even Wilder, prevents Axelrod "from attaining the distance we generally think of as being necessary for satire" (Corliss 1975, p. 93). But behind the idea of satire is the dream of reform. The satirist is a disappointed idealist, seeing mudholes, but dreaming of oceans. Axelrod, however, has no illusions about oceans. He admits he is not a moralist; reform is not his aim. His view is essentially black and amoral, believing that existence precedes meaning. He looks at life and finds the only way to cope with its absurdity is to laugh. His is a comic technique, but not necessarily a satiric one. Chaplin, with his moral outlook, growing from a belief that meaning precedes existence, was a satirist, but Axelrod believes that Chaplin destroyed comedy by incarnating the idea that there "has to be a tear behind snuggly love." He understands why, as a writer, he is often compared with Sturges, and admits he has a little of his quality, but "Sturges was wilder. I'm pretty wild," he says, "but my work grooves a little more on reality." For example, there are wild moments of extreme parody in *Bus Stop*, such as the exaggerated and unreal sequence when an exuberant and virginal Bo first encounters women and red lights on the streets of Phoenix. But there are also tender moments of real human contact, such as the scene where Virgil kneels next to the now battered and beaten Bo outside the bus stop and gently cools his injured face with snow. What Corliss calls Axelrod's "artistic schizophrenia" may be simply his ability to straddle both camps, and also, what can only be called his *serious* refusal to be serious: "I think most things are funny."

Axelrod says that the problem with the work of William Inge, the author of *Bus Stop*, is that it "took itself too seriously. It was like Chayefsky's." As an adapter, Axelrod feels no moral obligation to his source. "My obligation is to the film, not to the original work." *Bus Stop*, like any good adaptation, is extrapolated from its source. Movies, Axelrod stresses, "have a very specific medium of their own. You cannot literally transpose a play." Consequently, when he set out to do the screenplay for *Bus Stop*, he had no hesitation about rewriting dialogue, adding and eliminating characters, opening up the structure, and significantly changing the ending. The ending of the play is rather disconsolate, but Axelrod says simply, "I felt it should have a happy ending; it's a comedy."

For Inge, *Bus Stop* is a delicate look at the issues behind the quandary Cherie expresses in Act II: "I'm beginnin' to wonder if there *is* the kind of love I have in mind." The play explores love in various forms: the complexity of Shakespeare's *Romeo and Juliet*, "the animal passion" of Carl and Grace, the moving family bond between Virgil and Bo, and the idealistic images Cherie knows from the movies. She confesses, "Mebbe I don't know what love is," whereas Inge's point of view is expressed by the drunken and disillusioned professor, Dr. Lyman: "Maybe Man has passed the stage in his evolution where love is possible. Maybe life will continue to become so terrifying complex that man's anxiety about his mere survival will render him too miserly to give of himself in any true relation" (Inge 1958, pp. 187-88). The play ends bathed in this dismal light, on a note of solitude and resignation. Virgil recognizes that, with Cherie now a part of Bo's life, Bo no longer needs him. Like a parent who knows with sad wisdom that he must send his child from the nest, Virgil tells Bo to go on to the ranch in Montana without him. After the bus has left, Grace tells him that there will be another for Kansas City in a few minutes, but Virgil replies, "No thanks. No point goin' back there" (Inge 1958, p. 219). Next, with what may be the most resonant line of the drama, Grace says, "Then I'm sorry, mister, but you're left out in the cold," and she carries a can of garbage (a poignant visual metaphor that is not in the film because it would not reflect Axelrod's vision) out the back door. Left alone, Virgil mutters to himself the last line of the play: "Well . . . that's what happens to some people." As Grace silently closes up the bus stop, Inge's stage directions tell us, "One senses her aloneness" (Inge 1958, p. 219).

Axelrod is not tormented, however, like Ingmar Bergman, with the silence of God, nor is he pained, like William Inge, with man's solitary struggle for a meaningful existence. To him, *Bus Stop* is a romantic comedy. I didn't have to see it as a philosophical drama about true love. I thought it was a romantic comedy about a cowboy and a hooker. And comedies have happy

endings. In Axelrod's version, Virgil is still the archetypal
mentor/guide, leading his Dante through Hell (Phoenix),
Purgatory (the bus stop), to Paradise (Cherie). And like Dante's
Virgil, he leaves him at Paradise, but there is no shadow of Inge's
brooding and melancholy solitude. In an earlier stop at Grace's
diner (discussed below), Axelrod sets up a playful attraction
between Grace and Virgil, so that as we leave the two at the end
of the film, there is the strong hint that they are going "to have a
little bang." Axelrod says he did not want to play a poignant
scene with Virgil because that would have taken away from what
he sees as the main thrust of the film: the story of Bo and Cherie.
"I think the picture's over when Bo puts the coat around her.
And that's pretty romantic and nice." But the final wrapping on
the package is the impession that now Virgil and Grace might
have a little fun together, and Axelrod firmly insists that he
doesn't think the happy ending "compromised anything at all."
In terms of their world views, their concluding outlooks,
however, he agrees that *Bus Stop* the film and *Bus Stop* the play
are "entirely different things."

Axelrod's initial involvement with Inge's work came about
through Marilyn Monroe, with whom he had worked in *The
Seven Year Itch*. She was in New York, at the Actors' Studio, and
she suggested that he and Joshua Logan, who was to direct *Bus
Stop*, get together. "So, I met with Logan and we talked about it
and I said, 'It's a tricky thing because it's really, in God's honest
truth, not a very good play.'" Yet for adaptation, this could be an
advantage. "Well-constructed plays are almost impossible to
adapt." Part of the excitement of a well-structured play, as
opposed to a film, is its construction. "It's like packing a
suitcase, keeping everything tight and inside the seams at closing.
But when a play is loose and kind of lousy," Axelrod explains,
"it's much easier to adapt." Novels are intrinsically more suited
to the screen than plays; they are more alike; they both ramble.
To shape a screenplay is "a matter of finding walls and
constructing them. But I'm pretty good at that," Axelrod says,
"and I enjoy the challenge, perhaps because I love crossword
puzzles and that kind of stuff."

One of the clichés of adapation, of course, is that in doing a
play for the screen you "open it up." As A. R. Fulton has said,
"To be successfully adapted to the screen a play must give up its
characteristic unity" (quoted in Harrington 1977, p. 49). This
potential for expansion has influenced the way film views the

world: whereas drama usually sets man off *against* his world, film usually shows man *within* his world.² In drama, the world exists outside the play, and we know it only from what the characters tell us. Characters in film, on the other hand, move through the world, and we see them in relation to it. With a well-structured play, according to Axelrod, "it's very dangerous when you start unpacking, taking the stuff out of the suitcase and hanging it around the room. It's sort of like playing handball with no walls, you know, or squash with no walls. You have to build your own wall." He says, "There are no hard and fast rules, but generally speaking, I think it would be safe to say that the looser the play, the more effective it is as a movie, provided, of course, it's got interesting ideas and something to work with."

Bus Stop was particularly easy to open up, mainly, Axelrod explains, because "it was such a badly-constructed play and so much of the dialogue in the play itself as it was done on stage was exposition, explaining what had happened before. All I had to do was dramatize Bill's exposition. I mean, a rodeo is something you can hardly do on the stage, but it's a wonderful thing to shoot in a movie." And in fact, most of the rodeo scenes in the film are real—there was an actual rodeo in Phoenix.

The idea that Axelrod particularly liked in the play was "the waif, the wandering." It is Cherie's gradual journey west that caused him to change Joplin, Missouri, in the play to Lubbock, Texas, in the film. In both versions, she comes from the little town of River Gulch, Arkansas. Her background is the same. In the play, she wins second place in an amateur contest (first goes to two boys who juggle milk bottles) in Joplin, Missouri, and this success enables her to get a job at The Blue Dragon nightclub in Kansas City. But in the film, she wins that contest in Lubbock. The revision is due to her map, a structural invention of Axelrod's that serves visually to explain where Cherie has come from and where she hopes to go, a straight line drawn in lipstick from Arkansas to the dream factory of Hollywood. "The lipstick was good in terms of her character," Axelrod explains, "because Marilyn's mouth played the shit out of that part." The map also serves to dramatize the change in her destination as she crumples it up and throws it away when she decides to go with Bo to Montana at the end of the film. Lubbock is on that straight line between River Gulch and Los Angeles. As a typical New Yorker, Axelrod confesses that he knows, "that

Lubbock, Texas, and Joplin, Missouri, aren't exactly the same place," but, "I had no idea where either of 'em were; I just needed to accommodate the road map that she had."

In adapting a story for the screen, Axelrod says, "When I start a thing [what I do] is kind of give it a good shake and see what falls out. Most stories have a lot of padding in them." He stresses what he calls "the spine." If you get off the spine, the picture falls flat. "If the 'cutsie stuff' doesn't thrust the story forward, you've got to cut it." The analogy he uses is that of a Christmas tree. "You can have the most wonderful ornaments in the world—and I do good ornaments—but a bunch of ornaments without a tree is no good. You've got to have that tree, the thrust, the storyline, the spine of the thing has to be strong. Then you can hang any kind of goddamned thing you want, but always remember that the trunk of the thing is the tree, not the ornaments."

The subplot of Axelrod's *Bus Stop* turned out to be too ornamental. It took away from the thrust of the trunk, so as much of it as possible was cut from the film. The problem came up during a preview in San Francisco. "It seemed endless, endless, endless." Then it occurred to Axelrod that "once Marilyn starts with the boy, nobody gives a shit about Grace and the bus driver. That plot stops the action." Initially, in adapting the play, Axelrod combined the characters of the sheriff, Will Masters, and the driver, Carl, seeing no need for two of them. "It seems to me that anytime you can put two characters together, you should." Using two, where one will do, "dissipates the force of the thing." In combining them, Axelrod changed the personality of Carl, making him more pompous, "'I'm the Captain of the ship' kind of thing." And he stressed the sexual relationship between Grace and Carl, giving them a major scene where they go to the upstairs apartment and make love. As it was originally conceived, Betty Field, who plays Grace, regarded *Bus Stop* as her film "with Marilyn playing a little floosy." But to make the plot work, to eliminate its tedious "endlessness," much of the material between Grace and the bus driver had to be cut. The upstairs scene is hinted at in the film as it stands, but we do not see it. Field was furious, and, Axelrod says, "she never spoke to me again."

Paradoxically, however, the cutting of the subplot ends up hurting the film's structure. Inge's play is classically set in one location, a bus stop in Kansas, and all the action takes place in little more than four hours. But with film's ability to expand both time and space, Axelrod begins his *Bus Stop* with Bo at his ranch in Montana preparing for the rodeo. We then follow him and Virgil on their bus trip south where before they get to Phoenix they stop at Grace's bus station. But in the edited version of the film, this stop has no purpose. Axelrod's original plan was to use it to establish the bus stop and to set up Grace "because I felt at that time that Grace was a very strong character. I was trying to build because I thought Grace and the bus driver were going to be a second story, and I had to prepare for it . . . Had I known then what I knew by the time that preview was over, I wouldn't have done it." But it was too late to change, so the first stop at Grace's diner remains in the film although Axelrod admits that if he were to redo it today, he would cut it out, moving from the ranch straight to Phoenix and the rodeo.

Another change made in Inge's play which was afterwards edited so that it became superfluous was the addition of two children. "That was when I was in my cute period," Axelrod says. "I had a desperate idea that I wanted to have Marilyn play a scene with two little kids. I had a lovely scene where she's upstairs in her room with the kids reading to them. But the only thing she can find to read is *Confidential Magazine*, which was a glorious thing. We have this intimate, tender group of supine figures on a very plush couch, and the kids are goggle-eyed. But we had to cut all that out. Nobody was interested." The envisioned moment is typical Axelrod humor, undercutting sacred images of Americana—milk, mother, and children—with a dash of sex, but it was irrelevant to the thrust of the film.

We do see this kind of undercutting, however, earlier in the *Bus Stop* with Abraham Lincoln's hallowed Gettysburg Address. The germ for this idea, like so many in the adaptation, comes from a line in Inge's play. Bo tries to establish that he is not an illiterate rodeo star by admitting he can recite the famous speech, although he refuses to do it in public. Axelrod moves the incident towards the beginning of the film, the morning after Bo has met Cherie for the first time in The Blue Dragon. With unsuppressed exuberance, he bursts into her rooming house bedroom to take her to the rodeo parade. A standard, stuffy landlady protests that no male callers are allowed, but Bo persists with a shout that "we're getting married." Cherie is asleep and obviously naked underneath her light covers. Oblivious to this, Bo sits on her bed, grabs her, and begins to explain his plans. Stroking her soft, pale

shoulder, he explains that he is not ignorant and that he can
even recite the Gettysburg Address. We switch camera angles here
and view Bo and Cherie through the bars of the bed's headstead.
He seems to be on top of her, but totally unaware of any sexual
implications, as he begins, "Fourscore and seven years ago . . . ."
Cherie stirs and complains that she does not want to hear it, that
she does not want to go to the parade, that she is not going to
marry him, that she just wants to sleep. But Bo continues. The
camera angle again switches to what is now a medium close-up
level with one side of the bed as Bo, still stroking Cherie's
shoulder and arm, gradually begins to experience a sensation that
has nothing to do with literacy. He stumbles a bit as he says,
"rather it is for us, the living to be so concentrated and so
dedicated," and at this opportune moment the landlady comes in
to interrupt with a saving double entendre rooted in the natural
entwining of sex and history: "If you go any further, Mr.
Lincoln, you're going to miss the parade." For Axelrod, this was
"a creative way of taking an idea of Bill's and using it
dramatically." He admits, "I'm the funnier kid."

He has described his style as essentially that of parody: "I
always kick things as far as I can get them and have been known
on occasion to go too far. I love stretching the rubber band as far
as you can get it." But it had not occurred to him that his *Bus
Stop* might be a parody of itself. Richard Corliss has said that
Lord Love A Duck "almost *is* what it's satirizing" (Corliss 1975,
p. 95). Although this is not quite true of *Bus Stop*, the film does
parody the essential Axelrod theme of wish-fulfillment and want-
frustrations. Axelrod says he had never really thought about this
before, but with a little reflection it suddenly seems to him that
the film is "a parody of a western." Bo may have one foot in
reality, but from beginning to end, we can't take him very
seriously either as a cowboy or a lover. His romance with Cherie
is out of the comic books, and Marilyn herself, Axelrod explains,
"is bigger than life . . . . She's almost a parody of a blonde
herself." *Bus Stop*, Axelrod concludes, is a kind of "parody of
Foster's 'Heart of Gold' story. It doesn't take itself terribly
seriously."

This lack of seriousness may have been the cause of Inge's real
objection to the film. "I didn't take it with the kind of 'deadly
seriousness' that he did." He hated the picture and was angry
about it. Axelrod says "he got all hung up on Lyman, the major
character I cut out of the picture—the drunken professor." Inge

loved the brooding Professor, who was his spokesman in the play, who was himself. "Bill was such a depressed person. I mean, he committed suicide when he was sixty. He was a very downbeat guy. He claimed he was an alcoholic. He really wasn't. He spent all of his life wanting to drink. He was in Alcoholics Anonymous, and he had an unhappy sex life. He was always madly in love with Warren Beatty or somebody who wouldn't have anything to do with him. Very sad, very gloomy, sweet, dear man." But from Axelrod's point of view, this gloom had "no place in the story whatsoever." If Joshua Logan had had his way, the Professor would probably have stayed in. "Josh kind of liked it. He was a sucker for that kind of sentimental old drunk thing, since that's what he is, too. But no, he had to go."

In any adaptation, according to Axelrod, there are three phases, and each one brings changes. First, it's on paper, second you shoot it, and third, you see it in front of an audience. With *Bus Stop*, each phase "was a war." Although the film is "the best thing Marilyn ever did, it was hell getting anything out of her. She was fresh from the Actors' Studio where they pumped her full of such horseshit. Lee Strasberg did more damage to a generation of actors than anybody I know." Monroe's problem, at this point, was that she could not memorize. On the bus, after Bo has "kidnapped" her, there is a lovely scene between Cherie and Elma Duckworth [played by Hope Lange] in which she reveals her dreams about love. But she could not remember her lines, and she became more and more psychotic every time she blanked and Logan yelled, "Cut." So, he finally decided just to let the camera run, 900 feet of film, and with every other word, Joe Curtis, the dialogue coach, would have to yell, "and I really want love. I'm looking for love," and then she'd say, "I really want . . ." and stop. As Axelrod describes it, "Josh would then run in, so that to all of us, it looked like a love scene between Logan's ass and Marilyn. It took two days to do this goddamned thing. But somehow, it cut together like a dream. But you know, those terrible pauses, where it seems as if she's thinking and groping, what she's really groping for are words. She's looking at Joe Curtis to find out what she's supposed to say next. But the camera adored her."

Axelrod describes *Bus Stop* as Logan's "best work," even though it, too, may have been an accident. "He never looked through the lens. He was always directing on the side like a stage director. And he didn't have a clue about how to use

Cinemascope." At the time, one of the unexamined rules about "scope" was that you could not use it for close-ups. "Well, Josh did not know that. So in the final close-up with Bo and Cherie, we squeezed one of her eyes in that wonderful scene in the end where she drooled, and the drool comes out of her mouth a little bit." When Buddy Alden, the producer, saw the scene in the projection room, he said, "we gotta cut that." But Axelrod insisted, "If you cut that, you take my name off the picture. That happened, it's real. For Christ's sake, use it. You know," he says ironically, "I felt like Strasberg. But in this case Lee would have been right. That love scene shot in this funny way in Cinemascope, in close-up in Cinemascope, is the goddamnest thing. And Josh just didn't know what the hell he was doing. But it's just wonderful; it broke new ground."

Logan, Monroe, and Inge are all, in significant ways, creators of *Bus Stop*. But as an *auteur* screenwriter, Axelrod dominated all of them to create his own self-reflexive parody with a film that embodies both a comic distance from life and a compassionate embrace of it. *Bus Stop* encompasses a kind of ambivalent amorality that is a natural outgrowth of Axelrod's understanding of man's Janus-faced drives both to kill and to perpetuate himself. It took two years for Inge to forgive him for the transformations, the extrapolations, and the radical change of vision, but he finally conceded that it was a better movie than a play. "Bill said that *Bus Stop* should have been a movie. I mean, God meant that story to be a movie. A story about a rodeo cowboy, you know; it was a movie, not a play."

NOTES

1. All quotations from George Axelrod come from an interview the author had with him at his home on December 31, 1982.

2. For an elaboration of this argument, see Rudolph Arnheim, *Film as Art*, p. 22.

WORKS CITED

Arnheim, Rudolph. 1957. *Film as Art*. Berkeley: University of California Press.
Axelrod, George. 31 December 1982. Personal Interview.
———. 1971. *Where Am I Now—When I Needed Me?* New York: Viking Press.
Breton, Andre. 1966. *Anthologie de l'humour noir*. Paris: J. J. Pauvert.
Corliss, Richard. 1975. *Talking Pictures*. New York: Penguin Books.
Harrington, John. 1977. *Film and/as Literature*. Englewood Cliffs, N.J.: Prentice-Hall.
Inge, William. 1958. "Bus Stop." In *Four Plays by William Inge*. New York: Grove Press.

THE AUTHOR BEHIND THE AUTHOR: GEORGE CUKOR AND THE ADAPTATION OF *THE PHILADELPHIA STORY*

Gary L. Green

Previously the first concern of the film-maker was to disguise the theatrical origins of his model, to adapt it and to dissolve it in cinema. Not only does he seem to have abandoned this attitude, he makes a point of emphasizing its theatrical character. It could not be otherwise from the moment we preserve the essentials of the text.

André Bazin, *What Is Cinema?*

The Philadelphia Story (1940) fits squarely into what Gerald Mast defines as "the dialogue tradition" of film comedy, in which "the insight of the writers fused perfectly with the style and attitudes of the director, who expanded the sharp script into the full and final conception," a conception that had its source in "a unique aesthetic for destroying Hollywood assumptions while appearing to subscribe to them" (Mast 1979, pp. 249, 250). Of the many assumptions that characterized the Hollywood studio system, the almost guaranteed safety of the adaptation of a play to film was one of the most prevalent, one which George Cukor no doubt knew better than anyone working within the system. As a theatrical director, Cukor had been recruited to Hollywood at the advent of the sound era and subsequently became a director in the era of studio complacency over adaptation. After years of directing virtually word-for-word adaptations of plays, Cukor was perfectly primed to destroy the assumption about the relative ease of directing an adaptation, and *The Philadelphia Story* was the result of the urge to do so.

Because of his love for the theater, Cukor was always receptive to a script based on a play, for by working on such a project, he was in his true milieu, the world he knew best. In fact, of his 45 films, 22 are adapted directly from plays, and eight are actually set in the theater, not including the two pictures about the film industry, *What Price Hollywood* (1932) and *A Star Is Born* (1954).[1] Despite his working primarily with adaptations, Cukor was never constrained by them, as he makes clear in a 1970 interview with Gavin Lambert: "[The script] sustains me and frees me at the same time. . . . We all see things at a certain slant" (Lambert 1973, p. 14). This slant is precisely what defines

69

Cukor's success as an *auteur* of adapted material, a success clearly exemplified by *The Philadelphia Story*.[2]

Although Philip Barry's play, upon which the film is based, is an evening's worth of pleasant diversion, as evidenced by its success on Broadway, it is really nothing more than a strained comedy of manners, a form at which Barry seemed to excel. Gary Carey rightly describes the play, however, as purely an exercise "of a man with talent to amuse without the ability to make his audience care beyond the play's duration" (Carey 1971, p. 80). After having seen Katharine Hepburn's performance in *Holiday* (1938), a film directed by Cukor and itself adapted from a Barry play, the playwright approached Hepburn about the lead role in the play he was writing at the time, *The Philadelphia Story*. After hearing a basic summary of the plot, Hepburn eagerly agreed, and Barry set out to tailor the role of Tracy Lord exclusively for Hepburn. Tracy, the ice-goddess who stands in judgment of every character in the play, was the perfect role for Hepburn, who at the time had the reputation as "box office poison." For most filmgoers and critics in the late 1930s, Hepburn *was* Tracy Lord. Despite Barry's streamlining of Tracy, the role in the play is still relatively flat. After several laborious scenes in which Tracy manages to insult and alienate almost everyone on stage, she suddenly transforms herself into a warm and loving woman, due in large part to the rustic philosophy of Macauley Connor, the reporter/short-story writer. When finally she and ex-husband, Dexter Haven, are reunited at the end of the play, the manipulation in Barry's writing becomes all too obvious, and "the happy ending" comes off more as a cliché than as an organic result of the play's structure. Once outside the theater, no one in the audience really cares.

After Hepburn bought part interest in the play, including the film rights, she returned to Hollywood and convinced M-G-M to buy the property. She sold it, however, only under certain conditions: that she star, that Cukor (who had already directed her in four pictures) direct, that Donald Ogden Stewart write the script, and that she and Cukor have total control over the casting of the two male leads. Such a deal with an actor was certainly not part of the usual business practices of the studios, yet the *coup* Hepburn engineered granted almost total control of the project to Cukor, the only director Hepburn felt she could trust. This air of freedom that accompanied the production of *The Philadelphia Story* was the element that both sustained and freed Cukor's creativity, allowing him, in essence, to overthrow the conventions of the Hollywood dialogue comedy by making not only a film adaptation, but a self-reflexive film about writing and directing an adaptation.

Opening up a play for the screen was clearly the conventional approach to adaptation at the time of *The Philadelphia Story*, and even still is, but Cukor felt that an adaptation must be free to do more:

> "On the one hand you can't just turn out a photographed stage play; on the other hand, you can't rend the original property apart. If you don't preserve what was worthwhile in the original play when you create a different version of the material for the screen, you will suddenly find that you have nothing left. The trick is to subtly give the original play more movement on the screen that it had on the stage" (Phillips 1983, p. 36).

The success of this approach to adaptation rested, of course, with the screenwriter, whose work Cukor was quick to praise throughout his career, especially the script work of Donald Ogden Stewart.[3] To all appearances, Stewart's work on *The Philadelphia Story* should have been nothing more than "the gem-polishing of a gifted adapter" (xxiv), as Richard Corliss calls it, but the script is far more than that. Aside from rearranging some scenes, omitting and creating dialogue, and opening up the set, Stewart made one crucial change, one which illustrates perfectly Allardyce Nicoll's distinction between film and theater in terms of "film reality"; that is, "if the theater stands . . . for mankind . . . the cinema, because of the willingness on the part of the spectators to accept as the image of truth the moving forms cast on the screen, stands for the invidivual" (48). In eliminating the character of Sandy, Tracy's brother who appears in the play, Stewart added true dimension to the role of C. K. Dexter Haven, who becomes not only the truest individual in the film, but also the surrogate author-figure, one representing both screenwriter Stewart and director Cukor.

In the redesigned character of Dexter is located the fusion that Mast defines as the primary characteristic of dialogue comedy, for this new character is clearly the element in the script that both sustained and freed Cukor, allowing him to express his vision of life as well-produced theater, as performance, while at the same time pointing out the importance of the writer and director in the successful rendering of that vision. Dexter Haven, who stays primarily in the wings or on the fringes of both the action and the actual film frame, becomes the vehicle through which Cukor develops the vision, by consciously calling attention to the fact that *The Philadelphia Story* is filmed theater, a film in which we actually witness the scripting, production, and direction of a dialogue comedy, all through the point of view of Dexter, the writer- and director-figure. The end result is a film within a play and a play within a film, a double self-reflexive narrative form that comes together under the skillful hand of Cukor.

The nonverbal prologue to the film, which Cukor reveals he and Stewart designed *after* the film proper was finished, establishes the forthcoming structure and self-reflexive content of the picture. Dexter (Cary Grant) emerges from the front door of the Lord house carrying suitcases, followed almost immediately by Tracy (Hepburn) who holds his rack of pipes and bag of golf clubs. In the tradition of the romantic comedy, this opening leads the audience to the conclusion that Dexter is no doubt embarking on a working vacation and his loving wife is there to see him off. This assumption, however, is quickly undercut by Tracy's violent actions as she throws the pipes to the ground and grabs a golf club from the bag and breaks it over her knee, whereupon she spins around abruptly and marches back to the house. In a reversal of the opening shot, Dexter follows *her* this time, and after deciding not to act on his original instinct (to punch her in the face), he re-enacts the famous Cagney grapefruit-in-the-face routine (*sans* grapefruit) and pushes Tracy by the face into a sprawling pratfall.

This scene without dialogue seems somehow out of place in a dialogue comedy that rarely relies on slapstick, or at least not until Preston Sturges revived it in his great comedies of the 1940s. Yet, as Bazin points out, the origin of cinematic slapstick comedy, and actually of film itself, is in the theater, as the silent films of Keaton and Chaplin obviously remind us. Within the slapstick tradition, "the grafting together of cinema and comedy-theater happened spontaneously and has been so perfect that its fruit has always been accepted as the product of pure cinema" (Bazin 1967, p. 121), which is what Cukor and Stewart are stressing in the "silent" prologue to *The Philadelphia Story*. The scene returns to the roots of American film comedy in the theater, a point reinforced as action occurs both on a clearly defined stage (the front porch of the Lord house) and within the film frame (suggested by the front door, through which Dexter's slapstick revenge on Tracy is shot). Dexter's control of the stage is established at the outset, a control he will exercise throughout the film.

Dexter does not return in the film until after we learn what has occurred in his two-year absence, during which time, Tracy has secured a divorce from Dexter and is preparing to marry George Kittredge (John Howard), an Horatio Alger-type who wants to climb to the upper reaches of the American class system. Dexter has become a reformed alcoholic and has spent the years away from Tracy working in the Buenos Aires office of *Spy* magazine, a scandal sheet that relies more on pictures than words to satisfy its audience, and this reliance introduces the first motif of the self-reflexive film-within-a-film structure. *Spy*, which aptly describes the act of both the audience and the camera, is what sets the plot in motion, as Dexter agrees to cooperate in a blackmail scheme of the magazine's editor, Sidney Kidd (Henry Daniel), by covertly introducing Macauley Conner (James Stewart) and Liz Embry (Ruth Hussey), a staff writer and photographer, into the Lord house to cover what Kidd envisions as "the Philadelphia story," or more accurately an exposé of the frivolous life of the idle rich, of which Tracy's wedding will serve as a primary example. At this point, the film establishes Kidd as the writer of the scenario to follow; visually, however, Dexter will emerge as its true author.

Dexter's first appearance in the film after the prologue is again a silent one, as he follows behind and between Connor and Liz on their way to Kidd's office for their assignment. Dramatically, this shot appears to serve no function, but structurally it is critical, for it is a visual link to the prologue. In this scene, as in the first one, Dexter's control is manifested by his silence as Connor and Liz talk nonchalantly, completely unaware of his presence. Yet as we soon discover, Dexter is to become their director; he will assign them roles (as friends of Tracy's brother, Junius) in order to get them into the Lord house. And once they are inside, he will coach them on their performances. Their primary function, though, as he tells them, is to cover the wedding ceremony from as many angles as possible, with both words and pictures, or, essentially, they are to write a good script and convey it in pictures for the spectators of *Spy*.

The film's narrative emphasis shifts entirely at this point, toward the twofold stress on authorship (both Dexter's and Stewart's/Cukor's), which points to the power of the writer-director figure. Tracy, when faced with the prospect of having her wedding covered by *Spy*, declares in disgust, "Of all the filthy ideas, coming into a private home with a camera," which is, of course, the true function of the film author, and despite her successful destruction of Liz's camera, Cukor's camera remains, and it aligns itself firmly with Dexter's point of view. After establishing the motivation for his two principal actors (the director's function), Dexter again retreats into the wings, beyond the film frame, to coach the action silently, while the camera continues to invade the privacy just as if he were there.

A theatrical motif is introduced after Dexter reveals to Tracy the truth about Connor's and Liz's presence and their true roles as writer and photographer. Vowing to give them a "performance they'll never forget," Tracy retires to her bedroom to prepare for her part as the *terribly* sophisticated woman Connor and Liz will meet. Seated front and center in the parlor, the two unsuspecting reporters become an audience, a reversal of their original function. Enter stage right, Tracy's little sister, Dinah (Virginia Weidler), who first treats the two to a bilingual history of the Lord family and then to a burlesque show, capped off by a rousing rendition of "Lydia, the Tattooed Lady," preparing this "audience" for the comedy of manners that follows when Tracy makes her grand, sweeping entrance, again from stage right. Having exited from the door behind Connor and Liz, Dexter appears to have gone back stage, his directorial function having been utilized completely for the moment. Now the performers must carry off the production.

Dexter's services are again required in the next scene, when the plot becomes even more complicated as Uncle Willie (Roland Young) must suddenly shift roles and become Tracy's father. At the beginning of the scene, Dexter is seated off-camera, on the steps leading to the pool. However, when everyone becomes totally disoriented about who is who and how to react to this new plot twist, Dexter steps into the frame, onto the stage to attempt to sort out the conflict and reestablish the proper motivation for each character, verifying what he tells Tracy when she demands he leave. "I can't go, Red," he responds, "you need me too much." Working from the script in his head, Dexter refuses to leave until the production can be wrapped up to his satisfaction, and this will not happen until he leads Tracy to an understanding of her true essence as a human being, which in turn will allow him to engineer their remarriage at the end of the film.

Despite Dexter's smooth guiding hand in the events, he seems to have lost control as Tracy maintains her determination to marry Kittredge, an action in the plot that will severely undercut the happy ending Dexter has in his own script. Not surprisingly, it is Connor, the writer, who enables Dexter to rewrite the script, to regain control of the production. Sidney Kidd's exposé is suddenly inverted to become an exposé of Kidd himself, and this reversal removes the primary conflict in the blackmail plot. Because of his state of inebriation, Connor merely babbles about the facts that will lead to Kidd's downfall, while Dexter provides the real structure to the adaptation of Connor's story. Soon, he is the one dictating to Liz who types up his ideas to form the script that will release Kidd's stranglehold and simultaneously put Dexter, rather than Kittredge, at Tracy's side on her wedding day. Essentially, Dexter writes and directs what we come to see is the real Philadelphia story, a dialogue comedy of remarriage that appears to unfold of its own cinematic and theatrical volition, yet the presence of the author, Dexter, reveals just how staged the outcome actually is, as evidenced by the two final sequences of the film.[4]

The first sequence is set immediately after Connor has left Dexter's house to take a very drunk Tracy home. In a moment of boyish passion, he declares his love for her, which she temporarily accepts. His lines, however, are more or less revisions of what Dexter had earlier told Tracy—that she is a goddess, a queen, waiting for her prince who embraces the same impossibly high standards she does. Yet Connor reinterprets the lines, adding an emphasis on inner warmth, which Dexter had tried to convey to Tracy, but she was unwilling to accept the words from him. From Connor, however, she finds the essence of her character, what Dexter has wanted her to do all along. To celebrate the birth of this new Tracy, she insists on a purifying swim, almost in an attempt to leave the old Tracy behind and to emerge from the water as the woman she has discovered she can be. Again, though, Dexter steps in to handle the staging of this delicate situation, as Kittredge discovers what his bride-to-be has been up to in his absence. Even before Connor and Tracy make their entrance from the pool area, Kittredge is well on his way to drawing the worst conclusions, in spite of Dexter's attempts to prevent him from doing so. Instead, Kittredge chooses to follow Dexter's exasperated coaching: "All right," he tells Kittredge, "go ahead and think the worst," which is exactly what Kittredge does, and this fits quite conveniently into the scope of Dexter's script. The result is predictable as Kittredge waits for the moment to

punch Connor, but it is Dexter who steps in to do the job for
him, a critical moment when his directorial authority shifts from
that carried out behind the scenes or at the edge of the film
frame, to that which takes literal, physical control in changing
the action, forcefully adapting it to fit his own vision.

The vision reaches its fruition in the last sequence of the film
in which Tracy comes to the conclusion that she can't marry
Kittredge and that perhaps her feelings for Dexter have not
diminished in the two years they have been separated. She does
not come to this conclusion alone, however, for Dexter coaches
her with memories of "The True Love," the aptly named sailboat
he built for her as a wedding present, and which he gives her and
Kittredge earlier in the film in a much smaller size, again as a
wedding present. Feeding her the appropriate cues, Dexter
succeeds in creating the ending he has envisioned from the
moment of his reentrance into the film, for he has been unable to
forget what he has already confessed to Connor, "You might say
Miss Lord and I grew up together." Dexter has grown up
completely, and this is the experience and authority he brings to
his well-scripted transformation or adaptation of Tracy into a
warm and understanding adult.

In the climax of this scene, Tracy tells Kittredge she will not
marry him, which prompts the revelation of the true self-reflexive
nature of the film, opening with Kittredge's response to Tracy:

> Kittredge: "Possibly it's just as well."
> Dexter: "Yes, I thought you'd finally come to that conclusion."
> Kittredge: "I have a feeling you had more to do with this than anyone."
> Dexter: "Possibly, but you were a great help."

At this moment, Kittredge finally comes to realize his role in
Dexter's Philadelphia story, which indeed will be highlighted by
a wedding, but Kittredge will have no part. Once the self-
reflexive element of the film is revealed, Stewart and Cukor
exploit it for all its comic value, as Dexter moves closer to the
realization of his scripted happy ending. Now all he must do is
direct his own wedding.

When Tracy must explain to the wedding guests why she and
Kittredge will not be getting married, she forgets her lines, but
Dexter steps quickly to her aid. As Tracy stands framed in the
door leading to the parlor where the guests are assembled, she is
on stage to give the most convincing performance of her entire
social life. But she freezes and turns to her director for her cues,
and Dexter is right there, in the wings and in cinematic terms, he

is just beyond the film's frame, as he stands to the side of the door frame as the author/director, who, as Michel Foucault points out, "constitutes a principle of unity in writing where any unevenness of production is ascribed to changes caused by evolution, maturation, or outside influence" (Foucault 1978, p. 128), the function served by the film director. Unevenness certainly plagues Tracy's performance of Dexter's script, but Dexter provides the unity by telling her exactly what to say—that there will be a wedding after all. The expectations of the audiences (both that within and without the film) have been realized, but only because the scriptwriter and director of both Philadelphia stories allow this realization to come about.

A final irony awaits, though, as Cukor's directorial presence becomes intrusive in the very last shot of the film, usurping Dexter's authorship and putting it back in the director's chair, which sits to the side of the actual film frame. In the middle of the ceremony, Kidd reappears, with a camera, to finish the film he, in reality, instigated at the beginning. Dexter is not surprisingly more shocked than anyone, as his expression in the freeze frame indicates, for both he and we have been led to believe that Dexter has been in total control of this production. The last word, however, is Cukor's and not Dexter's, for the two freeze-frames before the end credits certainly do not fit into Dexter's vision. The wedding kiss in the final freeze is an incomplete one, in effect denying the audience the happy ending Dexter had in mind. Cukor will not give his surrogate author-figure the closing word; it is reserved for the revelation of the true authorship of the film. The author behind the author finally emerges.

Assessing the place of *The Philadelphia Story* in the history of film comedy and in terms of Cukor's career, Gavin Lambert claims that the film is "not only a very subtle, fluent adaptation of a play, it creates a genre all its own" (Lambert 1973, p. 119). This genre can perhaps best be described as a self-reflexive phase of dialogue comedy that emerges during the last years of the popularity of the screwball comedy in the late 1930s, a phase introduced by *The Philadelphia Story* and picked up in later films such as Hawks's *His Girl Friday* (1941), in which Cary Grant appears as a revamped Dexter Haven who writes and directs his reunion with Rosalind Russell; Lubitsch's *To Be or Not to Be* (1941), which is filled with a multilayered narrative concerned wholly with performance both on stage and in front of the camera; and Sturges's *Sullivan's Travels* (1942), which is oriented around virtually the same questions of authorship as Cukor's film, but in a much more obvious fashion. As the screwball comedy began to wear itself out, it had nowhere else to go but into the self-reflexive dialogue comedy tradition that would replace it in the 1940s.[5]

Gerald Mast's suggestion that Cukor's reliance on adaptations of plays makes him not "so psychologically perceptive as Hawks, so clever as Lubitsch, so parodic as Sturges, or so complex with structure as Wilder" (Mast 1979, pp. 278-79) begins to weaken when the very fusion Mast himself describes as the definitive element of dialogue comedy, in the case of *The Philadelphia Story*, the meshing of Stewart's and Cukor's sensibilities, resulted in the film that calls attention to itself as an adaptation within an adaptation, theater within film, and a film within a film, all three of which are regulated by the author (Stewart/Cukor) behind the author (Dexter). Within the very theatricality of *The Philadelphia Story*, Cukor pays homage to the roots of his artistic vision, reminding us, as Susan Sontag notes, that "cinematic virtue does not reside in the fluidity or the positioning of the camera nor in the mere frequency of the change of shots."

> Whether derived from plays or not, films with complex or formal dialogue, films in which the camera is static or in which the action stays indoors, are not necessarily theatrical. *Per contra*, it is no more part of a putative "essence" of movies that the camera must rove over a large physical area, than it is that movies ought to be silent (Cawelti 1985, pp. 345-46).

The "essence" of film for Cukor is in the word, the common denominator between theater and film and between the screenwriter/adapter and director, an essence he exploits lovingly in *The Philadelphia Story*. His camera remains stationary, indeed, appearing merely to film the theater of life, which is possible only because of the words and the director who turns the words into action, as both Cukor and Dexter do.

The major heresy of filmed theater, writes André Bazin, is "namely the urge 'to make cinema,'" a heresy deeply seated in "an inferiority complex in the presence of an older and more literary art, for which the cinema proceeds to overcompensate by the 'superiority' of its technique—which is in turn mistaken for an aesthetic superiority" over the theater, a heresy that has long governed theories of film authorship, shoving directors such as George Cukor into the background as merely skillful adapters, yet lest we forget the essence of cinema is in reality in the theater, *The Philadelphia Story* serves as a reminder that authorship is indeed common to both forms. Calling attention to this fact, as Cukor does so brilliantly, is perhaps the truest mark of pure cinema.

NOTES

1. The films adapted from plays are too numerous to mention here. For the best filmography, see Gene Phillips, *George Cukor* (Boston: Twayne, 1983). The eight films that feature the theater as a major setting are *Rockabye* (1932), *Sylvia Scarlett* (1936), *Zaza* (1939), *A Double Life* (1947), *The Actress* (1953), *Les Girls* (1957), *Heller in Pink Tights* (1960), and *Let's Make Love* (1960).

2. See Andrew Sarris's essay on Cukor in *The American Cinema* (New York: Dutton, 1968).

3. Stewart had written four scripts for Cukor up to the time of *The Philadelphia Story* and would write three more for him after. Cukor confessed his fondness and admiration for Stewart's talent and ranked him among the best of the writers with whom he had the opportunity to work. See Gavin Lambert, *On Cukor* (New York: Capricorn, 1973).

4. Stanley Cavell's essay on *The Philadelphia Story* in *Pursuits of Happiness* (1981) notes a similar function of Dexter Haven, but Cavell maintains that Dexter's authority is necessary for the propagation of a Utopian vision of America.

5. In "*Chinatown* and Generic Transformation in Recent American Films," John Cawelti notes that when any genre reaches its limits of development, it begins to transform itself in a number of ways, one of which is self-reflexivity. See *Film Theory and Criticism*, 3rd ed., Gerald Mast and Marshall Cohen (New York: Oxford, 1985), 503-520.

WORKS CITED

Bazin, Andre. 1967. "Theater and Cinema—Part Two." In *What is Cinema?* Vol. 1. Translated by Hugh Gray. Berkeley: University of California Press.

Carey, Gary. 1971. *Cukor & Co.* New York: Museum of Modern Art.

Cavell, Stanley. 1981. *Pursuits of Happiness: The Hollywood Comedy of Remarriage.* Cambridge: Harvard University Press.

Cawelti, John. 1985. "*Chinatown* and Generic Transformation in Recent American Films." In *Film Theory and Criticism: Introductory Readings.* 3rd ed. Edited by Gerald Mast and Marshall Cohen. New York: Oxford University Press. 503-20.

Corliss, Richard. 1975. *Talking Pictures.* New York: Penguin.

Foucault, Michel. 1978. *Language, Counter-Memory, Practice.* Ithaca: Cornell University Press.

Lambert, Gavin. 1973. *On Cukor.* New York: Capricorn.

Mast, Gerald. 1979. *The Comic Mind.* Chicago: University of Chicago Press.

Nicoll, Allardyce. 1936. *Film and Theatre.* New York: Crowell.

Phillips, Gene. 1983. *George Cukor.* Boston: Twayne.

Sarris, Andrew. 1968. *The American Cinema.* New York: Dutton.

Sontag, Susan. 1966. "Film and Theatre." In *Film Theory and Criticism.* 3rd ed. 340-55.

"NUR SCHAUSPIELER": SPECTACULAR POLITICS, *MEPHISTO*, AND *GOOD*

Harriet Margolis

In 1981, when István Szabó's *Mephisto* won the Academy Award for Best Foreign Film, attention was automatically drawn to Klaus Mann's 1936 novel, on which the film is based. *Mephisto's* protagonist is an actor, Hendrik Höfgen, who collaborates with the Nazis. In Mann's novel, he stands condemned for his selfish egotism, his overwhelming vanity, and, above all, his lack of conviction, which Mann attributes to his being an actor. In Szabó's film, Höfgen is not exactly whitewashed, but extenuating circumstances are argued: Höfgen, like all twentieth-century intellectuals and artists, is to some extent the victim of historical pressures.

The analysis of collaboration and the questions of collective and individual guilt that such an analysis raises have been a staple of twentieth-century art since the rise and fall of Italian and German fascism. In 1981, for example, C. P. Taylor opened a successful play in London called *Good*, which, not unlike *Mephisto*, shows the gradual downfall of a decent, talented individual who succumbs to the Nazi attraction. Even *Zelig*, according to Woody Allen, is based on "the idea of a chameleonlike personality" who gives up his "own personality so [he] can be part of the crowd—an attitude that, carried to an extreme, leads to fascism" (James 1986, p. 27). Despite their disparities, these works share a curiosity about how the individual becomes implicated in an overwhelmingly negative collective phenomenon.

When art addresses an issue like collaboration, its subject matter alone enters it into a debate associated with the names of Plato and Aristotle on the general relation between art and society. Mann focuses our attention on a particular facet of this debate, a subsidiary argument on the politics of representation, because his protagonist is an actor, who is furthermore modeled on an historically specific individual—Gustaf Gründgens, Mann's ex-brother-in-law. The extensive use of the arts for mass propaganda purposes, made possible by their increasingly sophisticated media, is a twentieth-century phenomenon. That

Mephisto's protagonist loans his artistic talents to the propaganda industry focuses the debate's attention on the artist's relation to ideology and ideologically determined representations. To the extent that *Mephisto* portrays the harm to society that an actor may cause, Mann's novel supports Plato's call to banish the artist. When the novel is brought to life on the screen, Szabó's visually striking images and Klaus Maria Brandauer's scintillating performance foreground the sort of harm an actor might do, for the twentieth century's awareness of the power of images is almost as great as its worship of stars.

On the other hand, works like *Good*, Szabó's *Mephisto*, and even aspects of Mann's novel support Aristotle's side of the debate because their authors hope the educational efficacy of their artistic production will beneficially affect society as a whole. *Good* and Szabó's film, as spectacles, come to life because of a pattern of interaction between performer and spectator that gives the performer a limited influence over the spectator. Through this medium, the Aristotelians argue, art can teach and inspire; their presumption is that truly good art will teach and inspire that which is good. In this tradition, through their presentation of an individual's reaction to a major contemporary crisis, Taylor's play and Szabó's film hope to evoke a collective and individual self-evaluation; at the very least, Mann's work asks for judgment. In so doing, these works follow the pattern of Greek tragedies as well as the Medieval and Renaissance morality plays.

Good's protagonist, a character named Halder, is a professor of literature, hence the intellectual par excellence. He also resembles another type, the classic Everyman. Unlike Everyman, though, Halder's ultimate rescue from evil by God is a most uncertain matter, for Taylor disallows the hope of rescue by God or by any other external force. At best, Taylor suggests, the possibility exists that individuals will choose well, that they will perhaps even be willing to forsake the good life in order to live a good life. Halder, however, is seduced by the Nazi incarnation of evil, philosophizing and equivocating every step of the way. He is more complex and self-conscious than the original flat-figured protagonists of the early morality plays, but the kinship remains.

Owing more than its title alone to *Faust*, *Mephisto* belongs with *Good* in this morality play tradition. Each work honors the family ties by treating good and evil as clearly recognizable, incarnate forces and by arguing mankind's relation to sin. Szabó and Taylor play on the dramatic potential of each moral dilemma experienced by their protagonists, because each conflict indulges the audience's desire to be reassured against evil. Will Halder/ Höfgen sell out his friend, his cause, his profession, his family? With each new problem, the audience yearns for the protagonist to make the right choice.

By denying reassurance that the protagonist will make the right choice and that therefore the audience too, if only vicariously, will make the right choice, Szabó and Taylor force the audience to consider carefully problems it might prefer to ignore. In combination with Mann's novel, these works challenge the audience to judge its own merits, individually and as a society. They embody Aristotle's response to Plato: "Art and literature give an imperative visibility to human problems which would otherwise remain in dark and spendthrift chaos" (Steiner 1986, p. 12). As an artist who believed that literature is "the comprehensive expression of human experiences" (Klaus Mann 1984, p. 117), Mann had necessarily to agree with Aristotle on art's potentially beneficial effects.

Nevertheless, Mann condemned the German film and theater world for reneging on its responsibilities. He argued that by staying in Germany and continuing to act, these artists supported the Nazis, despite the fact that they not only thought of themselves as apolitical but of art as existing in a vacuum (a position that Mann himself had once held). According to David Hull's history of Nazi cinema, though, bona fide Nazis in the industry were rare. The Weimar film and theater world leaned towards the fashionable Left, and when the Nazis took power this world remained a source "of limited resistance to the government" (Hull 1969, p. 7). Perhaps this is why, although aimed at a corrupt society, *Mephisto* must settle for a boomeranging attack on the weaknesses of individuals.

Upon its intitial appearance—after being printed in Holland, and smuggled into a Germany that banned its author (Hull 1969, pp. 91-92)—*Mephisto's* realistic account of real people produced near-mortal effects.[1] Mann wrote from the perspective of a political exile, working against the hated regime that controlled his homeland. Even if, as he implied in a disclaimer added only to the German edition of his novel, *Mephisto* was not directed against Gründgens specifically, it was certainly a missile aimed at the Nazi government, and it was recognized as such upon its initial appearance.[2] He had hoped to influence humanity en bloc with his art; instead, Mann threatened individuals with his gossip.

Removed from the context of immediate events, Szabó's
Mephisto is an adaptation; historical and textual fidelity matter
less than the universal issues evoked by Mann's work. Without
Mann's emotional investment in Gustaf Gründgens, Szabó avails
himself of typical rather than specific characteristics of
Gründgens's fictional embodiment, the actor Hendrik Höfgen. In
this, Szabó follows Aristotle's advice, but he is also the product of
historical materialism, and so he goes beyond Mann's concern
with one individual to stress the individual in relation to society
and history.

For example, had Gründgens had access to the international
acting opportunities that *Mephisto's* international éclat has
afforded Klaus Maria Brandauer,[3] many lives might have been
different. Not just an actor, not just Klaus Mann's brother-in-law,
Gründgens was also *Intendant*, or Director, of the State Theater
in Berlin during the Nazi regime. Effectively, he was "the leader
of theatrical life in the Third Reich" (Klaus Mann 1977, p. [5]),
and as such his image as a public figure took on an existence of
its own. If Gründgens is known in this country at all, it is for a
minor part in Fritz Lang's *M* (1931), for his interpretation of
Mephistopheles in *Faust*, and for his connection with Klaus
Mann. In Germany, though, he had a real social importance for
decades, even after the Second World War, and in practical terms,
he played a greater role in his country's cultural life than Klaus
Mann could claim.

Because he stayed rather than emigrate, however, Gründgens's
opposition to the Nazis was questioned. He answered that five
dependents lived in his Berlin household (including his parents
and sister), and that therefore he had to stay. Because he
continued to act, to harvest the rewards of staying, his support
for the Nazis was argued. He redistributed part of that wealth by
paying the salaries of employees he hired at the State Theater
who were unacceptable to the government and by providing food
and other necessities in the last years of the war when his artistic
colleagues were hardest hit. Once Gründgens became *Intendant*,
though, he and his support for the Nazis were condemned. As
Intendant, however, according to Gründgens, he could work to
salvage a remarkable theatrical tradition; he could do what he
could towards protecting the German theater from Nazi contami-
nation.[4] While he was about it, he used his various offices to
protect himself, his family and friends, and as many theatrical
artists as possible, from the Nazi regime and the more general
ravages of war.

Clearly, Gründgens was a collaborator, and yet he is not the clearcut case Mann presents him to be.[5] He may have acted always out of vanity and yet he often accomplished much good. Mann has Höfgen's wife, Barbara, exclaim in exile that every effort against the enemy is worthwhile, that every "millimeter" counts (208). Gründgens, after all, saved real lives, ameliorated the day-to-day deprivations of real lives. In these terms he is less to be condemned than Mann himself.

One reason for writing *Mephisto*, according to Mann, was that he thought it "necessary to expose and analyze the abject type of the treacherous intellectual who prostitutes his talent for the sake of some tawdry fame and transitory wealth" (Klaus Mann 1984, p. 282). He has Sebastian, his alter ego in the novel, condemn Höfgen because "he's always lying and he never lies.... He believes everything and he believes nothing. He is an actor" (Klaus Mann 1984, p. 130). Actors, in other words, lack all conviction.[6]

The difference is subtle, but when Szabó presents Höfgen as "highly ambivalent about what he is doing," it amounts almost to an exoneration rather than a condemnation. Both versions of *Mephisto* end with Höfgen's desperate cry that he is "only an actor." In the novel, Höfgen sobs into his mother's lap, retreating from his worldly responsibilities. Szabó has Höfgen, blinded and bewildered by Göring's floodlights, cry his declaration of ordinariness into an echoingly empty Nuremberg stadium. He suggests that Höfgen has an epiphany, a sudden realization

> that his pact with the Devil has brought him to the point where he cannot distinguish between reality and role. Or perhaps the role has become so overpowering that he must flee the stage. Or perhaps it is just the horrible glare of evil blinding him into the truth. (Hughes 1982, p. 16)

The implied comparison with Oedipus lifts Höfgen's story from the realm of a novel about a career (as Mann subtitled his work) to that of grand tragedy. It also points to allegorical elements of Szabó's message.

Mephistopheles, after all, is Goethe's representation of evil; as Gründgens/Höfgen plays him, he is a charming fellow, "highly complex, contradictory, and mercurial" (Erika and Klaus Mann 1940, p. 41)—above all, seductive. Mephisto, according to Mann, is the "typically German character," but according to Szabó, "the Germans were seduced by the Mephisto-consciousness. And this applies to other nations as well. The trick is to give people the appearance of security." Thus Szabó's "film is, among other things, about the ability to be seduced" (Hughes 1982, p. 15). In this light (the glaring light of that empty Nuremberg stadium), Höfgen's epiphany is a hopeful sign to the audience, that, however late it may be, it is never too late to attain consciousness, to see things clearly and to recognize evil for what it is.

History does not justify such hopefulness, though, as Taylor acknowledges in his play. The whole premise of *Good* is nevertheless that each individual can make a difference, that society stands or falls on the integrity of its individual members. Taylor speaks of the "lessons to be learned" from the "atrocities of the Third Reich" (Taylor 1982, p. 7), and suggests that if we do not learn these lessons we are doomed to obliterate ourselves through nuclear war. Szabó wants to know how the artist can "prende parte alla storia" (De Marchi 1977, p. 3); for himself he has chosen to "raccontare storie che raggiungano il piú alto numero possibile di spettatori" (De Marchi 1977, p. 3).

Perhaps *this* explains Szabó's emphasis on Höfgen's ambivalence, as though by stressing "the relationship between history and the individual"[7] Szabó can prevent a reductive perception of humans as being always either entirely good or entirely evil. This ambivalence suggests choice, and with choice comes the possibility of change. Szabó's sympathy for Höfgen is clear:

> In the end, things become too complex for him. Before . . . he lived for nothing but success. And now he has it, but is suddenly overwhelmed by the fire and brimstone of these terrifying spotlights that Goering, with demonic childishness, playfully shoots at him from every direction. (Hughes 1982, p. 16)

Szabó pictures a weak individual, flawed to be sure, beleaguered by forces larger than himself, and for this reason the Hungarian director concludes that Höfgen is no more evil than the rest of us.

In considering Höfgen's choices and comparing his situation with that of Gründgens, we enact Aristotle's justification for art and the artist. Plato, however, has yet to be heard, so let us turn now from art's useful effects to the harm it may cause through its agent, the actor.

Good faces the horror of collaboration through the eyes of a fictional participant who gradually realizes that his public actions no longer agree with the private image he harbors of himself. Like *Mephisto* the film and *Mephisto* the novel, *Good* uses the Nazi era in Germany as an emblem for evil incarnate and to stage an artistic discussion on individual responsibility faced by such evil. What is more, *Good*, like Szabó's *Mephisto*, takes as its subject an attractive intellectual who is seduced by Nazi power. Because such a protagonist "raises the horrible enigma of collaboration for current-day audiences" (Hughes 1982, p. 13), traditional identification with the protagonist turns into a potentially uncomfortable process of soul-searching. Szabó expressly desired such a reaction. Responding to criticism that he excised the real and novelistic sexual "perversions" of Höfgen/Gründgens, Szabó replied that he

> wanted the audience to identify with the hero of this film. . . . I wanted to evoke a collective sense of questioning among my audience: could they make the same mistakes, could they submit to evil in the same way . . . [sic] To achieve this goal, we could not have a hero who would divert attention into another area. . . . I didn't want to give people the chance to say, "This man is collaborating with the Nazis because he is a pervert and a fetishist; and since I am not a pervert and fetishist, I could not collaborate with the Nazis." (Hughes 1982, p. 17)

Identification, in contemporary film studies, focuses attention on the actor and on the influence that the actor can exert over the audience. This power is explained in terms of the politics of representation, or the persuasive power of images to modify our behavior. The discourse around the politics of representation analyzes the hegemonic control of the masses through ideological tools that not only persuade the masses to conform, but persuade them that they *want* to conform to the dominant model. "Spectacular politics," in this context, assumes that the image derives its power from the medium involved, the strength of the narrative, and the attraction of the star, among other factors.

A star, among other things, is an actor whose image has attained a certain power: the power to attract audiences predictably. One source of this power is the relationship between performer and spectator, which submits the spectator to passively experiencing events vicariously through the actor. When the performer enacts a character, the spectator is limited to that character's fixed (because necessarily consistent) point of view. Some author creates that point of view, making it that much further removed from the spectator's immediate experience. This relationship raises certain questions—overtly in Mann's and Szabó's works and discreetly in Taylor's play—about the moral status of the actor, or *Schauspieler*. More closely examined, how do we define an actor?

In German or in English it is possible to substitute *Spieler* or *player* for the word *actor*. For this aspect of the profession alone,

Plato held the actor in ill-repute. As though foreseeing the popularity of Mephistophelian figures, Plato notes (in Iris Murdoch's paraphrase) that "it is easier to copy a bad man than a good man, because the bad man is various and entertaining and extreme, while the good man is quiet and always the same (Murdoch 1977, p. 6). This makes Plato object that, being more likely to portray evil than good, art adds "to the sum of badness in the world." At best, art imitates the real, and thus the actor produces only shadows of the real. "Surely any serious man would rather produce real things, such as beds or political activity, than unreal things which are mere reflections of reality" (Murdoch 1977, p. 6). Perhaps, but can we really distinguish the "serious man" from the actor?

One of Gründgens's biographers cites Shakespeare: "All the world's a stage, and all the men and women merely players." Taylor's play makes the world a stage, the world of small individuals crushed by large events. The questions these actors confront on stage in their guises as characters are not unlike the questions the audience confronts throughout life as individuals. The artist, in this case at least, is thus no less serious, no less responsible, than any other individual. In fact, perhaps because of early theater's origins in religious ritual, actors are often held to be even more responsible. We expect actors to perform, to *represent* (or *personate*, as the OED would have it) the actions of *other* humans within an acknowledged environment[8] before an audience. Like a priest, the actor intervenes between the spectator and experience.

Gründgens, observers seem agreed, devoted a singleminded attention to the theater bordering upon worship. If his personal life was unsatisfactory, at night he received the audience's love and applause. If his personal life was chaotic, at night he found order on the stage: "Wenn ich auf der Bühne stehe, dann weiss ich, bei einem bestimmten Stichwort geht die Tür auf, und eine Frau kommt herein, die hat ein grünes Kleid an und sagt 'Guten Abend!' Was weiss man schon im Leben?" (Riess 1965, p. 62). His natural conclusion was that if the theater provided the order that was lacking in his everyday life, then his everyday life should be given over to the theater. And so, according to one of his biographers, "Gründgens war immer Schauspieler, auch ausser-halb des Bühnengeschehens. . . . Er selbst hatte nichts dagegen, für einen (Lebens-)Spieler gehalten zu werden. Er fand diese (Lebens-)Rolle sogar recht amüsant. . . . Sein Leben war acting, ein immerwährendes Spiel" (Goertz 1982, p. 8). For Gründgens,

the world and the stage were indeed synonymous; his defenders
can argue that he performed equally well before either backdrop.

Gründgens was not alone in the effort to impose an external
order on a chaotic life lived in a world perceived to be
fragmenting. Michael Holquist argues that many English mystery
novelists in the late twenties and early thirties tried similarly to
create on paper a reassuringly rational world that they could
superimpose over a threateningly multidimensional twentieth-
century world. Ironically, Gründgens's initial stardom came with
roles made possible by a growing audience for criminal fiction,
an audience amenable to less than honorable, less than noble,
protagonists.[9] In the early years Gründgens often found himself
compelled by financial need to play roles he disliked. The Nazis
made him wealthy, but they too had ways of forcing him to take
an unwelcome part. The worst of these was in *Ohm Krüger*; he
managed to avoid contact with *Jud Süss* through the power of his
office as *Intendant*.

Gründgens's anecdotes suggest that he recognized the resemblance between the Nazis and the questionable characters he often
played on stage and screen.[10] The best-known image from Szabó's
film may be a widely distributed publicity still, showing Höfgen,
still dressed in his black cape and white mask, shaking hands
with Göring (played by Rolf Hoppe), who is congratulating the
actor on his performance as Mephistopheles in Goethe's *Faust*. In
the novel, this scene occurs in a chapter entitled "The Pact with
the Devil," in which one also finds the following passage in
which Mann argues Höfgen's responsibility for the damage that
the latter's image has done:

> The first news that met Hendrik in Paris was the burning of the Reichstag.
> His long experience as a player of villains . . . left him in no doubt as to who
> had contrived and committed the outrage. Precisely those films and plays in
> which Hendrik liked to star had inspired the infamous, and at the same time
> infantile, cunning of the Nazis. . . . Without wanting to admit as much, he
> felt for the first time a mysterious connection between his own nature and the
> appalling mentality that could instigate such base acts as the burning of the
> Reichstag. (Klaus Mann 1977, p. 159)

This falls just short of accusing Gründgens of direct responsibility for the Reichstag fire, an absurd charge on the face of it, and
one that I can explain only with reference to the politics of
representation. If Gründgens "inspired the infamous," it was
because the glamor and fortune associated with the star's public
image validated the otherwise negative characters he so often
played.

Gründgens, of course, was just playing roles, roles that, let us remember, were written by various authors. Actors, artists in general, create worlds that do not exist, "arrogate to themselves, by imitative sleight of hand, a knowledge which they do not possess. Their imaginings are irresponsible because they entail no consequence in personal action" (Plato again, this time through the voice of George Steiner [Steiner 1986, p. 12]). These worlds and this knowledge evoke Bacon's Idols, or false illusions taken for real tings. Among the ways our perception may be deflected from the real, the Idols of the Theater seem especially pertinent.

Bacon describes these Idols of the Theater as "but so many stage-plays, representing worlds of their own creation after an unreal and scenic fashion" (35). Identification first with the character as well as with the star draws the spectator into these fictitious worlds. The ideological perspective apparent in the worlds that are represented, it can be argued, affects the individual's own particular perspective. Even if this artistic perspective is benign, its enabling mechanism is not. To quote Plato through Steiner again,

those who bestow on fictions . . . intense emotions . . . are dissipating those dynamics of consciousness which are vitally required for the right conduct of life in the city-state. The cry in the street becomes far less real to us, far less exigent of adequate response (and all true responsibility implies response), than does the scream in the tragedy which we are reading, in the novel, on the television screen. The imagination of the author, our facile entry into the warming grandeur of that imagination [—these things] debilitate. They devour, hence diminish, our resources for just perception and for the responsibility of the deed. (Steiner 1986, p. 12)

When the pattern of perspectives remains constant long enough, when the exposure to the pattern is frequent enough, the spectator cannot help but be affected, however immediate and impermanent the effect may be.

When Gründgens himself considered the stereotypical villains he had played, he spoke of their damage, not to his career (which they in fact made), but to his sensibilities, and to his image. "Ich bin manchmal ganz verblüfft," he said, "wie wenig das Bild, das man von mir hat, mit dem Bild, dass ich von mir habe, zusammenpasst," and he credited this discrepancy to "die Rollen, die das Bild von mir verfälschen." These, he claimed were the only roles he disliked (Gründgens 1967, p. 339). Not surprisingly, he did not speak of the potential harm that these roles may have done society, on the basis of which Mann could argue that Gründgens, through his stardom and through the roles which he played, contributed to the downfall of German society.

In one of Mann's autobiographical anecdotes, he addresses the criticism that his proper place as an enemy of the Nazis was at home in Germany fighting from within. Gründgens specifically compared the Manns' exile with his own case and concluded that, among other reasons, he was justified in staying because outside Germany he would have become only another helpless mouth to feed. Mann repeatedly acknowledged the blow that loss of one's native tongue must be for language-dependent artists. He himself was one of the few immigrant artists to achieve native fluency in a foreign language, helped, to be sure, by his early traveling opportunities, which were in turn facilitated by family connections. A key scene in both versions of *Mephisto* poignantly refers to the problem, but, like the industrious ant to the cricket, suggests that the artist should have prepared sooner. The great German-Jewish stage and film star, Elisabeth Bergner, did in fact carefully learn English in the years immediately before the Nazi takeover. When her fictional counterpart, Dora Martin, tells Höfgen that her future is set, that she has a contract in London, he unfortunately can only reply: "Ich brauche die deutsche Sprache." For Gründgens, whose initial, hard-fought success coincided with the coming of sound to film, acting outside German-speaking countries was not a happy prospect.[11]

Mann himself at one point advises the artist to "become addicted [to the theatre] as to a drug" (Klaus Mann 1984, p. 117). This advice sounds very much like a call to renounce the outside world for some more sequestered relation to reality—that for which Mann criticized Gründgens. When he switches from the theater to literature, though, Mann "stresse[s] the political responsibility of the man of letters." He admits that he himself "found it tiresome and depressing to delve into these matters in a sober and detailed way. Instead of facing the issue[s] squarely and tackling them realistically, I contented myself, in most of my political statements, with vague complaints and even vaguer suggestions" (Klaus Mann 1984, p. 168). It is hard, Mann must acknowledge, to satisfy one's responsibilities both as an artist and as a man of experience.

Occasionally Mann acknowledges that Höfgen might be merely the representation rather than the incarnation of evil. Sebastian's definition of the actor, however, resembles Mann's description of Mephistopheles, the Faustian incarnation of evil. Whether the actor, like Mephistopheles, should be considered a force for evil may depend upon personal standards. In relation to the spectator,

Mephisto—the force of evil—and the actor—Mann's representative of evil—do bear comparison: each presents a multifaceted
facade and a false perspective that lulls the spectator into a sense
of security.

It is hard, though, after learning how deeply embedded in
historical specificities it is, to read Mann's novel outside its
context in abstract terms. Its status as art, according to Aristotle's
definitions, is questionable. It looks, instead, like "a polemically
hateful portrait," as Szabó called it (Hughes 1982, p. 18). Still, in
the heat of battle it is easy and probably necessary to see people
in black and white terms. The unreproachability demanded by
Plato and Mann is unrealistic, more characteristic of the morality
play's flat figures than the rounded characters preferred by Szabó
and Taylor. Szabó and Taylor, on the other hand, have the
luxury of the philosopher, to consider things in hypothetical
terms. Ironically, although Szabó argues for consideration of
historical influences on individual behavior, it is his freedom
from the direct pressures of immediate events that permits him
this luxury.

Mann subtitled his autobiography *Thirty-five Years in This
Century*; the events of those years that formed his life will
overshadow the rest of this century. To quote George Steiner one
last time:

> The barbarism of the 20th century has given a new edge to [Plato's] challenge
> [to banish the artist]. Too many are the butchers and clerks of totalitarian
> rule who, in their personal and private lives, respond with cultured delight
> and genuine sentiments to the claims of fiction and the arts. We know now
> that a man can torture in the afternoon and be moved to truthful tears by
> Schubert or by Pushkin at nightfall (Steiner 1986, p. 12)

That man, however, was not Gründgens, just as, to the extent
that *Mephisto* expresses Mann's personal vengeance on
Gründgens, it is not art.

What Mann's portrait of Gründgens deemphasizes is self-
consciousness; for Gründgens was too intelligent and too talented
not to be self-conscious. It is this self-consciousness, this self-
awareness, that Mann denies Höfgen and that Szabó adds to the
character and that in some ways makes *Good*, with its unrelated
protagonist, the most thoughtful analysis of Gründgens's
character after all. And it is this self-consciousness and this self-
awareness that *Good* and the two *Mephisto*s provoke in us, their
readers and spectators, that finally refutes Plato and redeems the
artist. It may be, as Steiner notes, that self-consciousness does not
lead inevitably to good behavior; without it, though, we can *only*

hope for the natural selection of good over evil. In the twentieth
century, such a hope seems hazardous at best.

NOTES

1. "Das Erscheinen von Klaus Manns "Mephisto" in der Mitte der dreissiger
Jahre hatte eine schlimme Folge. Die Person von Erich Zacharias-Langhans, der
bis dahin unbehelligt geblieben war, gelangte durch diesen Roman ins
Scheinwerferlicht der Gestapo. . . . Als GG hörte, dass der langjährige Freund und
Mitarbeiter bereits ineiner Gestapo-Zelle sass, stellte er Göring folgendes
Ultimatum: wenn Langhans nicht frei käme, sähe, er, Gründgens, sich
ausserstande, weiterzuspielen. Dies war nun wahrlich keine einfache Situation für
Göring. Zwar war ihm Langhans und sein weiteres Schicksal völlig gleichgültig,
aber Gründgens wollte er nicht verlieren. Er liess sich also Langhans vorführen,
der, von zwei Gestapo-Beamten begleitet, erschien. Auch GG war bei dieser
Vorführung anwesend. Göring hielt eine grosse Rede—er schrie so sehr, dass GG
das Schlimmste befürchten musste—, in der er ausführte, Menschen wie Langhans
seien nicht wert, in Deutschland zu leben, und er verweise ihn daher sofort des
Landes. Wenn er nicht innerhalb von vierundzwanzig Stunden die Grenze
überschritten habe, würde er verhaftet und für immer eingesperrt werden" (Riess
1965, p. 156).

2. "Alle Personen dieses Buches stellen Typen dar, nicht Porträts" (Klaus
Mann 1981, p. 399) appears only in the German edition and was added at the
original publisher's instigation in order to forestall litigation over the similarity
between Hendrik Höfgen and Gustaf Gründgens (Gründgens 1967, pp. 18-20).
Roughly translated, the phrase means that all characters in the book represent
types rather than portraits. Predictably, the disclaimer met with disbelief, and the
book experienced a tumultous publishing history that only recently saw its legally
sanctioned appearance in West Germany.

The double banning of *Mephisto's* publication—first in Nazi Germany and
then postwar West Germany—resulted largely from Gründgens's direct and
indirect power to prevent that publication. (Gründgens forced the expurgation of
Mann's German edition of *The Turning Point* by threatening "a boycott of the S.
Fischer theater series" [Gründgens 1967, p. 11]). According to some observers,
Mann took his publisher's freedom to present *Mephisto* to the German public as a
symptom of that society's health. Mann's suicide in 1949 has even been attributed
to his bitter disappointment that postwar Germany had changed so little.

3. Brandauer and Szabó made another, less successful film, *Colonel Redl*, on
themes similar to those in *Mephisto*. Brandauer has also appeared in a James
Bond film, *Never Say Never Again*, and in the recently released *Out of Africa*.

4. *Meyers Enzyklopädisches Lexikon* states that "als Generalintendant des
Preuss. Staatstheaters (1937-1945) versuchte er, das Theater gegen direkte polit.
Zugriffe des Nationalsozialismus abzuschirmen." The Manns themselves quote a
friend remaining in Nazi Germany as saying that "'the most bearable productions
are at the Berliner Staatstheater. At any rate there's a producer there who knows
his job—Gustaf Gründgens'. We both burst out laughing," they write in *The
Other Germany* (Erika and Claus Mann 1940, p. 111).

5. In *Gründgens: Schauspieler, Regisseur, Theaterleiter*, K. H. Ruppel
reminisces about speculation on Gründgens motives: "Wir fragten uns, was einen
intellektuellen, hochsensiblen und nervösen Schauspieler, einen Regisseur von
artistisch perfekter Formbetontheit wie Gustaf Gründgens bewogen haben mochte,

sich im Bewusstsein dieser Diktatur und in der Erkenntnis ihrer unvermeidlichen Konsequenzen an die Spitze ihres (mindestens nach seinem Ruf und Rang inder Vergangenheit) exponiertesten Theaters zu stellen. Dass er der nazistischen Kunstideologie von Natur und Charakter aus feind sein musste, wussten wir. Dass er als Retter des deutschen Theaters auftreten wollte, dafür hielten wir ihn für zu unpathetisch. Dass er Glanz auf sich ziehen wollte, der in rings hereinbrechender Verdüsterung billig zu haben war, widersprach seiner Distinktion und seinem Geschmack. Schliesslich fanden wir einen Zug heraus, der uns einen Schlüssel zu dem psychologischen Problem zu bieten schien—eine Eigenart, die schon früh bei Gründgens hervorgetreten war und seine Karriere als Schauspieler schon in den zwanziger Jahren mitbestimmt hatte: Seine Lust am riskanten Spiel" (Rischbieter 1963, pp. 17-18).

6. Mann's negative feelings about actors appear in his selection of a line from Goethe's *Wilhelm Meister* as epigraph for his novel: "Alle Fehler des Menschen verzeih' ich dem Schauspieler, keine Fehler des Schauspielers verzeih' ich dem Menschen" ("all men's failings I forgive in actors; no actor's failings will I forgive in men").

7. According to Szabó, *Mephisto* delineates "a universal problem concerning twentieth-century intellectuals: the relationship between history and the individual" (Hughes 1982, p. 18).

8. A proscenium theater, a cinema screen, for example; cf. *The Purple Rose of Cairo*.

9. "Am 23. Oktober 1928 wurde Gustaf Gründgens auch für Berlin entdeckt, jedoch in einer Rolle, die ihm wenig behagte....Spielte er den sadistischen Homosexuellen Ottfried Berlessen in der Uraufführung von Ferdinand Bruckners "Verbrecher"....Dieser glatte, eiskalte, zynische, in seiner Abgefeimtheit funkelnde, scharf artikulierende Typ war neu für Berlin. Von seinem Ottfried an war Gründgens Berlins meistbeschäftigter Schauspieler und Regisseur, und fast alle Stücke, in denen er spielte, inszenierte er selbst. Er wurde Spezialist für leichte Stücke, Revuen und, im Film, für Schurken mit Krawatte, für Gentleman-Verbrecher" (Goetz 1982, p. 26).

10. Curt Riess recounts the following story: "Eines Tages—es war vor der Besetzung Prags—war GG bei Göring, als Hitler gemeldet wurde. Göring schob ihn schnell zur Tür hinaus und verschloss sie. Es handelte sich um eine Doppeltür, und GG musste feststellen, dass auch die andere Seite abgeschlossen war, so dass er wie in einem Käfig gefangen sass. Er hörte die ganze Unterhaltung mit an. 'Diese Leute machten also Weltgeschichte. Aber sie sprachen darüber wie Bierkutscher. Ich erinnere mich noch, dass Hitler sagte: >Denen werden wir es geben...< Kein Wort von der wichtigen politischen Entscheidung, die jetzt fiel, von den möglichen Folgen, die sich ja auch bald einstellten. Nur die kindische Freude am Augenblickserfolg'" (Riess 1965, p. 158).

11. Gründgens and Mann both sought their fame and fortune in the theaters of Weimar Germany. Where Gründgens had to struggle, though (and for an account of the hard work which typified an actor's life in the time period with which we are concerned, see Werner Krauss' autobiography, *Das Schauspiel meines Lebens*), Mann's family connections smoothed the way, as they did again in the thirties when Mann became a refugee.

WORKS CITED

Bacon, Francis. 1939. *Novum Organum. The English Philosophers from Bacon to Mill.* Edited by Edwin A. Burtt. New York: Modern Library.

De Marchi, Bruno. 1977. *István Szabó.* Il Castoro Cinema 37. Firenza: Nuova Italia.

Goertz, Heinrich. 1982. *Gustaf Gründgens.* Hamburg: Rowohlt.

Grundgens, Gustaf. 1967. *Gustaf Gründgens: Briefe, Aufsatze, Reden.* Edited by Rolf Badenhausen and Peter Gründgens-Gorski. Hamburg: Hoffmann and Campe.

Holquist, Michael. 1971. "Whodunit and Other Questions: Metaphysical Detective Stories in Post-War Fiction." *New Literary History* 3:135-56.

Hughes, John W. 1982. "*Mephisto*: István Szabó and 'the Gestapo of Suspicion.'" *Film Quarterly* 35:13-18.

Hull, David Stewart. 1969. *Film in the Third Reich: A Study of the German Cinema 1933-1945.* Berkeley: University of California Press.

James, Caryn. 1986. "Auteur! Auteur!" *New York Times* 19 Jan., sec. 6:18-30:

Krauss, Werner. 1958. *Das Schauspiel meines Lebens.* Edited by Hans Weigel. Stuttgart: Henry Goverts.

Mann, Erika, and Klaus Mann. 1940. *The Other Germany.* New York: Modern Age Books.

Mann, Klaus. 1981. *Mephisto: Roman eine Karriere.* München: Spangenberg.

———. 1977. *Mephisto.* Translated by Robin Smyth. New York: Random House.

———. 1984. *The Turning Point: Thirty-Five Years in This Century.* New York: Markus Wiener.

Murdoch, Iris. 1977. *The Fire and the Sun: Why Plato Banished the Artists.* Oxford: Clarendon.

Riess, Curt. 1965. *Gustaf Gründgens: Eine Biographie.* Unter Verwendung bisher unveröffentlichter Dokumente aus dem Nachlass. Hamburg: Hoffmann and Campe.

Rischbieter, Henning, ed. 1963. *Gründgens: Schauspieler, Regisseur, Theaterleiter.* Hannover: Friedrich.

Steiner, George. 1986. "Language Under Surveillance: The Writer and the State." *New York Times* 12 Jan., sec. 7:12+.

Taylor, C. P. 1982. *Good: A Tragedy.* London: Methuen.

BERTOLUCCI'S ADAPTATION OF *THE CONFORMIST*: A STUDY OF THE FUNCTION OF THE FLASHBACKS IN THE NARRATIVE STRATEGY OF THE FILM

Peggy Kidney

"Da buon seguace della teoria dell'autore ritenevo che il montaggio non fosse che una logica conseguenza del modo di girare,... (invece) ho capito che è un'altra scrittura, che si può montare un film anche *contro* il modo in cui si è girato, *contro* quello che si è girato."

Bernardo Bertolucci

("As a loyal believer in the Auteur theory I felt that editing was but the logical consequence of the way in which one shoots ... [instead] I understood that it is another writing, that a film can even be edited *against* the way in which it was shot, *against* what one has shot."
Author's translation; see footnote 8)

Bertolucci's *Il conformista* (1970; English title, *The Conformist*) is not just the cinematographic adaptation of Moravia's novel (1951),[1] as the title of the film suggests, but a rewriting of the widely known historical event of the Rosselli murders, the June 1937 political assassination of Carlo and Nello Rosselli, two antifascist brothers who were murdered near Paris by order of the Italian Foreign Office.[2] The film is also a rewriting of the novel that is based on the Rosselli case.[3] In his rewriting of the novel, Bertolucci abandons Moravia's chronologically developed narrative in favor of a discourse built on anachronous sequences, in this case on flashbacks or *analepses* (see Chatman 1978, p. 64, for a discussion of *analepses*). This is a fundamental change instituted with respect to the novel and is also the key to the film's independence from it. Although the basic story remains unaltered in the text of the film, it is the discourse (for a discussion of story and discourse, see Chatman 1978), the new textual arrangement of the plot that gives rise to a psychological and highly subjective text. The new text is no longer presented through the "objective," rational point of view of an omniscient narrator who controls the narrative, the implied author of the novel, but through the point of view of the protagonist himself, Marcello Clerici. The point of view adopted by Bertolucci is thus internal and subjective, and expressed through the flashbacks.

The flashbacks portray the character's psychological state as a product of past events that are continuously present. They correspond to a narrative strategy aimed at creating a structure that encourages the lack of differentiation between past and present, suggesting that the past is an integral part of the present. The flashback structure also reinforces the psychological nature of the character's entrapment in a system that he himself has created.

On the level of viewer participation, the flashbacks function to increase the viewer's involvement, because the viewer naturally seeks the reorganization of events presented initially without causal and chronological coherence. The viewer must rearrange the scenes mentally, according to a rational progression in order to reconstruct the chronology of the narrative and the sequence of events that have led to the protagonist's problematical situation. The final reorganization of all events in their proper sequence can occur only at the end of the film when the action develops strictly in the present and is no longer interrupted by flashbacks. Some of the flashbacks, the flashbacks that contain other flashbacks (flashbacks within flashbacks), present a special problem because the viewer must reconstruct not only the external, overall chronological sequence of the flashbacks in real/ historic terms but also the internal chronological sequence of the flashbacks within flashbacks in order to establish the actual sequence of events. The complex structure of Bertolucci's film requires an active role on the part of the viewer, a much more active role than that required of the reader of Moravia's linear text because the viewer is called on to interpret what appears on screen.

Whereas Moravia's narrative begins with the description of Marcello as a child and then follows the character's development, Bertolucci's narrative begins *in medias res* in the Paris hotel room on the morning of the murder of Professor Quadri and his wife. The first sequence takes place in the hotel room as Marcello prepares to go out; the second sequence portrays Marcello as he leaves the hotel, and the third shows him getting into a car driven by special agent Manganiello, Marcello's assistant.[4] From this point on, the narrative follows two directional lines: one chronological, which frames the narrative and represents the present (and which is reinforced by a musical leitmotif), and another that depicts past events with the introduction of flashbacks. Schematically, the narrative development follows a linear progression associated with the car that Marcello and Manganiello are riding in, and which is moving continuously in time and space toward the scene of the murder, and a nonlinear progression that includes ten breaks in the linear development or ten moments of *analepsis*, which occur while the car is traveling. These breaks, which can be considered ten incidents of ellipsis because "the discourse in the present halts, though time continues to pass in the story" (Chatman 1978, p. 70), are more important obviously than the framing device of the traveling car. The viewer in fact is left to assume that Marcello and Manganiello continue their journey in the car while the flashback sequences are presented on the screen. This structure emphasizes the importance of the psychological effects of past events on the character and the workings of his mind, his thoughts and recollections, even his dreams (vertical development) while downplaying the role of objective considerations linked to the plot (horizontal development). Kline points out that the first scenes of the film (in which Marcello is portrayed at various times dozing in both the car and the flashbacks) operate on principles of "condensation, displacement, projection, and doubling—all techniques of what Freud has termed the latent dream work" (Kline 1981, p. 231).

In diagram form, the structure of the film is as follows (*analepis* breaks by number):

#1   #2   #3   #4   #5   #6   #7   #8   #9   #10
car .. car .. car .. car .. car .. car .. car .. car .. car .. car ... car→ X =
Murder scene→ end

X = point of convergence
elimination of flashbacks (*analepsis* breaks)
elimination of framing device (the car)

The *analepses* are presented both as *single* flashbacks followed by a return to the present action within the traveling car (a device that is employed six times) and as *composite* flashbacks, in other words, flashbacks within flashbacks (a device that is employed four times). In the second case, the composite structure produces a "mise-en abîme" effect that functions to confuse the chronological order of the actual events presented. The action in fact does not return to the present after each flashback to establish the distinction between the past and the present but continues instead with another flashback, creating internal relationships between various levels of time in the past. From one moment in time in the past, the narrative moves either to another moment in the more distant past than the initial flashback sequence or closer to the present with respect to the preceding flashback, but still in the past. As the number of flashbacks increases so does the number of internal relationships produced because these are tied to the positioning of each event with respect to the other on an ideal chronological time-line. For example, in the second break in the linear development, Bertolucci offers the viewer a composite flashback that contains four distinct flashbacks. The first (f_1) is a continuation of the first flashback in real/historic terms, which portrays events at the radio station and to which I have assigned the value (f_0). (f_1) is followed by three other flashbacks (distinguished from each other by a film cut) in which the events of (f_2) occur in film time *after* (f_3). The last flashback, (f_4), in this sequence occurs in real or historic time after (f_3) but in film time *after* (f_2). The sequence produced is thus: f_1, f_3, f_2, f_4.

In diagram form, the *analepsis* breaks (by number) appear as follows:

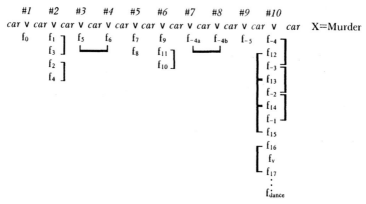

(For the individual identification of the flashbacks presented in this diagram see note 5)

This use of a nonchronological ordering of the flashbacks is repeated in the *internal* structure of the 6th and 10th breaks in the narrative and in the *external* relationships between narrative breaks themselves in terms of the chronological gap *between* breaks #6 and #7 and breaks #9 and #10. The most complex narrative break is the last one, break #10. In this composite flashback, which, after four sequences of internal *analepsis*, develops according to a chronological scheme, there is the greatest chronological gap between single flashbacks. The arrangement, repeated several times, juxtaposes some of the earliest historical events of the narrative (f_{-4}, f_{-3}, f_{-2}, f_{-1}) and the most recent events expressed in flashback form (f_{12}, f_{13}, f_{14}, f_{15}), which are the scenes of Marcello's confession. This arrangement brings Marcello's past to bear as openly as possible on his present situation and suggests the existence of an initimate relationship between past and present in which past events are not relegated to the memory of the past, but play a vital role in shaping the present, and in fact are part of it. It is important to note not only the duration of the confession flashbacks and the insistence upon the confession sequences themselves (presented four times in the film) but also the importance that the sequences acquire because of their positioning in the narrative development. They are in fact placed immediately preceding the chronological development in the last part of the flashback sequence, which also immediately precedes the return to the present and the crucial murder scene. The repetition of the confession sequences suggests Marcello's preoccupation with the idea of making amends for the past and settling the score with it through the murder of Professor Quadri.

Break #10, the last break preceding the crucial murder scene, is not only the most complex from the point of view of its *internal* structure and the nonlinear presentation of the events, but also the most interesting as far as the *external* structure of the *analepsis* breaks is concerned. In fact, break #10 presents events that chronologically precede all events presented thus far in the narrative (with the exception of f_{-5}), with the suggestion that the time factor in no way minimizes their bearing on later developments. The earlier events of the narrative are placed in the same *analepsis* break in which the last flashback of the narrative (the dance scene) is presented. The dance represents the furthest chronological development of the flashbacks, the moment of the past which is closest to the present, in reality, the events of the night before. After the dance scene (f_{dance}) the narrative catches up with the present and integrates itself with the linear development that has been used as a framing device for the discourse. From this point on, there are no flashbacks; the past is incorporated in the present, and the action coincides with the movement of the car in which Marcello and Manganiello are riding to the scene of the murder.

The presentation of the flashbacks does not follow a rational chronological order, but a subjective point of view that is internal to the events. It is the point of view of Marcello himself. The apparently chaotic presentation of the flashbacks suggests the workings of Marcello's own mind. While Marcello is in the car on the way to the murder scene, he thinks about past events and these are presented on the screen in the order in which he recalls them. As Lopez states:

In Bertolucci's *The Conformist* time becomes telescoped and reordered. It is compressed into memory based on Marcello's personal experiences, and thus becomes internalized and more real in the sense that the years that intervene between one significant event and another do not necessarily have to be accounted for in the viewer's mind as we accept (due to our own experience) the selective, sifting process of memory. (Lopez 1976, p. 306).

The sequence that I feel best demonstrates this concept occurs in breaks #7 and #8, which basically contain elements of the same flashback. In these two mini-flashbacks (f-4a) and (f-4b), which have in fact minimal screen duration, Marcello, who has temporarily gotten out of the car that Manganiello is driving, recalls getting into Lino's car as a child (the character of Lino in both the Moravia novel and Bertolucci's film is the chauffeur who attempted to seduce Marcello and who Marcello believed that he had killed). The recollection is triggered by the visual parallel offered by the car that Manganiello is now driving behind him and Marcello's own ambivalent feelings about wanting or not to get in. The cutting in these two flashbacks scenes and the minimal duration of the flashbacks themselves suggest not only Marcello's recollection of the events but also his reexperiencing of them as in a "déjà vu." The *analepses* are separated by an extremely brief period of story-time creating the overall effect of what Chatman calls "discontinuity between discourse-time and story-time," which underscores the importance of story-time over discourse-time and the lack of a rational chronological structure to the presentation of events past and present.

In Bertolucci's *Conformist* the discontinuity between discourse-time and story-time increases the lack of distinction between the structures of time and encourages the perception of time and events in the character's past as indistinct from those of his present. The *analepsis* breaks, with their internal and external nonlinear structure, present Marcello's point of view on a narrative level. Nowhere is the break from Moravia's story more evident in fact than in the murder scene. In Moravia's novel, Marcello is not present at the scene, but reads about it in the newspapers at the office. In Bertolucci's film, Marcello is at the scene, inside the car that holds him captive and from which he never emerges. The murder scene is not shot completely from Marcello's point of view; in other words, the scene is not shot strictly through "Marcello's eyes" with the camera being placed at his eye level, but the camera focuses on his eyes three times, suggesting that the scene is witnessed from his point of view. Shots of his eyes precede in fact both the professor's getting out of his car to investigate what has happened to the driver in the car that is blocking the road, the arrival of the fascists from behind the trees, and Anna's desperate call for help outside his car window. Marcello's physical presence at the scene, his role as indirect participant,[6] not just spectator, as evidenced especially in the shot in which Anna bangs on the car window and he fails to respond, along with the overall subjective structure of the film create the perception of a presentation of events from his point of view. Bertolucci thus demonstrates that point of view in cinema can be achieved not only cinematographically with the use of the camera, which suggests the identification with the character, but through narrative structure as well.

The murder scene is important structurally because it signals the moment in which past and present coincide. It is the central scene of the film in fact because the function of the narrative thus far is to present the events and the reasons that have lead Marcello to his involvement in the murder of Professor Quadri. Bertolucci's murder scene is a rewriting of the Moravia text not only because the director places Marcello at the scene and presents it from his point of view, but because the violence of the scene, Professor Quadri's lengthy and repeated stabbing and Anna Quadri's chase in the woods and eventual murder with the shot that disfigures her beautiful face reinscribe the political aspects of the historical account into the scene, which thus becomes an indictment of the violence of fascism.

Whereas in Moravia's novel the narrative signals an ideological change that has shifted the emphasis from political history to psychological, sexual, and social questions, Bertolucci's film reintroduces the political question, thus integrating two texts and producing a third, highly subjective text. The film as I have already suggested is thus a rewriting of both the generally accepted historical text of the Rosselli murders (subtext$_1$) and the Moravia text of Marcello Clerici (subtext$_2$). Although Bertolucci introduces other elements such as the psychoanalytic code,[7] the fundamental change that he brings to the Moravia text is structural in nature, and it is a change that affects the entire narrative and the conclusion of the story. In the novel, in fact, Marcello is eliminated in the implied author's "deus ex machina" strategy of an air raid in which Marcello, his wife, and daughter

are all killed, whereas in the closing sequence of the film
Marcello is presented in a self-reflexive mood, as he attempts, it
seems, to face his homosexual tendencies, the root of all his
troubles. He looks at the naked body of a young male prostitute
barely visible in the shadows, and from whom he is separated by
a symbolic series of bars through which he glances, still a
prisoner of himself. In Bertolucci's film, the past and its
problems reerupt tragically in the present and Marcello's
problematical situation, dilemmas, and reflections about his
actions and condition continue unresolved.

In conclusion, the difference between the two texts, the tension
between Bertolucci's film and its subtext, Moravia's novel, is not
just a formal difference: it is the critical difference, a difference
that is the expression of the ideological concerns of Bertolucci's
text. The adoption of the intricate system of flashbacks functions
to present the subjective point of view of the protagonist instead
of the implied author's objective viewpoint. It is the subjective
viewpoint that frames the narrative and influences the discourse.[8]
Although, as other have demonstrated, Bertolucci's *Conformist* is
a visual rewriting of Moravia's novel that includes the development of other codes, it is the structural rearrangement of the
original narrative that is the key to the film's independence of the
original text.

NOTES

1. The English version of the novel is entitled *The Conformist* (Moravia, 1953).
2. See Mack Smith, 1976, p. 104.
3. The story of Moravia's novel is closely related to the story of the Rosselli
case. In the novel, Moravia changes the historical events of the murder by
introducing a husband-wife team (Professor Quadri and his wife Lina) in place of
the Rosselli brothers and by concentrating not on them directly or on their
murder, but on the person responsible for arranging it. The story of Marcello
Clerici thus represents the fictional development of an *implied text* of the event,
the story of the organizer of the crime.
4. For a discussion of the changes that Bertolucci makes with regard to the
names of the Moravia characters, see T. Jefferson Kline, "The Unconformist:
Bertolucci's *The Conformist*," and D. Lopez, "Novel into Film: Bertolucci's *The
Conformist*." No one has remarked upon the resemblance between Manganiello's
name and the Italian word for "manganello" or billy club, symbol of the fascist
"squadristi" and their punitive attacks. Even Giulia in the film comments on the
comical character of the name: "Che nome buffo, Manganiello." Bertolucci's
intent was clearly ironic and the choice of name appropriate.
5. The flashbacks presented in this diagram can be identified as follows:

   f_0 Radio station visit with Italo Montanari
   f_1 Continuation of f_0 at radio station

f_2 At the Minister's headquarters: "The Office of the Minister!"

f_3 Continuation of f_1 at radio station

f_4 Continuation of f_2 at fascist HQ; Marcello is accompanied to the Minister

f_5 Wall with names (cemetery?); Marcello with flowers on way to Giulia's

f_6 Continuation of f_5

f_7 At Giulia's for lunch

f_8 Marcello and Manganiello at mother's house

f_9 Continuation of f_8 at mother's house

f_{10} Back from visit to asylum

f_{11} Asylum visit with father

f_{-4a} Shot of Lino's car from behind with child on side (part of f_{-4}; to be repeated)

f_{-4b} "Stop!" by Marcello as a young boy (part of f_{-4}; to be repeated)

f_{-5} Children around Marcello on the ground

f_{-4} Children around Marcello; continuation of f_{-5}; Marcello gets up and gets into Lino's car. Flashback contains previous f_{-4a} and f_{-4b} segments

f_{12} Confession

f_{-3} Marcello with Lino outside villa and in Lino's room

f_{13} Confession: "Then what happened?"

f_{-2} Back to Lino's room. Scene on bed (with sound of the confession)

f_{14} Confession: "Are you sure you are telling the truth?"

f_{-1} Back to Lino's room: "Shoot, shoot, kill the pretty Butterfly"

f_{15} Confession: Marcello talks about repaying society and is absolved

f_{16} On train with Giulia. Giulia begins to explain why she is unworthy of him

f_v Ventimiglia: Marcello walks behind a painting that turns into reality. Visits fascist leader who gives him new orders.
Note: the chronological positioning of this event is extremely difficult because f_{17} continues as if there had been no break although the train's arrival in Ventimiglia had been announced by the conductor at the end of f_{16}.

f_{17} On train. Continuation of f_{16}. Action begins where f_{16} left off. Giulia tells Marcello about Uncle Perpuzio, and he reenacts the scene described, taking on the role of the uncle.
Henceforward to f_{dance} the action develops chronologically; then it returns to the present, to the traveling car that is following Prof. Quadri and his wife.

One should note the binary links between all flashbacks except for f_7 and f_v and the increasing complexity of the correspondences between single flashbacks. The last *analepsis* break is the longest and most complex with regard to the temporal correspondences in the alternation of the flashbacks.

6. It must be remembered that Marcello is responsible for setting up the murder of Professor Quadri.

7. For a discussion of the psychoanalytic code as it is used by Bertolucci in the film, see Kline.

8. It is interesting to note that Bertolucci, in an interview with Enzo Ungari published in *Scene madri di Bernardo Bertolucci*, 1982, p. 73, states that he shot the film leaving open the possibility of ordering it in a chronological manner, but that in the editing room he discovered the possibilities for the vertical

development obtainable through montage. From the very beginning, however, he admits that he was fascinated with the idea of using the trip in the car as the "present" of the story, the container of the story while the protagonist travels also in the past. (The translation is my own.) On the importance of the montage and Bertolucci's work with Kim Arcalli, see Franca Faldini and Goffredo Fofi, 1984, p. 143. The quote on the title page is taken from this source.

WORKS CITED

Chatman, Seymour. 1978. *Story and Discourse*. Ithaca: Cornell University Press.

Faldini, Franca, and Goffredo Fofi. 1984. *Il cinema Italiano d'oggi 1970-1984 raccontato dai suoi protagonisti*. Milano: Mondadori editore.

Kline, T. Jefferson. 1981. "The Unconformist: Bertolucci's *The Conformist: Modern European Filmmakers and the Art of Adaptation*. Edited by Andrew Horton and Joan Magretta. New York: Ungar.

Lopez, D. "Novel into Film: Bertolucci's *The Conformist.*" *Literature Film Quarterly*. 4.4:303-12.

Moravia, Alberto. 1953. *The Conformist*. Translated by A. Davidson. London: Secker and Warburg.

Smith, Denis Mack. 1976. *Mussolini's Roman Empire*. Middlesex: Penguin.

COLLABORATION, ALIENATION, AND THE CRISIS OF IDENTITY IN THE FILM AND FICTION OF PATRICK MODIANO

Richard J. Golsan

One of the most highly regarded and controversial movies to appear in France in 1974 was Louis Malle's *Lacombe, Lucien*. Taking place in Southern France under the German Occupation in 1944, the film follows the adventures of a seventeen-year old peasant boy, Lucien Lacombe, and his involvement with a band of French collaborators working for the German police. As the film progresses, Lucien, politically ignorant and morally naïve, becomes as callous, mercenary, and brutal as his older cohorts.

For the most part, critics of *Lacombe, Lucien* have focused their attention on the motivations of the young collaborator and on the film itself as a "long, close look at the banality of evil" (Kael 1974, p. 94). Most have concluded that Lucien is an adolescent on the make, looking for action, driven by a burgeoning sexuality that translates into a thrist for power (Altman 1974, pp. 549-550; Westerbeck 1974, p. 215). He falls in easily with the pro-Nazi thugs not because he is motivated by any political belief of ideology but because, like his fellow collaborators, he is morally vacuous and completely indifferent to the sufferings of others. Charles Altman sums up the film's protagonist as "raw id without compensating superego" (1974, p. 550).

These assessments of the young collaborator and the film that tells his story are not inaccurate, but they tend to focus too exclusively on the nature of evil as it is presented in *Lacombe, Lucien* and the misguided energies of the adolescent boy. Malle's film is also a meditation on the social and political realities of collaborationist France and a study of the alienation and loss of identity suffered by Frenchmen as a result of their devastating defeat at the hands of the Germans in 1940. Unfortunately these interlocking aspects of *Lacombe, Lucien* have been overlooked largely as a result of two factors. The first is that the manifestations of evil are so dramatically presented and the character of Lucien so disturbingly engaging that they tend to overshadow the rest of the film. Secondly, few critics of the

107

movie, at least in this country, have paid much attention to the fact that the screenplay was coauthored by the young novelist Patrick Modiano.[1] In many ways, *Lacombe, Lucien* is simply a transcription into the medium of film of a Modiano novel, and examining it in relation to the writer's other fictional works helps to illuminate some of the film's more understated themes. This is especially true in the case of the movie's treatment of collaboration, alienation, and the crisis of identity and their tragic inseparability. The examination of these themes, moreover, ultimately sheds light on the problem of evil and its sources in the lives of the collaborators and in the life of the French nation as a whole during the Occupation.

One of the most significant traits shared by all the heroes of Modiano's novels is an anguished awareness of their lack of roots, their lack of a past, in short, the absence of any real sense of their own identity. They are orphans, as in the case of one of the adolescent heroes of the recent *De Si Braves Garçons*, or as in the instance of another boy in the novel, children whose parents have rejected them, even going so far as to rent them their own apartment so that parent and child can live separate lives. In other works such as *Livret de famille*, they are individuals whose parents, and fathers in particular, are little more than ghosts. The latters' names do not appear on their children's baptismal certificate, and they are described as "des hommes de nulle part" (Modiano 1972, p. 157) by other relatives. The hero of Modiano's most ambitious and critically acclaimed novel to date,[2] *Rue des boutiques obscures*, is even more radically uprooted and cut off from his past. He is an amnesiac who has lived in ignorance of his former life for over ten years. His resulting sense of alienation and loss of identity is expressed in the opening sentence of the novel where he states: "Je ne suis rien. Rien qu'une silhouette claire . . ." (11).

With few exceptions, the plots of these novels are constructed around the protagonists' efforts to recover their identities and recapture the past. In some instances, they attempt to accomplish these tasks by searching for lost fathers or mothers who have disappeared. In other cases, they delve into their parents' histories in order to know and understand them, in the hope that solving the riddle of their elders' identity will furnish them with roots and a past and make self-definition possible. For the hero of *Rue des boutiques obscures*, the task is more difficult, because an amnesiac whom no one recognizes can hardly know where to begin his search.

Whatever the object of their quest, their voyage into the past, all of Modiano's heroes are led inexorably back to the nightmare years of the German Occupation. Described as a "troubled time," a "disquieting epoch," or even "the deluge," the Occupation is not simply the period during which the individual protagonists' pasts disappeared and their identities evaporated. It is also a time when, as one of the characters in *Rue des boutiques obscures* notes, it was common practice to live under an assumed name or carry false papers (Modiano 1978, p. 181). In short, it is that moment in history when Frenchmen as a whole were deprived of their roots, their pasts, and their traditions and were forced to wonder who and what they were.[3] Given these circumstances, it is not surprising that Modiano's heroes ultimately fail in their personal quest for identity, because the rootlessness and aliena-tion that haunt them affect the nation as a whole. The recovery of their own identity hinges upon the restoration of the nation's identity, and, in Modiano's fictional universe, the Occupation has made this all but impossible.

Two novels in particular furnish memorable portraits of France during the Occupation and situate the problems of alienation and loss of identity directly in relation to this historical context. In both works, the collaborationist *milieu* serves as a metaphor for French society as a whole and what it has become under the heel of the German occupant. The protagonists of the novels are both adolescents who have been deprived of their past or some part of it, whose quest for self-definition leads them into the heart of the corrupt, pro-fascist camp.

Swing Troubadour,[4] the hero of *La Ronde de nuit*, is a young man who suffers constantly from feelings of aimlessness, emptiness, and alienation. To borrow an expression from Sartrean existentialism, he is painfully aware of his own contingency. Having no relatives to speak of except a mother who has moved to Switzerland to escape the Occupation, he has surrounded himself with a surrogate family consisting of two aging misfits, in the hopes of providing himself with a makeshift identity and roots. Swing also imagines himself the favorite son of a certain M. de Bel-Respiro, whose vacated home he has taken over during the Occupation. The resulting ephemeral sense of belonging that these dreams afford provides him with one of the few pleasures he has.

Swing's quest for an identity or, failing that, some niche or purpose in life, eventually leads him into contact with a gang of collaborators headed up by a man known simply as Le Khédive.

Le Khédive and his fellows are only too happy to welcome the young man into their group and to give him a mission. They want him to infiltrate a resistance network, and after having gained the confidence of its members, to betray them. Swing is happy to oblige because as he explains: "Ne me sentant aucune vocation particulière, j'attendais de mes aînés qu'ils me choisissent un emploi" (Modiano 1969, p. 93).

Troubadour's newfound vocation does not provide him with the sense of self or purpose he had longed for. In fact, it only exacerbates his identity crisis and feelings of contingency. He finds himself drawn to the resistance fighters not so much because their cause appeals to him but because they, too, offer him a "vocation" and an identity. Soon he is no more than a "un papillon de nuit/qui/voletait . . . d'un lustre à l'autre . . ." (Modiano 1969, p. 140) unable to settle on either. Ultimately, however, he does betray the resistance fighters, largely out of bitterness that he can never achieve their sense of purpose or self-possession. As Swing realizes at the end of La Ronde de nuit, his quest for an identity and a mission that would fulfill him has failed. He now recognizes that "Je n'avais ma place nulle part" (Modiano 1969, p. 140). Summing up his position, he affirms: "Je n'ai jamais eu de carte d'identité" (Modiano 1969, p. 119). The novel closes with Swing fleeing Le Khédive and his cohorts, who wish to kill him now that he is no longer useful.

The collaborationist *milieu* into which Swing's quest for an identity and a purpose in life leads him is certainly incapable of providing him with what he seeks in the first place. It is a world turned upside down, where authority is no longer vested in legitimate social and political institutions and respected members of the community, but is instead in the hands of the dregs of society. Le Khédive and his cronies, the self-styled "kings of Paris," are miscreants of every kind: drug addicts, pimps, whores, swindlers, killers and ex-policemen dismissed for misconduct. They are vacuous individuals who, like Swing himself, possess no identity of their own and spend their time trying to appropriate the identities and qualities of others. Le Khédive, for example, is a convict intent upon becoming Head of Police and commanding a respect he doesn't merit. Two other members of the group, Lionel de Zieff and the baroness Lydia Stahl, are phony aristocrats with spurious titles. All three, like their protégé, live in houses that belong to others and drive stolen cars. Even their power and authority are not really their own; they exercise it only by the grace of their Nazi masters. As Swing so accurately describes them, they are simply "des rats qui prennent possession d'une ville après que la peste a décimé ses habitants" (Modiano 1969, p. 24).

The world that the collaborators have created for themselves is one in which all social, cultural, and spiritual values have disappeared. It is a dog-eat-dog world in which all social intercourse occurs in the drunken, debauched atmosphere of the nightclubs that have proliferated since the Nazi victory. Constructive, creative activity is a thing of the past, as the collaborators amuse themselves by listening endlessly to German popular music, playing hide-and-seek, or simply drinking. All that is left of the transcendant, the sacred, are the astrological predictions and hocus pocus of the self-styled magus Ivanoff, which the others take quite seriously.

All sense of decorum and all observance of traditional moral and ethical values have been swept away as well. The captured resistance fighters are tortured upstairs while the collaborators happily drink, play games, or apply makeup downstairs. Sexual perversions abound, and lewd behavior is the rule and not the exception. Le Khédive makes passes at Swing Torubadour while Lydia Stahl and Frau Sultana openly pursue their lesbian relationship in the parlor. Zieff fondles a woman's breast in full view of everyone, and those present simply laugh at the woman's protests. When the collaborators have nothing else to do, they attack and vilify each other.

Given these circumstances, it is not surprising that Swing does not find an identity of a purpose in Le Khédive's circle. The collaborationist *milieu,* as it is depicted in *La Ronde de nuit,* is an inauthentic world in which life is experienced vicariously, and in which all of man's actions spring not from values or beliefs but from instincts, whims, or base impulses. Swing himself describes it as a world from which "la Morale, la Justice, l'Humain" (Modiano 1969, p. 68) have disappeared, and he understands by the end of the novel that all those who live in such an environment are eventually stripped of these qualities as well.

Les Boulevards de ceinture, Modiano's third novel and winner of the French Academy's *Grand Prix du Roman* in 1972, differs from the earlier *La Ronde de nuit* in that the collaborators depicted are for the most part only thinly disguised historical figures. The leader of the collaborationist group, a certain Jean

112   FILM AND LITERATURE

Muraille, is a newspaper editor who got his start before the war working for cheap, sensationalist newspapers specializing in rumor, innuendo, and blackmail. He has taken advantage of the Occupation, or "[le] désordre de la nuit" (Modiano 1972, p. 68) as the young narrator/protagonist describes it, to rise to a position of prominence in the Parisian press, and he dreams of becoming head of the Paris Press Corporation. Like Le Khédive in *Le Ronde de nuit,* he aspires to a position of authority and respect that he doesn't merit and that he could not have hoped to obtain before the war.

Among the members of Muraille's group is his daughter, the movie actress Annie Muraille, whose only credit seems to be the leading role in the film *La Nuit des rafles* or "Night of the Roundups." Although the subject matter of the movie is not revealed, the title is a less than subtle reference to the roundup of Jews in Paris and elsewhere in France during the Occupation. Annie is also known for her sexual promiscuity and her penchant for wearing furs in August.

Anyone familiar with the Occupation period would recognize this couple immediately. Jean Luchaire, on whom the character of Muraille is clearly based, was a second-rate journalist who became head of the Paris Press Corporation under the Nazis. Corinne Luchaire, his daughter and the inspiration for Annie Muraille, was a minor movie actress before the war who became a luminary of Parisian high society during the Occupation. After the Liberation, Luchaire was condemned to death and executed, and his daughter was sentenced to ten years of national disgrace, which entailed the loss of all civil rights and privileges.[5]

Several other members of Muraille's entourage are easily recognizable as thinly disguised historical figures as well. François Gerbère, who is the most celebrated columnist on Muraille's newspaper *C'est La Vie,* is obviously inspired by the infamous pro-Nazi journalist Robert Brasillach who, like Luchaire, was condemned for treason and executed after the war. He has the same boyish appearance and sports the same hornrimmed glasses. His columns are mostly antisemitic, pro-Nazi tracts, and like the real Brasillach, his obsession with virility and force is a front for his homosexuality. His last name, Gerbère, would appear to be a wordplay on the name of one the most famous pro-collaborationist newspapers, the Nazi-sponsored *La Gerbe.*[6]

Two of Gerbère's colleagues on *C'est La Vie* are also clearly bases on well-known collaborationist journalists. A certain

Maulaz's name which differs only slightly from that of Charles Maurras, the right-wing leader and long-time editor of *Action française*.[7] Another journalist, identified simply as Suaraize, pronounces his name the same as the editor of the pro-Nazi newspaper *Aujourd'hui*, George Suarez, although the spelling is different.[8]

Modiano's intention in creating a fictional collaborationist *milieu* that is hardly fictional at all becomes clear when one realizes that there is very little difference between this semi-fictional milieu and the more imaginary one described in *La Ronde de nuit*. Both are valueless, amoral, and sterile worlds whose denizens live vicariously off the power and influence of the Nazis. Both are peopled by individuals who are nothing more than their crass façades, as in the case of Annie Muraille, who wears her furs year round, or figures who conceal what they are behind images intended to delude others as well as themselves, like François Gerbère. In either case, all authenticity is lacking, and the artificial, morally vacuous universe of collaborationist France is not one in which man can find meaningful action or come to any real understanding of who he is. By establishing so close a link between fiction and historical reality in *Les Boulevards de ceinture*, Modiano reminds the reader that the nightmare of the Occupation is not simply the frightening but harmless product of the writer's imagination but part of France's past as well.

When the young narrator/hero of the novel enters Muraille's collaborationist circle, he identifies himself as Serge Alexandre,[9] an aspiring writer. Unlike the protagonist hero of *Le Ronde de nuit*, he is not seeking an identity or a vocation for himself, but is instead looking for his father. As it turns out, he has come to the right place, because his father, who does not at first recognize him, is one of Muraille's intimates. The father's name and title, the Baron de Deykecaire, recall the phony aristocrats of *La Ronde de nuit*, and like them he has borrowed his noble identity as well as the house in which he lives. He participates in the group's profiteering, but he is abused and humiliated by Muraille and his fellows because, either out of timidity or some vestige of a moral code, he refuses to join in the group's debauchery. Like the collaborators of *La Ronde de nuit*, Muraille and his fellows spend their time in the seamy nightclubs so prevalent in Occupation Paris or indulging in orgies in which all sexual practices, including incest between the journalist and his daughter, are considered acceptable behavior.

It is not difficult to recognize in the situation just described the allegorical structure that underlies *Les Boulevards de ceinture*. Serge Alexandre, symbolic of French youth cut off from its traditions and its past as a result of the defeat of 1940, sets out to rediscover his roots. His quest leads directly to the heart of collaborationist society, where the Baron de Deykecaire, his father and the symbol of the nation itself, is consorting with the enemy. The fact that Deykecaire does not recognize or acknowledge his son until late in the novel is suggestive of France's abandonment of its youth and its future in its choice of collaboration during the early years of the war. Only when a German defeat appeared to be a real possibility after the events of 1942 did Frenchmen in large numbers take up arms against their oppressors in an effort to regain control of their own destiny.[10]

Without wishing to press this sort of interpretation too far, we might note as well that the father's choice of collaboration not only deprives the son of his roots but damages him in other ways as well. In the amoral ambiance surrounding Muraille's set, Serge soon finds himself losing his grip on his own morality. Like the others, he begins to drink heavily and sleep with prostitutes. He eventually agrees to write for *C'est La Vie*, and the titles of his journalistic endeavors are suggestive of his gradual debasement. He writes serials whose titles, "Confessions d'un chauffeur mondain," "Via Lesbos," and "Les Dames des studios" (Modiano 1972, p. 133), confirm his newfound vocation of pornographer.

Experiencing within himself the "crise de valeurs sans précédent" (Modiano 1972, p. 108) that he finds all around him, Serge begins to lose his sense of who he is. Borrowing an expression from the protagonist of *Le Ronde de nuit*, he affirms that he has lost his identity papers. In a desperate attempt to reappropriate his past and his sense of self and in an effort to strike back at the individuals and the situation that have deprived him of these necessities, he kills Gerbère and convinces his father to flee with him. Although he himself escapes, and perhaps France's future along with him, the Baron de Deykecaire, symbol of the nation's past, is captured by the Gestapo and led away to be executed.

* * * * *

At first glance, *Lacombe, Lucien* appears to differ significantly from Modiano's novels in its evocation of the Occupation years, its portrayal of the hero, and its overall tone. There is an attention to historical accuracy and detail in the film that is absent in *La Ronde de nuit* and *Les Boulevards de ceinture* and that attracts the attention of the audience in the very first scene. Lucien is emptying slop buckets in a home for the aged while the camera casually pans the room. It pauses on a prominently placed photograph of Marshall Pétain, head of the Vichy government and architect and proponent of the policy of collaboration. Over the noises of Lucien working and the murmurs of the old people, one hears a radio address by Philippe Henriot, propagandist for Vichy France and pro-Nazi zealot. The photograph and the address situate the story that is about to unfold squarely in the Occupation period and, combined with the obvious resignation of the old folks and the indifference of Lucien, suggest an acquiescence to the Nazis and their French minions that typified many Frenchmen during the period.

Lacombe, Lucien also treats the question of antisemitism and the persecution of the Jews in a much more direct and precise fashion than do Modiano's novels. Lucien becomes involved with the Horn family, Jews fleeing Paris and hoping to escape to Spain. Although he sleeps with the daughter France Horn, his callous indifference to the family's plight throughout most of the film recalls the tragically pervasive attitude in occupied France during the early 1940s.

Lucien's callousness is just one form of antisemitism treated in the film. The vicious and murderous racism of Faure, the fascist zealot of the collaborationist group with which Lucien becomes involved, manifests itself most strikingly when Horn comes to find Lucien. After comparing Jews to rats and implying they must be exterminated (Malle and Modiano 1974, p. 122), Faure turns Horn over to the German authorities who deport him.

The servant who seduces Lucien just after he joins the *collabos* also turns out to be infected by the disease of antisemitism. When Lucien shows up with France Horn at a party thrown in honor of one of the collaborators who had decided to leave for Spain, the servant, maddened by jealousy, attacks France publicly, repeatedly calling her a "sale Juive" (Malle and Modiano 1974, p. 99). The scene frighteningly conveys the irrationality of racial hatreds and the manner in which they crop up in situations in which race, religion, or cultural differences are not really at issue at all.

More striking, perhaps, than the differences in representation of the Occupation years in *Lacombe, Lucien* and in Modiano's

novels is the sharply divergent portrayal of the respective heroes
of these works. As noted earlier, Lucien is a mischevious
adolescent with an overabundance of energy, sexual and
otherwise, and an apparent lack of morality. He is a sly,
pragmatic peasant boy who, it would appear, is not subject to the
moral and ethical quandries of the more intellectually developed,
city dwelling narrator/protagonists of *La Ronde de nuit* and *Les
Boulevards de ceinture.*

Appearances can be deceiving, however, especially when one is
comparing the different media of fiction and film and when the
tone of the works in question is so sharply divergent. Modiano's
first-person narratives are by and large internal monologues. All
observations of external reality are filtered through the narrator's
selective eye and mediated by his anguished emotions. By
contrast, in *Lacombe, Lucien* the camera strives to be comprehensive, objective and impersonal, in short, an accurate recorder of
reality down to its minutest details.[11] It catches photographs of
Pétain while the soundtrack picks up a speech by Henriot
without interrupting the narrative flow. Such a task is much
more difficult to accomplish in a novel and especially in first-
person narratives like *La Ronde de nuit* and *Les Boulevards de
ceinture.* Malle's camera attempts also to mirror accurately the
characters' feeling and emotions, without necessarily commenting
on them or attempting to explore them in depth. This is certainly
not the case in Modiano's fiction, and it goes a long way towards
explaining why Lucien seems so different from Swing Troubadour and Serge Alexandre.

Although the different media of fiction and film tend to
highlight the divergences between Modiano's novels and
Lacombe, Lucien, there are strong similarities between the works
that confirm their intertextuality and reveal the hand of their
common creator. For example, the collaborationist *milieu*
presented in *Lacombe, Lucien* is almost a carbon copy of its
counterparts in *La Ronde de nuit* and *Les Boulevards de ceinture.*
Lucien's cohorts include Tonin, an ex-policeman dismissed for
misconduct before the war but reinstated by the Nazis; Jean-
Bernard, a decadent aristocrat of dubious extraction; and Betty
Beaulieu, a small-time movie actress who, like Annie Muraille in
Les Boulevards de ceinture, is an oversexed, overdressed manne-
quin. She resembles Annie as well in that she too has starred in a
film entitled *La Nuit des rafles.*

Like Le Khédive, Muraille, and their groups, the collaborators
in Malle's film amuse themselves by drinking, baiting each other,

and indulging their cruelest and most inhuman whims. When Lucien brings France to the party, the aging alcoholic ex-cycling champion Aubert asks her to dance and then proceeds to fondle her in front of the entire company. With the exception of France and Lucien, no one seems to be shocked or offended in the least. Betty Beaulieu, when not complaining of the inferior quality of the *Dames Roses* she drinks, amuses herself by watching captured resistance fighters tortured. All the collaborators are busy absconding with the possessions of others, and all delude themselves with feelings of self-importance.

A subtler and ultimately more significant link between *Lacombe, Lucien* and Modiano's novels concerns similarities in plot structure and allegorical intention. Lucien falls in with the Nazis only after being turned down by the resistance and, more importantly, only after being banished from his own home. Early in the film, he goes home for a vacation only to find part of the farm inhabited by strangers making use of dishes and other items that he angrily asserts belong to his father. He then discovers that his mother has taken a lover whose name, Laborit, as Charles Altman notes, is an obvious wordplay on col-laborat-or (Altman 1974, p. 550). Laborit now runs the farm in the place of Lucien's father, who is a prisoner of war. Moreover Laborit, as Mme. Lacombe tells her son, no longer wants the boy around.

The situation, as Altman correctly asserts, is a "thinly veiled allegory of the French political situation" (Altman 1974, p. 550) during the Occupation, and when Lucien sets out from the farm, he has been deprived of his roots, his past, his identity. He falls in with the collaborators because they provide him with a new identity and purpose, and the power that he experiences through them commands the respect of others, a respect that he craves after his humiliation by Laborit at home.

Later in the film, when Lucien forces himself into the Horn family, his actions can be construed as stemming from not only his desire for France but also an unconscious attempt to provide himself with a family, a set of roots to replace the ones he has lost. In this he resembles Swing Troubadour of *La Ronde de nuit,* who has also adopted a surrogate family. One does not question Lucien's sincerity when he tells Horn: "Vous savez, monsieur Horn, je vous aime bien . . ." (Malle and Modiano 1974, p. 115). His rescue of France and the old grandmother at the end of the film is the protective gesture of a young man who has assumed the responsibilities of the absent father after Horn's deportation. Lucien's obvious happiness and peace of mind at the

end of the film, when he is providing for his adoptive family in
the wilderness, suggest that this is the situation he has been
striving for all along.

If Lucien's most telling trait is that, like Swing Troubadour
and Serge Alexandre, he has been deprived of his roots and his
identity and if his actions derive from a conscious or unconscious
desire to recover both, then the problem of his immorality or
amorality needs to be considered in a new light. The protagonists
of *La Ronde de nuit* and *Les Boulevards de ceinture* are not
predominantly evil or immoral at the outset of the two novels,
but they succumb to the immorality or, more accurately, the
amorality of the collaborationist *milieu* as the novels progress.
Similarly, the protagonist of *Lacombe, Lucien* is not necessarily
an evil individual at the outset of the film, although much has
been said of his killing a bird with his slingshot in the opening
scene, and later of his slaughtering rabbits on a hunting trip
(Kaufman, 1974, p. 18; Altman, 1974, p. 554). In the first
instance, it could be argued that the shooting of the bird is
simply the action or instinct of a wily peasant hunter testing his
skills; in the second case, Lucien's killing spree can be seen as a
means of striking back indirectly at Laborit and the others who
have taken what is rightfully his and denied him his birthright. It
should be noted that the scene involving the killing of the rabbits
occurs almost immediately after the sequence during which
Lucien discovers his family home inhabited by strangers and his
father's place taken by Laborit. It is only when he joins up with
the collaborators that Lucien's violent impulses are turned toward
other men, and this occurs primarily because such murderous
behavior is condoned in the vicious, sterile and inhuman world
of Tonin, Betty Beaulieu, and their like. Pauline Kael points out
correctly that Lucien might well have been a decent, respected
member of his rural community with a natural outlet for his
violence, had the war not taken place (Kael 1974, p. 94).

In this light, the evil in *Lacombe, Lucien* is less the evil of a
particular individual than that of a *situation*. In a world turned
on its ear, where accepted social norms no longer apply, and
where traditions and values have been undermined, man loses
sight of who he is and becomes capable of anything. For
Modiano and Malle this *is* the world of the Occupation, and
Lucien Lacombe, like Swing Troubadour and Serge Alexandre,
should be viewed more as a *victim* of evil rather than a
manifestation of it.

There is one final point of convergence between *Lacombe, Lucien* and the fiction of Patrick Modiano. Before the film begins, a statement by the philosopher Santayana flashes on the screen. It reads: "Those who do not remember the past are doomed to relive it." At the end of *Les Boulevards de ceinture*, the narrator returns years later to the hotel where Muraille and his fellows used to hang out. The bartender, who happily served the collaborators and who now just as happily serves his new clients, tells him to forget the past and look instead to the future. The message in both instances is clear, and it is perhaps the final message Patrick Modiano wishes to convey to his countrymen. One cannot and should not forget or ignore the horror and tragedy of the Occupation. Only by facing it clearly and keeping it constantly in view can French society recover from it and avoid its recurrence.

NOTES

1. In his review of the film in *The New Republic*, Stanley Kaufman mentions the fact that Patrick Modiano coauthored the script with Malle, but he fails to identify Modiano or mention his fiction. In her review, Pauline Kael states that Modiano has written novels about the Occupation, but does not touch on their importance vis-à-vis the film. Jay Cocks, Bea Rothenbuecker, and Colin Westerbeck completely ignore Modiano and his contribution to *Lacombe, Lucien* in their reviews.

2. *Rue des boutiques obscures* was awarded the 1978 Prix Goncourt, France's most prestigious literary prize.

3. The sense of shock, dismay, and especially *déracinement* experienced by the French as a result of the defeat of 1940, is described in numerous histories of the period and especially in works such as Marc Bloch's *Strange Defeat* (see in particular Chapters One and Three). It is also evoked in films like *Le Chagrin et la pitié* and the more recent *M. Klein*.

4. The name Troubadour itself, of course, is suggestive of the character's rootlessness, because the troubadours were wandering poets and minstrels who traveled and performed in the south of France and especially in Provence from the twelfth to the fourteenth century (see Adam, Lerminier, Morot-Sir, *Littérature française*, pp. 12-13).

5. For a discussion of the career of Jean Luchaine during the Occupation, see David Pryce-Jones, *Paris in the Third Reich*, pp. 49-50 and Pierre Assouline, *L'Epuration des intellectuels*, pp. 126-127. For Corinne Luchaine, see p. 349 in the notes of Céline's *Castle to Castle*.

6. Brasillach's life and journalistic carrer are examined in detail in Robert Tucker's *The Fascist Ego: A Political Biography of Robert Brasilach*. The book also contains an excellent photograph of its subject. For a discussion of *Le Gerbe*, see Bertram Gordon, *Collaboration in France During the Second World War* 86-88.

7. The most complete discussion of Maurras's career and the *Action Française* movement is contained in Eugen Weber's *Action Française: Royalism and Reaction in Twentieth-Century France*.

8. For Suarez's career before and during the Occupation, see David Pryce-Jones, *Paris in the Third Reich*, p. 53.

9. The narrator's real name is never given. He uses the alias "Serge Alexandre" when he registers at the Inn where Muraille and his cronies hang out. His choice of alias is of interest, since Serge Alexandre was also as alias used by the infamous swindler of the 1930s, Sacha Stavisky. Stavisky's dubious dealings and mysterious death in 1934 implicated a number of government officials and provoked a scandal that led eventually to the fall of the Chautemps government and the right wing-inspired riots of February 6, 1934 (for a complete account of the Stavisky affair, see Weber pp. 319-40).

There are interesting parallels to be drawn between Modiano's protagonist and the historical figure Stavisky, but there are important distinctions to be established as well. Like the narrator in *Les Boulevards de ceinture*, Stavisky was a rootless outsider given to using phony identities. Like his fictional counterpart, he was involved in what Weber describes as "that shadowy half world where fashionable people, crooks, adventurers and politicians mixed . . ." (320). Unlike Modiano's hero, Stavisky was not simply a naïve youth corrupted by right-wing extremists. As a matter of fact, the majority of Stavisky's political (and jounalistic) connections were on the left instead of the right. Given the contradictory nature of these comparisons, Modiano's reasons for providing his hero with such a provocative alias remain unclear.

10. For a brief discussion of the German setbacks of 1942 and the subsequent growth of the Resistance movement within France, see Pierre Miquel, *Historie de la France* 228-236.

11. In her review of the film, Pauline Kael describes Malle's camera as a purely "investigative instrument." She continues, "[Malle's] technique is to let the story tell itself while he searches and observes" (94).

WORKS CITED

Adam, Antoine, George Lerminier, and Edouard Morot-Sir. 1972. *Litterature francaise*. Vol. 2. Paris: Larousse.

Altman, Charles. 1974. "*Lacombe, Lucien*: Laughter and Collaboration." *French Review* XLIX: 549-558.

Assouline, Pierre. 1985. *L'Epuration des intellectuels*. Brussels: Editions Complexe.

Bloch, Marc. 1968. *Strange Defeat*. Translated by Gerard Hopkins. New York: W. W. Norton.

Celine, Louis-Ferdinand. 1968. *Castle to Castle*. Translated by Ralph Manheim. New York: Dell.

Cocks, Jay. 1974. Review of *Lacombe, Lucien*. *Time* 14 Oct. 4, 8.

Gordon, Bertram. 1980. *Collaboration in France During the Second world War*. Ithaca: Cornell University Press.

Kael, Pauline, 1974. Review of *Lacombe, Lucien*. *New Yorker*. 30 Sept.: 94-100.

Kauffman, Stanley. 1974. Review of *Lacombe, Lucien*. *The New Republic* 5 Oct.: 18, 33.

Malle, Louis and Patrick Modiano. 1974. *Lacombe, Lucien*. Paris: Gallimard.

Miquel, Pierre. 1976. *Histoire de la France* 2. Paris: Fayard.

Modiano, Patrick. 1972. *Les Boulevards de ceinture*. Paris: Gallimard.

———. 1982. *De Si Braves Garcons*. Paris: Gallimard.

———. 1977. *Livret de famille*. Paris: Gallimard.

———. 1969. *La Ronde de nuit.* Paris: Gallimard.

———. 1978. *Rue des boutiques obscures.* Paris: Gallimard.

Pryce-Jones, David. 1981. *Paris in the Third Reich: A History of the German Occupation 1940-44.* New York: Holt, Rinehart and Winston.

Rothenbuecker, Bea. 1974. Review of *Lacombe, Lucien. Christian Century* Nov. 13: 1074, 1076.

Tucker, William. 1975. *The Fascist Ego: A Political Biography of Robert Brasillach.* Berkeley: University of California Press.

Weber, Eugen. 1962. *"Action Francaise": Royalism and Reaction in Twentieth-Century France.* Stanford: Stanford University Press.

Westerbeck, Colin. 1974. Review of *Lacombe, Lucien. Commonwealth* 29 Nov.: 214-215.

WRITING WITH THE INK OF LIGHT:
JEAN COCTEAU'S *BEAUTY AND THE BEAST*

Lynn Hoggard

"Vive la jeune Muse Cinéma car elle possède le mystère du rêve et permet de rendre l'irréalité réaliste."

—Jean Cocteau, 1959

When in 1757 Madame Leprince de Beaumont published "La Belle et la Bête," she was drawing on sources of the fairy tale that go back ultimately to Apuleius's Cupid and Psyche myth in the second century. She probably drew from a seventeenth-century French tale by Charles Perrault called "Riquet à la Houppe" about a brilliant but misshapen man who makes a beautiful girl appear witty, while her love for him allows her to see him as splendidly handsome (Bettelheim 1977, p. 304). By the eighteenth century, this animal-groom fairy tale centers on the harmonious integration of head and heart and the proprieties of social education. For purposes of comparison with Cocteau's film adaptation, let us briefly review Mme. de Beaumont's polished tale.

A wealthy merchant tries to provide his six children with the best education possible. Two of his three daughters are selfish and vain, whereas the third, Beauty, likes to read good books and doesn't want to marry, preferring to stay by her father's side. The father loses everything, and the family is forced to live on a farm, where Beauty becomes the servant and is the subject of her sisters' abuse. Hoping to reclaim one of his ships, the father returns to the city, bearing requests for lavish gifts from his daughters, except for Beauty, who asks only that he bring her a rose. Disappointed in his hope, and once again left with nothing, he wearily turns his horse toward home. On the journey he loses himself in a magic forest, feasts at an empty castle, is provided with bed and clothing, and, upon leaving the forest, picks a rose to bring home to Beauty. At this point appears a Beast "si horrible que [le marchand] fut tout prêt de s'évanouir," who demands the father's life or that of one of his daughters in exchange for the plucked rose (Mme. de Beaumont 1979, p. 9).

Sick at heart, the father returns to tell his family the bad news. Beauty, of course, calls it her "joy" to be able to save her father and show him her love, preferring, she says, to be devoured by this monster than to die of grief over her father's death. Reluctantly, the father agrees. Once at the Beast's castle, Beauty finds everything arranged for her pleasure. During her first night a fairy appears in a dream, telling her that her good deed will be rewarded.

The Beast, never physically described, visits Beauty, watches her eat, describes himself as having a good heart but no wit, and asks her to marry him. She refuses, but tells him that there are many men more monstrous than he, men with handsome faces but corrupt hearts. For three months, the two live harmoniously, the only pain to Beauty being the Beast's daily request of marriage. Then, through an image in her magic mirror, Beauty learns that her father is dying of grief over her presumed death and asks permission to visit him for a week, a request that the Beast reluctantly grants.

Beauty consoles her father and learns that her two sisters have married foolishly, one marrying a handsome man, "beau comme l'Amour," who is in love with himself, and the other, a man of great wit who enrages everyone, beginning with his wife. The sisters, jealous of Beauty's happiness, conspire to make her break her promise to return to the Beast at week's end. After ten days' absence and a warning dream, Beauty does finally return, deciding that she will marry the Beast because she respects him. She finds him lying by a stream in the garden, dying of a broken heart. There she throws herself upon him, puts water on his head to revive him, and discovers that she loves him deeply. As soon as she speaks her love, the Beast is transformed into a prince "plus beau que l'Amour," who thanks Beauty for breaking an evil spell cast on him by a wicked fairy. He was allowed to show no wit and could return to his native form only if a beautiful woman agreed to marry him.

The pair return to the castle to find all Beauty's family united with them, along with the good fairy from Beauty's dream. The fairy tells Beauty that because she chose virtue over beauty and wit, she has merited having all three qualities united. The two sisters are turned into statues on the castle gates, prisoners to witness Beauty's happiness until such time as they acknowledge their faults. Then, with a flick of the fairy's wand, the entire ensemble is transported into the prince's realm, where Beauty and the prince are married and live in a happiness that is perfect because it is, as the last line tells us, "fondé sur la vertu" (de Beaumont 1979, p. 45).

A tale for children, "Beauty and the Beast" works at a psychological level as well as a narrative one, as Bruno Bettelheim has pointed out in *The Uses of Enchantment*. It is a tale about sexuality, portraying a successful oedipal transfer from father to lover and a coming to terms with sexuality in a way that leads to happiness for everyone. In fact, as Bettelheim notes,

> No other well-known fairy tale makes it as obvious as "Beauty and the Beast" that a child's oedipal attachment to a parent is natural, desirable, and has the most positive consequences for all, if during the process of maturation it is transferred and transformed as it becomes detached from the parent and concentrated on the lover (Bettelheim 1977, p. 307).

"Beauty and the Beast" deals in an indirect way with a child's inchoate fears of sexuality. The rose that the father plucks, for example, becomes a symbol of both father's and daughter's fears of lost maidenhood. Pointing up its sexual nature, the Beast is given the body of a snake in certain earlier versions of the tale; it confesses that the spell was cast when, as man, it had seduced an orphan. Having used a helpless victim to satisfy its lust, it can be redeemed only by unselfish love (Bettelheim 1977, p. 306).

These sexual fears, however, prove unnecessary when Beauty discovers that the Beast is kind and honorable. "While sex may at first seem beastlike," Bettelheim notes, the child comes to understand that "in reality love between woman and man is the most satisfying of all emotions, and the only one that makes for permanent happiness" (Bettelheim 1977, p. 306). At first Beauty feels her love for her father and her attachment to the Beast as opposing pulls. As long as the sexual longings are fixed on the father, the Beast is perceived as repugnant. When, however, in an *epiphanous* moment Beauty realizes that she loves the Beast, his sexuality is no longer odious to her. She has successfully made the transfer of love from father to lover, giving her father the type of love most beneficial to him, and giving the Beast his human form, thereby making a life of happiness possible for the two of them (Bettelheim 1977, p. 308). In psychoanalytic language, Bettelheim calls the marriage of Beauty and the Beast "the humanization and socialization of the id by the superego" (Bettelheim 1977, p. 309).

Mme. de Beaumont's story works also at the mythic or metaphysical level. Simple in its profundity, it tells us something we need perpetually to re-learn—that a thing must be loved before it is loveable. As in "Cinderella" love has the power to transform life in mysterious ways. Beauty's love is a gentle wisdom that brings wholeness, giving the Beast wit and beauty.

In alchemical terms, love is the philosopher's stone that helps turn baser elements into gold, beasts into men, and cinder-gatherers into beauties. As we'll see, both the psychological and mythic levels of the story undergo transformation in the twentieth-century adaptation.

Almost two centuries later and again in France, in August of 1945, Jean Cocteau began filming his version of the tale, a version that some judges at Cannes in 1946 said would go right over the heads of kids and would seem childish to grown-ups (Cocteau 1951, p. 76). Others criticized Cocteau for having imposed his personal mythology on a story that wasn't his, but Cocteau responded by saying that he chose the story *because* it corresponded to his personal mythology, adding: "le plus drole est que tous les objets et actes virés à mon compte se trouvent dans le texte de Mme. Leprince de Beaumont" (Cocteau 1951, p. 76). Cocteau's changes in the story resulted in a visual fairy tale for adults whose dimensions are rendered more mythic and more ambiguous than those of the earlier tale. Before examining the work as film, let us first note those changes.

First of all, Cocteau does away with the moralizing geography of the narrative that has Beauty succeeding because of her virtue. As if in the same stroke, Cocteau also eliminates the fairies from the landscape. Instead of a world split between good fairies and corrupt cities, we have in Cocteau's treatment the world of the real, represented by the father and his children in their country house (we never see them in the city), and the world not of fairies but of the imagination or the surreal, represented by the magical forest where branches part to let one pass by, and by the castle, where doors and mirrors speak, where sheets turn themselves down and rugs unfurl, where caryatids follow humans with their eyes and emit vapor from their mouths, where a disembodied arm pours wine from a decanter, where tears turn into diamonds and mirrors shatter from grief—in short, a primordial place where everything lives and wants to become (Cocteau 1970, p. ix). Beauty's bedroom is as lush and verdant-seeming as the gardens surrounding the castle in this other-world of imagination where, as André Breton has said of surrealism, "tout cesse d'être perçu contradictoirement."

The worlds of real and surreal, as Cocteau presents them to us, are complementary. The Beast tells Beauty that his night is not hers. When it is night in his domain, it is morning in hers. Cocteau has multiplied the magical elements that allow for movement from one world to the other, adding to the truth-telling mirror and the rose of the original story the talismans of horse, glove, and golden key.

Also, he has streamlined the plot. One effect of the streamlining is to give the film greater psychological credibility. In the story, it seems odd that the father, so fond of Beauty, should agree rather quickly to let her take his place as the Beast's victim. The film eliminates this awkwardness by having Beauty slip away without the father's knowledge or consent. Likewise, the story has the father falling ill for love of a daughter that he has willingly turned over to the Beast; the film shows the father's illness as being complexly tied to both the redemptive love of one of his children and the ignoble actions of the other. After Beauty's departure, her brother Ludovic uses his father's possessions as collateral on a gambling debt. When he is unable to pay, the family's furniture is taken. With only his bed left as a courtesy, the father lies dying in an empty house, whispering Beauty's name.

Although the literary version tells of a development in the relationship between Beauty and the Beast but doesn't show it, the film takes great care to shape the couple's contacts into poetic images that reveal an increasing intimacy, which operates in tension with the characters' restraint. We see Beauty begin to anticipate the Beast's arrival; we note her comment that his voice seems softer, just as we note their first moments of physical contact, then their walks, her hand resting on his, through the garden. In one of the film's later scenes, Beauty gives the Beast water to lap from her hands, showing no repugnance at his animal ways. If love is, as St. Exupéry has suggested, a process of taming, then the film's images would suggest that the Beast has tamed Beauty into needing him.

In addition, Cocteau has done away with two of Beauty's brothers, leaving only a carousing brother, Ludovic, and his sidekick Avenant (whose name in French means *pleasing* or *handsome*), a suitor to Beauty. The addition of a boyfriend, by positing an alternative to father and Beast, mutes the earlier story's oedipal tones. Avenant (played by actor Jean Marais, who also plays the role of the Beast and, at film's end, Prince Ardent), though amazingly handsome, is violent and brutal. His character is revealed in the opening "shot" of the film, as Avenant and Ludovic shoot arrows at a target. Ludovic accuses Avenant of cheating and pushes him, causing Avenant's arrow to stray toward the house, penetrating the room where Beauty works. Later he brutally insists that she marry him ("Epousez-moi," he says, trying to force her to kiss him), whereas the Beast in his turn will gently say, "La Belle, voulez-vous être ma femme?"

Although Mme. de Beaumont's characters Beauty and Beast remain abstractions, Cocteau's are a physical glory. The Beast is dressed in the clothes of a great lord and has exquisite manners, along with the enormous, terrifying head and paws of a lion—the latter requiring five hours of makeup per day to achieve. Although no serpent, the Beast is intensely sexual. He watches Beauty dine with an appetite bordering on the sexually ravenous and lurks both outside and inside her bedroom, once ordering her harshly: "Fermez votre porte . . . vite, vite!" Never violent in her presence, he seems never to be other than violent away from her. When he hears an animal sound in the distance, his ears quiver and perk. He returns to the castle from the hunt steaming and covered with the fresh blood of his victims. Beauty spies on him once and watches in wonder as he laps water from a pool like a feline (preparing for the later scene in which she gives him water from her own hands). Being a creature both noble and murderous who is torn by conflicting desires, Cocteau's Beast achieves tragic dimensions. He is the glory and disgrace of man himself— capable of everything, and of its opposite. Until Beauty's love is freely given, however, he will remain prisoner to his despair.

Beauty too is prisoner, more to her own perceptions even than to the Beast. She must tread the difficult path that leads from sexual repulsion to abandonment. She has already rejected Avenant, yet it will be even harder for her to love the Beast, so different from anything she has known. Cocteau presents actress Josette Day, like the Beast, in distinctly physical, even sexual, terms, at the same time showing her as Beauty to be an extraordinarily beautiful but down-to-earth country girl, bewildered but steadfast in her loyalties. Her bodice untied in a way that partially exposes her breasts, she is unselfconsciously voluptuous. The eyes of the castle feast greedily on her as she moves from place to place, the statues as well as ourselves becoming erotic voyeurs.

Cocteau's most dramatic change in the fairy tale is in the addition to the Beast's castle of a secret, glass-covered Pavilion to the Goddess Diana, the place where all the Beast's treasures lie hidden, a place to which even he does not have access. When Beauty leaves him to visit her father, the Beast gives her the

Pavilion key, which she slips into her bodice. He gives it as a sign of his love and trust, for it is the most sacred thing he possesses. Viewed psychologically, the Beast has given Beauty his manhood, his sexuality; her response is a nurturing one. But the imagery of the film carries us beyond the psychological. Viewed mythically, which is where the film locates itself, the Pavilion is the sacred center of creative life. Avenant and Ludovic, along with Beauty's two sisters, conspire to steal the key, hoping to carry off treasures for themselves. Avenant gets the key and finds his way to the Beast's castle; once there he decides not to use the key and shatters the glass dome of the Pavilion. As Avenant hangs from the ceiling in preparation for dropping to the floor, the statue of Diana that guards the temple comes to life and shoots an arrow (much like the one Avenant shoots in the opening scene) that strikes Avenant in the back, killing him. The attempted rape of the chaste goddess's treasure again contrasts sharply with the Beast's reverent behavior toward Beauty, suggesting that force at whatever level can never bring about the surrender of love or mystery. The insertion of the scene at Diana's Pavilion, which in the film is spliced into the scene of the Beast's death, also sets up the most crucial visual message of the film, a message we will discuss shortly.

Rounding out the changes Cocteau made is the film's ending. The couple is not reunited with family and then transported to the prince's kingdom. Beauty does not save the Beast by agreeing to marry him. The Beast, in fact, *dies*. But before his death, he has received a look of love from Beauty (the lover's gaze having as much power in this film as in troubadour poetry) that allows him to be reborn as Prince Ardent. He was changed into a beast, he tells Beauty, as punishment to his father who didn't believe in fairies. Only a look of love can transform him into the figure of his beloved's dreams. Alone, the two lie down on a magic cape to leave for a perfect realm. As they prepare to leave, Beauty tells Prince Ardent, "J'aime avoir peur . . . avec vous." What has happened between them is not a domestication of the id by the superego, as in Mme. de Beaumont's version, but something more complex. Returning too late from her father's to save the Beast, Beauty had cried out as she fell to his side, "C'est moi le monstre!" Beauty has been transformed. She has embraced the strangeness, the awesome sexual wilderness of the Beast, as part of herself, just as the Beast at the end has become as fair of form as Beauty.

By not insisting on a nuptial agreement, and by allowing a *look* of love to suffice, Cocteau has lightened the social and moral burdens of Beauty's mythic journey into the realm of love. Cocteau has also done something else that is highly significant for the medium of film: he has taken out words and in their place substituted a picture—*le regard*—a visual image with a visual message all its own, completely bypassing the intellect.

Summarizing the changes Cocteau made, we see that he played down the oedipal nature of the heroine, provided adult credibility for the characters' behavior, and, by adding Avenant, made the heroine's conflicts an adult's conflicts rather than those of a child. The Beast in Cocteau's treatment becomes a major, multidimensional figure rather than a foil. The tale is still about sexuality, but Cocteau has made sex both more obvious (because more physical) and more subtle (with the opulence of decor and costuming reminiscent of Vermeer, Rembrandt, and Gustave Doré, and the inclusion of the treasure-dome as a collective image-center). The film version suggests a powerful and pervasive sexual awareness, but it is about more than sex; it is about the unconscious, where sex and poetry and creativity lie buried, as if sleeping, to surface for most people only in the most fragmentary ways. Cocteau's Beauty and Beast are like twin Sleeping Beauties who must somehow, somnambulant, find their way to each other to be whole.

Cocteau had more in mind, however, than a pyschological study of human sexuality, no matter how perceptive those insights might seem. His ultimate aim was *poésie,* which is what Cocteau called all his writing, including that writing he said was done with the "encre de lumière," meaning, of course, cinema. "Je crois que le grand privilège cinématographique de la France c'est la poésie," Cocteau writes (Gilson 1964-1969, p. 116). As he defines it, poetry is that "something else" in great art that moves us, something that is not of the art itself. It has nothing whatsoever to do with the poetic. In fact, the artist ought not to try to create poetry: "Ma méthode est simple: ne pas me mêler de poésie. Elle doit venir d'elle-même" (Cocteau 1946, p. 14). Instead, Cocteau beguiles the muse: "Je laisse les événements suivre la route qu'ils veulent. Mais au lieu de perdre tout contrôle, comme il arrive dans le rêve, je célèbre les noces du concret et de l'inconscience, qui mettent au monde ce monstre terrible et délicieux qu'on appelle *Poésie*" (Gilson 1964-1969, p. 126). Poetry comes, Cocteau believes, through rigor, order, natural invention, beauty, and simple lines—in other words, through precision (Gilson 1964-1969, p. 56).

Pacing and lighting in the film deserve particular attention in that both are arranged to highlight the poetic theme without being used "poetically." The scenes at Beauty's home are paced briskly, with a stationary camera (Cocteau felt a moving camera annulled movement) and with frequent changes of angle, giving the sense of constant motion with many points of reference. Likewise, the lighting is fuller in the shots at Beauty's home, but becomes progressively darker as the story moves closer to the Beast's castle. In the family scenes at Beauty's, light hits the characters' faces clearly and evenly. We sense order, proportion, clarity.

On the other hand, from the moment we enter the forest, we leave behind the world of proportion whose contours are known. Lighting is uneven, although never fuzzy or misty. The chiaroscuro technique may boldly highlight a hand or a neck while leaving a face in shadow. Shadows, in fact, begin to behave as if they too were characters with parts to play. The father climbs the steps to enter the Beast's castle and is terrified by his own immense shadow, which looms menacingly toward him. Background often is as brightly and unevenly lighted as foreground; a door, a bannister, or a flight of stairs competes with characters for importance. We have entered a dream world where perspective has no importance, where forces other than reason hold sway.

The intensification of dark and light imagery at the Beast's castle illustrates the contrast between the worlds of real and unreal. The rose, a symbol of Beauty herself, lights up like the sun when the father first sees it, and the petals seem to unfurl. The characters often are seen moving from areas of shadow to areas of blinding light, as when, at one point, the Beast carries Beauty up a flight of stairs into a light so white that both totally disappear. At its peak, the cinematic ink of expression vanishes, leaving nothing but imageless light.

The pacing also changes once we are at the Beast's castle. The shots become longer, many lasting twenty or more seconds, again with a stationary camera. Moreover, several shots are even taken in slow motion, such as the one of Beauty running through the Beast's castle. With no hard cinematic editing to jolt our minds into alertness, we are beguiled into the slow, sensuous rhythms of the film's poetry; we fall more deeply into the waking dream.

Cocteau sees art at its best as able to transcend itself and lead us to glimpse the mystery and marvel of life. When it does this, art has achieved "le réalisme irréel," unreal realism (Cocteau 1951, p. 76), the state of the waking dream. Cocteau's method is to focus relentlessly on the realistic detail, but his goal is for *vérisme*, a truth that, because it combines consciousness with unconsciousness, becomes "plus vrai que le vrai" (Gilson 1964-1969, p. 119). To achieve this higher truth within the medium of cinema, Cocteau claims to use any method he can, including his justly famous trick shots (as when, for example, to intensify the eerie grace of Josette Day as Beauty moving through the Beast's castle at night, Cocteau had the actress pulled along on a dolly, creating an effect of Beauty floating rather than walking). Verism, Cocteau feels, is uniquely suited to cinema because in film one *sees as fact* not only the world of the real, but that of the unreal as well. As the most accessible of the senses, sight carries an authority of belief that the written word cannot equal. It also bypasses the more intellectual circuitry of language, which Cocteau, though poet, novelist, and playwright himself, believes removes us from the most immediate and therefore most powerful apprehension of poetry. Study of the filmscript of "Beauty and the Beast" reveals consistent effort by Cocteau to transfer verbal narrative into visual form. There is no voice-over narration in the film. Instead, the images, a small amount of dialogue, and judicious transitions and editing convey the narrative thrust. Spoken lines by the characters are consistently pared, to the point that the actors complained that they didn't have enough to say. As mentioned earlier, Beauty's words of love were changed to a look of love. Like other surrealists, Cocteau wants to bypass reason and reach emotion with the force of surprise.

With Cocteau, the eye of the camera becomes our eye in the most intense way. His knowledge of the conventions of theater assists him in recognizing where the spectator is and how the angle of the shot would affect him. "J'insiste sur le mot: *indiscret*," he writes. "La caméra est l'oeil le plus indiscret et le plus impudique" (Cocteau 1951, p. 106). Cocteau's most daring shots, as critic André Bazin has noted, are founded on an unerring knowledge of our reactions as ideal spectators (Gilson 1964-1969, p. 148). Thus, when Beauty's father is about to pluck the forbidden rose in the Beast's garden, we realize suddenly, watching the father as if through a tiny keyhole, that we the audience are the Beast looking at the father as potential prey. The effect is unsettling, as it was intended to be. We have become intensely an Other.

François Truffaut has said that cinema is first and foremost two shots that follow each other well. Cocteau adds the flavor of his own style to Truffaut's idea. "Le cinéma exige une syntaxe," he has said. "Cette syntaxe n'est obtenue que par l'enchaînement et par le choc des images entre elles" (Cocteau 1951, p. 13). Contrary to having a film flow, Cocteau's aim, he insists, is to prevent the images from flowing; instead, he wants to oppose and separate them (Cocteau 1951, p. 15). He insists that editing is style, and that any filmmaker who doesn't do his own editing is translated into a foreign language (Gilson, 1964-1969, p. 112).

Cinema to Cocteau is the means to an end, the end being not narrative or psychological study, but poetry. Cinema is the Zen finger pointing to the moon, the medium leading to, but not synonymous with, the message. It isn't magic, but suggests that life, could we see it whole, is indeed magical. Like all the surrealists, Cocteau is in sensibility very much within the Romantic tradition. But in method, which consists in delving into the interior of the psyche and bringing back insights that are at once deeply personal and broadly mythic, and in the freshly innovative ways he chose to do this, Cocteau stands in the avant-garde of twentieth-century art.

His unique contribution to cinema stems, in fact, from his surrealism. By probing the human unconscious for images of itself and by putting those private but universal images before us, he *rei*fies our interior world, thereby giving it tangible reality. This process of transformation is the essence of surrealist art. In the service of an artist, cinema is the ablest of the art forms to transform the fantastical elements of the human mind into concrete and mobile images—to make the unreal real. When the archeology goes deep and the vision is of a high order, the result is surrealist cinema; outside of Cocteau, Buñuel, and a very few others, such surrealism in cinema remains an unmet challenge. "La Muse Cinéma," Cocteau saw clearly, "est trop riche, trop facile à ruiner d'un seul coup" (Cocteau 1951, p. 10).

Cocteau's personal, poetic style of writing in this "encre de lumière" made him a natural precursor to the *Auteur* movement in French cinema, which also embraced the idea of cinema as a kind of writing (*caméra-stylo*) that is both creative and personal. Cocteau's adaptation of *La Belle et la Bête* suggests that he clearly understood that his film should not seek to recreate the literary experience, but to reflect it from a different angle.

The scene of the Beast's death near the film's end suggests perhaps better than any other Cocteau's theme and method. I would like to conclude with a brief discussion of it. As Beauty leans over the dying Beast, attempting to revive him, the scene is cut and spliced into a simultaneous scene, that of Avenant and Ludovic breaking into the Pavilion of Diana. The Beast dies of a broken heart at the precise moment that Avenant is executed for rape. As the camera, our eye, studies Avenant's dead face, a change occurs. Avenant's face becomes that of the Beast, the Beast's face becomes Avenant's. The Beast is not transformed or resurrected. Instead, phoenixology occurs: Rising from the corpse is neither Beast nor Avenant, but Prince Ardent, a new character, noble as the Beast and beautiful as Avenant, but more than either. Because of the visual simultaneity of the images, Cocteau's resolution is temporally different from the Hegelian dialectic of Romantic literature. As a result, the cinematic experience is different from the literary one. To our eye, there are not three phases occurring, but one. The Taoist symbol of the yin/yang comes closer to suggesting the dynamic visual interplay of opposites that Cocteau postulates. Avenant has added the light of his beauty to the dark of the Beast's surface; the Beast has replaced the violence of Avenant's character with its own depth of soul. Out of that union comes a perfect whole that lives and moves. Having found themselves in finding each other, the Prince and Beauty do not return to family and castle. Through Cocteau's art, they have left the worlds of real and surreal behind. On the ink of light, they fly away to live on in the magic of cinematic poetry.

WORKS CITED

Bettelheim, Bruno. 1977. *The Uses of Enchantment.* New York: Vintage Books.
Cocteau, Jean. 1970. *Beauty and the Beast.* New York: New York University Press.
———. 1951. *Entretiens autour du Cinmatographe.* Paris: Editions André Bonne.
———. 1946. *La Belle et la Bête: Journal d'un film.* Paris: Janin. de Beaumont, Madame Leprince, et d'Aulnoy, Madame. 1979. *La Belle et la Bête et autres contes.* Paris: Le Livre de Poche.
Gilson, René. 1964-69. *Jean Cocteau. Cinéma d'aujourd'hui, 27.* Paris: Seghers.

THE PLIGHT OF FILM ADAPTATION IN FRANCE: TOWARD DIALOGIC PROCESS IN THE *AUTEUR* FILM

Ghislaine Géloin

> Literary forms have to be checked against reality, not against aesthetics—
> even realist aesthetics.
>
> Brecht, *On Theatre*

Considering the recent spate of film adaptations of well-known literary works, such as *Under the Volcano* (Huston 1983, novelist Malcom Lowry), *The Bostonians* (James Ivory 1983, novelist Henry James), *Passage to India* (David Lean 1984, novelist E. M. Foster), in the USA; *Swann in Love* (Schlöndorff 1984, novelist Proust), in Germany; and in France, by Bertrand Tavernier, *Clean Slate* (1982, scenarist Jean Aurenche, novelist Jim Thompson), *A Sunday in the Country* (1984, late novelist and former scenarist Pierre Bost)—there seems to be a renewed interest in producing films based on liteary works. In the eighties, the filmmakers seem no longer to have any compunction about telling stories of the past and to reconnect, at least, in the case of France, with the old style of "quality films" of the fifties that the New Wave hated and ridiculed so much. The phenomenon has caused the old contentions, prejudices, and polemics of the fifties against film adaptation to resurface. In France, Tavernier won't fail to be criticized for doing away with New Wave film progress and revolutionary practices, since Pierre Bost and Jean Aurenche were the very names of the scenarists' team that became the prime target of the film Avant-garde's attack.

If reactions have been superficially the same in the USA and in France, viewers and critics have demonstrated cultural biases that have something to do with each nation's particular attitude toward its literary legacy. This attitude, in turn, has mapped out a history of different and distinct relationships between literature and cinema in the two countries. In France, film has always had an ambiguous relationship to literature, a relationship charged with a love-hate tension, as film continues to claim at the same time its affinities to and independence from literature. It was partly to regain their artistic freedom that the Cineasts of the 60s—the *Auteur* Film in general—turned against the film

135

adaptations of the fifties, for they found the philosophy implicit
in making them unacceptable. This attitude was best exemplified
by Godard's cinema which, time and again, proclaimed outrage-
ously, "No more stories" (of any kind).

It is film adaptations of literary works that cause old passions
to flare up again. Resistance is still staunchly alive in the French
mentality. France's literary legacy still tends to represent a sealed-
off cultural universe intent on maintaining its hegemony by
dictating rules, one of which is that aspects of the novelistic
experience are not translatable from the printed page to the
screen. It recognizes an unwritten law: the more "literary" or
well-known a novel is, the less "filmable" it is. Indeed, film
adaptation has been the Achille's heel of the cinema. Unavoida-
bly it offers itself for the kill. Such a film suffers a bad reputation
even before the shooting has begun. A recent case in point is
Swann in Love. Proust has always carried a legendary reputation
of being "unfilmable" and has been the "untouchable" of
literature. When Visconti conceived such a project in 1962, he
eventually had to yield to some unclear pressures and abandoned
his project. When Schlöndorff brought the first realization of
Proust to the screen, the endeavor was even more disconcerting
because it meant that a foreigner was daring to adapt a
masterpiece of French cultural heritage. The cineast, aware of the
losing battle, is reported to have said jokingly that he would slip
out of France during the Parisian premiere to avoid being
lynched by the French.

I am acknowledging here the new spate in film adaptation to
reassess its historical plight and raise again some vital issues. Are
we witnessing another age of adaptation, a nostalgia for (high)
literary culture, for literary classics, which had found their way
after the fifties into TV serials, into "TV art drama," like
Masterpiece Theatre, as part of a cultural commodity, consumerism? Do these films intend to foster a cultural memory and
reinforce the cultural-ritual baggage of a nation, with some
educational stimulus? Or is film now better armed to rival with
the novel?

If we look into the reception that these film adaptations have
had, we notice the same attitudes from critics and sophisticated
viewers that were voiced previously: the film is still compared to
its source, the film's achievement gauged with that of the novel.
In a way, novel and film look at each other and judge each other.
At best, the filmmaker will share credit with the author's

achievement, and will also have to account for every deviation from the novel. At worst, the film is measured against the novel, accused of leveling off the novel's content, of "desecrating" and vulgarizing it. The film is never judged in its own right, and the original forsaken. In almost every case, the final verdict is returned: "*It is not* the novel."

If we return, however, to the case of the Proust adaptation and examine the media reaction, there seems to emerge slowly a new national mentality, a new sensibility toward film adaptation. *Swann in Love* caused a mini-event on the national cultural scene and became a heated issue in the media during February 1984. The influential *Le Monde* titled the event "the end of a taboo" and well-known writers were asked to give their opinions on their own visualization of the Proustian world. Actually the question was a devious way to lead the writers to argue on the filmability or the unfilmability of the Proustian world. Philippe Sollers took sides with the film and preremptorily stated that it was breaking a formidable taboo (which we can add was long awaited). His arrogant article brought an immediate ironic reproof from one of the main leading cinema magazines, *Positif*. He was accused of cultural consumerism. I wonder if the polemics of the debate meant to allude to the lifting of a taboo for film adaptations of literary works in general or to herald officially the beginning of a new area, long sought after and practised all along, though in a devious way, by the New Wave. A writer seems to have summed up the core of the contention when, in the guise of a conclusion, he declared that Schlöndorff had at least "the courage to end a terror of cinema: that of *writing* on a film based on the novel by Marcel Proust (*Le Monde* 23 Feb. 1984). In other terms, is literature finally ready—film as well—to be "penetrated" according to a new concept of adaptation of literary works?

The writer's remark leads us indeed to the dialogic process in the *Auteur* cinema, which originated in the sixties. The dialogic practice—taken from Bakhtin's theories on "Discourse in the novel" in *The Dialogic Imagination*—is only the extreme point of film adaptation, its deconstructive aspect. It has mainly remained unnoticed, or at best been cursorily acknowledged to be dismissed under the label of Homage, and as a gratuitous and irritating cultural idiosyncrasy of the French filmmakers. This cinema is often accused of being literary, with all of the derogatory connotations that such a term conveys. It has finally

138 FILM AND LITERATURE

been taken for a trademark of the French film, which is referred to also as a cinema of quotations. Yet the dialogic process, as a new perspective in adaptation, introduces a revolutionary use of literature, a revenge from the varied experiences and mishaps that the French cinema has suffered from its involvement with literature. The study of these relationships might help us understand the concept of resistance that film and literature have held against each other, or more precisely, literature has fostered against cinema, while the latter was constantly reaffirming its affinities but always placing them "elsewhere."

The inevitability of a dialogic process in the *Auteur* films can be understood best if we first analyze and reassess the true nature of the rivalry between the two arts and their respective languages, if we explain the positions taken by the filmmakers of the New Wave in the polemics that ensued, and show what was at stake in the conflict.

From the very start, because of its aesthetics principles, narrative cinema, consciously or unconsciously, grounded itself in literary fiction, mainly in the literary realist tradition. Eisenstein, referring to Griffith, summed up this strong involvement in literature:

> Our cinema is not altogether without parents and without pedigree, without a past, without the traditions and rich cultural heritage of the past epochs. It is only thoughtless and presumptuous people who can erect laws and an esthetic for cinema, proceeding from the premises of some incredible virgin-birth of this art. (Eisenstein 1949, p. 323)

Griffith affirmed that he proceeded in the same way in his films as Dickens did in writing his novels and that the only difference between them was that the story was told through images instead of words. From first to last, Griffith and Eisenstein studied Dickens's literary techniques to find equivalents for their cinematic techniques. According to Eisenstein, Dickens's works became the pivotal point between a literary past and the art of cinematography. He finally praised Griffith for having grounded his cinematic craftmanship, and film craftmanship in general, in Dickens.

French narrative cinema resumed this direction and grounded itself in the rich legacy of fiction, turning almost exclusively to the literary realist tradition of the novel that it judged it could serve best because of the power of the camera to capture elements of reality as had never been done before. It contended that the novel could best represent reality, under the assumption that the camera permitted the conquest of the real. For the first time, film was bringing to the screen a perfect equation with the real. Realism became identified with its cinematographic representation. Because the moving image conveyed a greater impression of reality, duplicated—and even simulated—reality was, indeed, the real itself; it could restore to the literary work its ideal form, the complex fabric of the objective world. André Bazin saw in the evolution of cinema, drawing from "Stroheim-Murnau trend," "the secret of the regeneration of realism in storytelling." For him "only an increased realism of the image [could] support the abstraction of montage," and because the image was "founded on a much higher degree of realism it has at its disposal more means of manipulating reality and of modifying it from within." Consequently, he concluded "the film-maker is no longer the competitor of the painter and playwright, he is, at last, the equal of the novelist" (Bazin 1967, p. 142); therefore, the cinema was brought irrevocably in the site of the novelistic discourse.

Film put itself in a double bind: mimesis of the real; it needed literary fiction—that is a prior language and form—as a guarantee for artistic enterprise. In so doing, it became mimesis of literature. This period was that of a cinema that put itself slavishly to the service of literature—unwittingly paying lip-service to it—on behalf of a literary truth that had already distilled reality. French narrative cinema extended nineteenth-century fiction, the literary realist tradition. It appropriated the fiction that seemed to work the closest to "the thing." Zola's works were cannibalized on the screen, were the object of a series of adaptations, each in an ever-increased effort to reach "The Language of Truth" by putting itself above the other languages of truth, in an attempt to recover the original meaning, to be the *Same*. Cinema was the realization of the grand utopia of realism, of a literature becoming the world. Because of its technical ability to produce what Bazin called "l'effet du réel" (reality-effect), the film had recovered the presence of the world captured in the transparency of the visual image, better, of the real. Both had become in the process the *Same*.

Truffaut initiated the polemics against literary adaptations in 1954 in an article, "A certain tendency in the French Cinema," starting with his famous outcry "Down with literature." He denounced the servility of the classical cinema—the cinema of "quality"—toward the novel and the inadequacy of a system intent on reproducing, on appropriating the original. The

scenarists' team: Pierre Bost and Jean Aurenche became the butt
of Truffaut's vengeful attack. He asked in a rage whether there
was one literary work of art in the national heritage that had not
been spared. His cinema would reaffirm its affinities with
literature but would involve it this time, however, at another
level.

Truffaut also became the true exponent of "Le Manifeste de la
Caméra-Stylo" (Astruc 1948)—literally "the Camera-Pen." It
claimed that writing with one's camera was in no way different
from writing with one's pen. The programmatic article drew the
film in its novelistic royal path. It prophesied optimistically a
new age by developing a language, a supple *écriture*, that would
write with "nature in the raw," which would not merely reflect
reality but interrogate it. So far film had confessed the difference
between describing and writing (in French *d-écrire* and *écrire*).
The camera was to become the "pen" of the twentieth century,
and there would be no field that it could not master. The
Manifesto was to become very influential in the *Auteur* theory of
the New Wave, which made the filmmaker an artist engaged in
forging a personal style like every writer. As early as 1957,
Truffaut predicted that the film of tomorrow seemed to him even
more personal than a novel, individual and autobiographical,
like a confession or a private diary. It was again to reassess film
as a modern novelistic discourse; however, Auteurism was linked
to a romantic ideology of art-as-expression. It had for polemic
value to reclaim for cinema an artistic enterprise and to suggest
that self-expression occurred not only in content but above all in
cinematic form.

Though New Wave screenwriters preferred to write directly for
the cinema, they did experiment with adaptations in accordance
with their theories. It was as if they wanted to challenge the deep-
seated opinion and the novel on its own ground. They took as a
model Bresson and the *Dairy of a Country Priest*, 1951. The film
became a sort of *cause célèbre* and inaugurated the true practice
of an art of adaptation. For the first time a revolution in the
standard practice of adaptation had been achieved, a novel "in
sight and sound" had been translated in the language of cinema.
The "film of literature" had put itself to the service of literature,
served its cause, by finding a cinematic style worthy of the
original. There could be an art of adaptation when it was given
to a true art of the cinema. André Bazin talked about the
achievement as "a dialectic between the cinema and literature":

It was not a question of free inspiration with the intention of making a
duplicate. It is a question of building a secondary work with the novel as
foundation. In no sense is the film "comparable" to the novel or "worthy" of
it. It is a new aesthetic creation, the novel so to speak multiplied by the
cinema . . . . The aesthetic pleasure we derive . . . includes all the novel has to
offer plus, in addition, its refraction in the cinema. (Bazin 1967, pp. 39-40)

In his first film, *Les Mistons*, 1958, Truffaut attacked, in an in-
joke, the adaptation of the cinema of "quality" and mocked
ferociously its scenarists (here, Jean Delannoy). He set about to
show what a true adaptation was about and opted for a free
adaptation by "stealing" from three novellas by Maurice Pons.
Free adaptation is a matter of knowing how to "steal," in a series
of transactions, exchanges, metamorphoses, by exploiting fully
the language of cinema. *Jules et Jim*, 1961, also became a model
of the art of adaptation. The film was a rare occurrence of the
fusion of two temperaments into one vision, a rare empathy of
thought and sensitivity between two authors, sharing the same
"elective affinities," alluded to in the film by having the
protagonists share the Goethe book. The enterprise is then always
semi-auto-biographical, for adaptation always implies a reading
of the original; therefore it is always a discourse that brings in
the process a dialogic dimension.

Then, in 1963, Godard took his own stance in *Le Mépris/
Contempt*, and brought the inevitability of a dialogic process in
the two arts one step further. The film's subject matter is about
adaptation—the rewriting of *The Odyssey*—and is itself adapted
from the novel *Il Disprezzo* by A. Moravia. More precisely, it is
about the impossibility of adaptation and brings forth the
concept of difference. A filmic adaptation differs necessarily from
the original if the potentialities of the medium are to be fully
exploited. It is necessarily an interpretation. It always contains an
internal (or explicit) criticism of the original (like the act of
reading itself). This time literature and its language are
scrutinized and judged coldly by the cinema. Godard's intentions
in this film are highly strategic. His cinema has started to
function as an "agent provocateur," refusing to remythologize in
another language and incorporating disruptive points of view to
decenter the ideological world in which literature (and traditional
film, by the same token) has inscribed itself. The stratified novels
and film bringing a new context, become the site of a struggle.
The film, in its attempt to return to the first *récit*-in-the-world,
realizes that it has to deal with a language that Bakhtin described
as "overpopulated with the intentions of others." The story can

lend itself superficially to the appropriation and transformations into another language, but, along the way, "many words stubbornly resist, others remain alien, sound foreign in the mouth of the one who appropriates them and who now speaks them." Godard, through Fritz Lang's voice, can come only to the liberating realization that "[the words] cannot be assimilated into his context and fall out of it; it is as if they put themselves in quotation marks against the will of the speaker" (Bakhtin 1981, pp. 293-94).

It is therefore appropriate that Godard's cinema has been called a cinema of quotations, because quotations are the core of his strategy. The film, by being constantly situated at the intersections of other language systems, of different kinds of discourses already saturated with prior meaning, by necessity possesses a dialogic dimension. Writing for Godard always occurs within and against a hostile linguistic (or other) environment; *his* is always a subversive writing:

> (an) heteroglossia that rages beyond the boundaries of such a sealed-off cultural universe, a universe having its own literary language. . . . It is necessary that heteroglossia wash over a culture's awareness of itself and its language, penetrate to its core, relativize the primarily language system underlying its ideology and literature and deprive it of its naive absence of conflict. (Bakhtin 1981, p. 368)

The above-mentioned films heralded the political program of the New Wave, especially after 1968. The creative adaptation picks up from the formula "inspiré par" of Renoir who, in his artistic humility, had understood that adaptation of the novel and the novel itself are two different practices and consequently he opted for free adaptations. Instead of trying to replace the novel, film and novel exist side by side and are to be judged on their own terms. Nevertheless, critics continued to use literary criteria, and film continued to suffer from the plight of adaptation and continued to be seen as imitation, reproduction and, as with every imitation, inferior to the original, merely a "viewer's digest" of literature. This plight mainly comes from the concept of classical texts conceived as closed texts—as "readerly texts" (to use Barthes' terminology in *S/Z*)—that the reader approaches as a consumer, with little freedom to invent. It also comes from the staunch hostility of literature to deal as equal to equal with an artistic cinema conceived as an art of self-expression.

Meanwhile film was ready to assert its independence: it owed it to its literary formation. It took the form of a slow apprenticeship of its narrative potentials grafted on an alien context. It is as if the cinema had to discover its own language in someone else's language, that of the novel. It is in this constant imitation—and confrontation—with literary forms and structures that film has gradually evolved from a dramatic art and slowly matured as a narrative art. Its dual literary and cultural heritage has allowed film to develop subtle narrative strategies that have mapped out cinematic forms. First alienated in the dominant cultural universe of the book, it has spoken the voices of others in a muted speech. Its love for fiction has worked out to eliminate differences in the vain ideological hope of becoming identical. But it has along the way freed itself from slavishly imitating the novel and consequently from the entrapment of the reproduction of the real, which Bazin considered as "its vocation on the service of realism." Then comes the time for narrative self-invention, for writing with the specificity of its own language. Bresson had prophetically defined cinema, in the late fifties, as an *"écriture* (writing) with images in movement and with sounds." The film was led to redefine itself, to invent the ground of its own desire, its "otherness." As Bakhtin argued, any discourse *"lives* as it were, on the boundary between its own contexts and another alien context (Bakhtin 1981, p. 282).

With the New Wave, literature loses its monologic status and is brought down to earth. Fiction is no longer a closed system, but is simultaneously open and closed. From now on, the literary work is conceived as an open text with no definite meanings. More precisely, every fiction is an amalgam of both the "readerly" and the "writerly." In *S/Z*, Barthes defined the "writerly text" as the operation of rewriting the text in the process of reading it:

> the writerly text is *ourselves writing*, before the infinite play of the world (the world as play) is traversed, intersected, stopped, plasticized by some singular system (Ideology, Genre, Criticism), which reduces the plurality of entrances, the opening of networks, the infinity of languages. The writerly is the novelistic without the novel . . . production without product structuring without structure. (Barthes 1970, pp. 299-300; my translation)

In France, culture has been secularly and primarily literary. But, since the second half of the twentieth century, instead of being seen as instructing us about the real world to a point of being confused with the real, literary/cultural models are seen as interpretive models fraught with social, moral and aesthetic intentions that inform our culture. For the New Wave, the emphasis in adaptation is essentially on the writerly. This emphasis represents the political modernism of the artistic text and is an entirely strategic enterprise. By its writerly side (or rather, by fractioning it into disparate fragments that can still be of some use) fiction becomes marked by limitless plurality of meanings, open to new intentions and change. These texts are taken in a dialogic process with the fiction of the film, with the intention to write from radically different perspectives. The book becomes endlessly reusable, accessible to new discourses—multi-discourses. It "compels them," as Bakhtin said, "to serve new intentions, to serve a second master" (Bakhtin 1981, pp. 299-300). The process of the transformation is necessarily dialogic—that is, it involves a dialectical interaction between two fictions, between two styles, two languages, points of view woven into a new plot, new contexts, reinterpreted by the author. For instance, this is the case of Truffaut's series of *The Adventures of Antoine Doinel*. It is a cinema written in the practice of intertextuality, the modern writing *par excellence*.

The film is caught in this double bind. By its vocation "in the service of realism" that film retains at its core—the reality-effect that film fosters, and which has long been considered its plight—the camera has become the apparatus of the twentieth century with which to spin stories, to fictionalize the world with "nature in the raw." In so doing, it continues to cater to the desire of Fiction that is inherent in humanity. Greimas has revealed the natural propensity of the real to be narrated, that is to become intelligible. The oldest operation of humanity is to have imposed on the world narrative patterns that articulate the world, give it order, and are precursors of knowledge. Thus the world has become saturated with languages. As a full-fledged narrative art, cinema by necessity has to feed on fiction. But also, by its literary formation, film has to compose with a prior language that we call literature, and which is the secular narrative art-form (the novel/the book), with all the tales written, and which have allegedly screened "reality." It has to come to terms with the stories-in-the-world in an artistic reworking, itself in search of a new narrative that would return to the real but without relinquishing the textual-effect. The New Wave's cinema challenges the view of reality imposed by a prior language, for cinema exists in this dilemma, in these multifold boundaries. At the heart of the debate lies an "ontological"/ideological tension. If cinema has to deal with the real, and because the real is always pre-ordered by previous discourses, its task is to rupture this order, to search for a more accurate way of looking at the world; in so doing, it discloses the way that culture informs the word.

Faced with the necessity of borrowing from other languages (by its popular French abbreviation and false latin etymology: ciné=siné=without), the modern film, which reflects back on its aesthetic principles, assumes the act of reading prior discourses and speaks with the cultural residues. The expropriation of the language of others is part of the phenomenon of the modern artistic enterprise, of the pluralistic worldview of our contemporary culture. It is embedded particularly in the nature of cinema. In Sade, Fourier and Loyola, Barthes defined the locus of modern writing as follows:

> In fact, today, there is no language site outside bourgeois ideology: our language comes from it, returns to it, remains closed up in it. The only possible rejoinder is neither confrontation nor destruction, but only theft: to fragment the old texts of culture, science, literature, and change its features according to formulate of disguise, as one disguises stolen goods. (15; my translation)

This is exactly the lesson that Antoine Doinel learns in *The 400 Blows*, the fictional autobiography of Truffaut, when he steals from Balzac the content of his essay without disguising it. It seems to be also the lesson that the New Wave gives us as often as not in its films. By disclosing here and there fragments of texts, its films place their own narrative intentions in diagolue with other discourses that already mediate the world. These cineasts make former texts slough off their old skins in order to look at them differently: these are recognized or not. the reinscription of literature as language is not a sign of weakness, but is part of the cinema's ability to signify, that is, its ability to play with, to control, to restructure, to disrupt prior fictions. Cinema takes pleasure in reworking old meanings, but it does not insist that a particular truth be established. Finally, the viewer is left to sew the pieces into a whole, encouraged to search for new answers while the film warns him to resist reinterpretation.

By using "ready-made" intertexts, the incorporated texts lose their own status as a signified entity to be approached as new signs that launch again, in a new context, a signifying process. Film and novel become the site of a struggle, the locus of an act of aggression, as if they were in an Oedipal crisis. The film puts itself in a dialectical tension of involvement, as the protagonists are ruled by an obsessive mimetic desire, and disengagement from literature, as the filmmaker establishes some wrongdoing in literary discourse. The meaning of the film exists somewhere in the gap, or *differance* (to use Derrida's term which enables writing to be), between the world (the reference to reality that film is allegedly closer to) and the art form that articulates it (reference to cultural signs). In this double allegiance, the filmic text shies away from its two determinations, redirecting its intentions always somewhere *between*. Eventually, the book is brought to trial, as many half-lies or illusions structuring our world. Referentiality on either side of the coin is thrown into doubt. Finally, filmic texts mainly address their operation to spectator-text relations in order to reexamine with him the structuring of subjectivity, the fictionalization of reality. The process is always an act of reading at the core of which lies questioning, critical judgment, disclosing by the same token our propensity to mythmaking.

The New Wave is a deconstructive cinema. It uses explicitly antirealist and anti-illusionist—mainly Brechtian—strategies to put our cultural forms (and older practices of the cinema) into question. These stylized techniques disengage us from the processes of identification. The cineasts of the sixties became the investigators of our culture at every level. The world's cultural forms are seized, appropriated, analyzed, relativized, taken apart, transformed, and redefined, to subvert them in order to change the world. This was Rimbaud's poetic program, the one that Godard reinscribes in its filmic text, starting with *Pierrot le fou*, 1965. These films usually do not have beginning and end, because they refuse to remythologize. The text is left open in the instability of its meaning. Forging an alliance with the book, the film becomes the site both of challenge and "otherness." In the dialogic process, the intertext, summoned to explain itself, is freed to speak once more. The aggression is always an act of writing. It challenges the view of reality that prior languages represent, passing themselves off as the real and demystifying them. The film itself, as another language of the real, brings another's voice, exposing the difference.

No matter what the multifold manifestations of the dialogic process, its stakes and its various forms of aggression, it comes from one passion, that of literature. This love can be denied, corrected, seen from other disruptive points of view, but it will remain forever an unforgettable—if unrequited—love. This was the passion of the films of the New Wave, of the *Auteur* Film in general.

APPENDIX

Some French *Auteur* films that use the dialogic process.

1—The dialectical relationship between life, reading, and writing:

L'Homme qui aimait les femmes (*The Man Who Loved Women*), Truffaut 1977.
This is the story of a man who also loved books narrated by his woman publisher. The reader-turned-writer realizes at a certain point that he cannot narrate his life unless he turns to other narratives in order to compare his autobiography and model his own writing to them. The film reveals more than the book-within-the-film it documents. More particularly, it highlights the "blind spot" of his written autobiography. By depicting a scriptorial and visual record of events that do not totally mesh, the film aims at reflecting reality more closely.

Le Genou de Claire (*Claire's knee*), Rohmer 1970.
Rohmer's protagonists act usually as if they were characters in a novel. Here, the protagonist's life becomes the project of a novel designed by his woman-friend writer. He surrenders himself willingly to the plot.

There are three conflicting points of view in the film with their many displacements and illusions:

1) The novelist becomes the film's primary narrator. But life intrudes and the novelist's plot falls short.

2) Then the protagonist takes his "novel" into his own hands and becomes his own "hero" and teller of his own story. Along the way, he realizes that he needs to spin a fine story-thread to enhance the real-life experience. But the protagonist loses his credibility while the woman novelist acts as the arbiter of events.

3) The camera documents both points of view, but also, by its own narrative power, gives another perspective on the events. The viewer is put in the unstable position of having to constrast the different structuring patterns in order to reach a better appreciation of what has really happened.

Providence, Resnais, 1977.
The title symbolizes the Providence of Writing. The film takes place in Providence where Lovecraft used to live. Resnais was an ardent reader of Lovecraft, and he uses him as the literary model for his writer-protagonist. Despite all the references, however, the symbolic network remains limited.

The film shows how the literary imagination is sometimes rooted in reality and how it sometimes plays tricks with reality and with itself. The audience is left to sort out what reality is and what is pure fabrication of the mind.

L'Histoire d'Adèle H (The Story of Adèle H), Truffaut 1975.
The film embodies the passion of writing from a (neurotic) romantic perspective. It is the writing of the libido supplementing an existential inadequacy. Adèle H (Victor Hugo's daughter) transforms her life into a text that becomes *The Story of . . .* and it will end up in madness. The film reveals how writing can be a snare and focuses on the process of self-destruction and devastation by a romantic passion.

2—The books as the structuring device: their introjection and projection onto the world

Ma Nuit chez Maud (*My Night at Maud's*), Rohmer 1969.
Clermont Ferrand: Pascal's birthplace. Philosophical concepts of Luck, Chance, Providence, Grace, and Choice, taken from Pascal's theory of the Wager and reinterpreted, are transferred to secular decisions, to the narrator's fear of marriage and several restrictions in his life. They become easy alibis to assuage his qualms of conscience and end up in Jesuitic hypocrisies.

The Pascalian text here is revived and seen against a Marxist context. The viewer experiences the conflict between the protagonist's behavior and a barrage of dubious motivations. His series of intellectual principles have offered him tailored responses to conduct his life and marriage but at the expense of truth. But actually they have only been a way of shutting out the difficulties of his own circumstances.

Les Aventures d'Antoine Doinel, Truffaut.

The 400 Blows, 1959. The Balzacian subtext *A la Recherche de l'Absolu* is inscribed in this film and the passion for Balzac discovered.

Stolen Kisses, 1968. On being discharged from the army, A. Doinel reads *Le Lys dans la vallée* (Balzac). The novel is immediately introjected into the protagonist's inner world and then becomes a structural force that forms the very core of the self. Part of the story will be transferred to his first love affair.

In *Domicile Conjugal,* 1970, A. Doinel has become an amateur novelist and continues his search for the Absolute by experimenting on carnations. The protagonist will learn how to "get the facts right" and to adjust to life contexts.

Paris nous appartient (Paris belongs to us), 1960; *Out One Spectre,* 1971-74, Riveti.

The mythical Paris, seen through literary texts by Balzac, H. James, Proust, etc., does not match the present Paris. The attempt to structure Paris through the conspiracy of literature fails. Literature, with the delirium of interpretation that it fosters, always deceives and misguides us. Reality, with its changing circumstances, does not lend itself to mediation by earlier literary discourses.

Pierrot le fou, Godard, 1965.

The protagonist is a modern version of Don Quixote. He lives in the world of books, the "best of all worlds," indulging in his travel in the demon of analogy, in a concatenation of supplementary literary mediations. But the literary does not participate in the world. The adventure ends up in a flight into madness.

Deux Ou Trois Choses que je sais d'elle (Two or Three Thing that I know of her) Godard, 1966.

Godard explores the cultural phenomena of the modern French society. Several studies of the famous *Idées* collection are brought to testify and become the "chapters" in the film. These books already structure our modern society and propose solutions. They are not to be taken as truth, however, but as tools, methods, for further investigation into ever-changing phenomena.

WORKS CITED

Bakhtin, M. M. 1981. *The Dialogic Imagination.* Translated by Caryl Emerson and Michael Holquist. Edited by Michael Holquist. Austin: University of Texas Press.

Barthes, Roland. 1971. *Sade, Fourier, Loyola.* Paris: Seuil.

———. 1970. *S/Z.* Paris: Seuil.

Bazin, André. 1967. *What is Cinema?* Essays Selected and Translated by Hugh Gray. Berkeley: University of California Press.

Brecht, Bertolt. 1978. *On Theatre.* Edited by J. Willett. London: Eyre Metnuen.

Eisenstein, Sergei. 1949. *Film Form.* Edited and Translated by Jay Leyda. New York: Brace Jovanvich.

GREENE'S FICTIONAL TREATMENT:
AN EXPERIMENT IN STORYTELLING

Edward A. Kearns

The Third Man is the story of a decent, intelligent man who finds himself vaguely split between his faith in rationality and his fascination with intuition, between his belief in facts and his attraction to fictions. His world is also variously splintered: Vienna has been quartered into postwar administrative zones and divided between the old, civilized Vienna with its "bogus easy charm," and the new Vienna, war-torn, bombed out, the Vienna of black markets in which integrity and corruption seem to go hand-in-hand. There is the above-ground Vienna and a subterranean one, a "strange world unknown to most of us," a "cavernous land of waterfalls and rushing rivers, where tides ebb and flow as in the world above" (Greene 1977, pp. 454-55). He is likewise attracted to the world of the unconscious, with its angels and demons, its energies and powers, but he has devoted himself to the conscious world of experience, of "reality." He distrusts romantics and their childlike notions of good and evil, their willful innocence; he has little, if any, time for women and is suspicious of those who do. Yet he envies the romantics, the lovers, and those people who have somehow kept their instincts and imagination alive. Thus, he writes a story and in doing so rediscovers his own reservoirs of imagination and compassion.

If the above summary of Graham Greene's *The Third Man* seems a bit tilted or out of focus, it is because it describes the fictional treatment of the story, not the film. For the novel is Calloway's story; he narrates it, and the very process of storytelling allows him to resolve the conflicts noted above and to reunite his divided self. The film is, however, the story of Holly Martins; it begins with the narrative voice of Joseph Cotton, and although that voice gives way to the omniscient vision of the camera, the film remains Martins's story.

According to Greene, *The Third Man* was never intended for publication, but it had "to start as a story before those apparently interminable transformations from one treatment to another" (Greene 1977, p. 368). Thus, to understand what he regarded as "the finished state of the story," i.e., the film, we must first

149

understand Calloway's narrative of it, and we must recognize that
many of its thematic conflicts remain in tact from one treatment
to another because its seemingly disparate central characters have
in fact much in common. Martins willfully clings to naive
notions of himself, his past, and his chum, Harry Lime; he
deceives himself. But Calloway is equally deceived by his
insistence on a rational, factual, "adult" mode of perception.
Neither character sees the full truth of things; the one risks never
growing up, whereas the other risks growing much too old and
cynical. The one must restore a balance that the other has yet to
achieve.

Moreover, both are psychologically divided, split apart from
their own unconscious, from its restorative, creative, and
"feminine" powers—from what Carl Jung called the "anima."
For Martins, the problem is embodied in his numerous and
unsatisfactory affairs with women. For Detective Calloway, it lies
in powers of perception, in truth and falsehood, and hence at the
core of his storytelling, which, as we shall see, he regards
ultimately as feminine.

Calloway assures us early in the novel that "I have
reconstructed the affair as best I can from my own files and from
what Martins told me. It is as accurate as I can make it—I haven't
invented a line of dialogue, though I can't vouch for Martins's
memory . . ." (Greene 1977, p. 370). That's rather a heavy claim—
and disclaimer—at once. It should put the reader on guard—as
should Calloway's belittling of his own inventiveness: "I haven't
enough imagination" (Greene 1977, p. 370). These claims, and
his spoofing of cheap novelettes during his first interview with
Martins, suggest a no-nonsense fellow who puts little stock in
anything but facts, and who enjoys pooh-poohing those who put
it in anything else.

Yet he tells us in the second sentence of the story that, when he
first saw Martins, he made this note about him:

> In normal circumstances a cheerful fool. Drinks too much and may cause a
> little trouble. Whenever a woman passes raises his eyes and makes some
> comment, but I get the impression that really he'd rather not be bothered.
> Has never really grown up and perhaps that accounts for the way he
> worshipped Lime. (Greene 1977, p. 369)

That's a remarkable note to make about a stranger first seen at a
funeral; that it proves to be accurate merely underlines Calloway's
unreliability as a narrator. Either he has more faith in
impressionistic judgments than he would have us believe, or he's
doctored the files from which he has reconstructed "the affair."

Obviously, then, what we know of Martins and his memory we know only through Calloway's narrative. Calloway notes the split in Martins's character between "the absurd Christian name and the sturdy Dutch surname" (Greene 1977, p. 373), and he tells us further, "Rollo looked at every woman that passed, and Martins renounced them forever. I don't know which of them wrote the Westerns" (Greene 1977, p.. 373). But the split he sees in Martins reflects the division in himself, for Calloway is far more attracted to writers of fiction—even cheap fiction—than he admits. Toward the end of his narrative, as he and the other police enter the sewers, chasing Lime, he remarks, "If you have ever read the adventures of Allan Quartermain and the account of his voyage along the underground river to the city of Milosis, you will be able to picture the scene of Lime's last stand" (Green 1977, p. 455). This blending of fiction and reality, and the very language of it ("adventures," "Lime's last stand") seems peculiar to one who scoffs at Westerns.

More subtle evidence of Calloway's attraction to fiction and imaginative writing occurs still later in the chase scene, as he tells us, "We moved slowly on, our revolvers trained for a chase, and Lime turned this way and that way like a rabbit dazzled by headlights . . ." (Greene 1977, p. 457). It is Martins, of course, who finally puts Lime out of his misery and who is the only witness to Lime's last moments and last words. According to Calloway, Martins gave a full description of the situation, but one should note Martins's language: " . . . [Harry] was in great pain, and just as an animal creeps into the dark to die, so I suppose a man makes for the light. He wants to die at home, and the darkness is never home to us." It's possible, of course, that a dime-store novelist thinks and speaks this way, but the lines sound more like Calloway than Martins, and they are certainly out of idiom with Martins's final remarks, made only moments later:

> [Harry] was trying to speak, and I bent down to listen. 'Bloody Fool,' he said—that was all. I don't know whether he meant that for himself—some sort of act of contrition, however inadequate (he was a Catholic)—or was it for me—with my thousand a year taxed and my imaginary cattle rustlers who couldn't even shoot a rabbit clean? Then he began to whimper again. I couldn't bear it any more and I put a bullet through him. (Greene 1977, p. 458)

Surely the allusions to Harry as an animal—and to that particular animal—should give us pause, for it was Calloway, in the passage cited earlier, who first likened Lime to a rabbit. The

animal imagery is not fortuitous. Calloway embellishes much of
his story with it, and it is perfectly suited to a man seeking to
reunite his rational faculties with instinctive ones.

More evidence of Calloway's grudging admiration for imaginative writers and their instinctive powers lies in his admission that
Martins, for all his wild-west, romantic naïveté, manages to
"prove me to be a fool" (Greene 1977, p. 383). The admission
appears at the beginning of the third chapter, and shortly
thereafter, as Martins first reveals his suspicions about Lime's
first, false death, Calloway remarks, "It was a shot in the dark,
but already he had this firm instinctive sense that there was
something wrong . . ." (Greene 1977, p. 391). It is that instinctive
sense that Calloway admires, and the links among animal
imagery, instinct, and Calloway's being proved a fool are drawn
together not only by the echoing of the rabbit image, but also by
Lime's last words—"Bloody fool." On the final page of
Calloway's narrative, the game is complete, as Calloway,
speaking to Martins, echoes Lime and himself once more, "You
win, you've proved me a bloody fool" (Greene 1977, p. 459).

Calloway's early claims to accuracy and to factual detail
demonstrate the consciousness that he has brought to the task—at
the same time that they hide his transforming a report into a
story. In the end, he seems equally conscious of the transformation from fact to fiction, as he describes Martins's meeting with
Anna following Lime's final—and real—funeral:

> I watched him striding off on his overgrown legs after the girl. He caught her
> up and they walked side by side. I don't think he said a word to her: it was
> like the end of a story except that before they turned out of my sight her hand
> was through his arm—which is how a story usually begins. (Greene 1977, p.
> 459)

Fans of the film will immediately recognize how radically
different this ending is from that of the film, as well as the extent
to which Calloway's narrative has become a story, and a romantic
one, at that.

Still, Calloway is not quite done with us. He says, as Martins
and Anna stroll away, "And Crabbin? Oh, Crabbin is still
arguing with the British Council about Dexter's expenses." Film
viewers will recall that Mr. Crabbin, having heard that "B.
Dexter" is in town, solicits the famous writer for a lecture, on the
assumption that he's discovered Benjamin Dexter, rather than
Buck—Martins's pen name. The result of this one example of
mistaken identity (a significant motif in the story) is little more
than a comic interlude in the film—i.e., *in Martins's story*. Why

does Calloway feel the need to refer to it and sum it up at the end of his?

Well, it is not merely a comic interlude for him. As he tells us at the time of it, "I am a great admirer of Dexter . . . Dexter has been ranked as a stylist with Henry James, but he has a wider feminine streak than his master—indeed his enemies have sometimes described his subtle, complex, wavering style as old-maidish" (Greene 1977, p. 385). Calloway's own style may avoid the extremes of the "feminine streak," but readers should not ignore his admiration of it. Nor should they overlook the odd appearance of yet another animal immediately after the disastrous lecture. The treatments of the incident in both the film and novel are similar—Martins escapes into a dark room where he hears odd sounds, human sounds; in the novel they are described by Calloway as "like somebody whispering—a long continuous monologue in the darkness" (Greene 1977, p. 422). And, still in the novel, Sergeant Paine opens the door, switches on the light, and retrieves Martins, who, with a backward glance, sees "the eyes of a parrot chained to a perch staring beadily back at him." Martins apologizes to Paine, "I lost my way."

The significance of the incident lies in something earlier—a dream that Martins purportedly mentioned to Calloway, a dream in which Martins found himself "walking through a dense wood, ankle-deep in snow. And owl hooted, and he felt suddenly lonely and scared" (Greene 1977, p. 386). He had an appointment to meet Lime under a tree, saw a figure whistling a familiar tune, and ran towards it. Then,

... the figure turned and it was not Harry at all—just a stranger who grinned at him in a little circle of wet slushy melted snow, while the owl hooted again and again. (Greene 1977, p. 386)

We must be careful to note the associations mounted here—dim and imprecise as they may be. In the dream, Martins mistakes a stranger for his friend, Lime, whereas in the Consulate lecture he is mistaken for someone else. The owl, obviously, anticipates the parrot. The slush surrounding Martins's feet in the dream anticipates the muck of the sewers, and, according to Calloway, who claims to quote Martins, as Martins approached the dying Lime, Harry whistled his theme song. Martins says, "What made him whistle that absurd scrap of a tune I'd been fool enough to believe he had written himself?" (Greene 1977, p. 458). None of these incidents has particular significance for Martins's story; their importance lies in what they reveal of Calloway's developing imagination and narrative.

Thus, in summary of the case I may say that the novel's narrator is a hardened detective who has grown weary with the world and finds himself uncomfortably on the brink of cynicism; he has little faith in anything but facts and reason. But this dedication to facts has proved him a fool, and he clearly envies the intuitive, feminine capacities of Henry James and Benjamin Dexter—as well as the instinctive powers of Martins, a third-rate writer and would-be detective. Calloway is divided against himself, but insofar as he recognizes these powers in others, he retains a trace of him himself, and insofar as he can transform them into a creative act, the division can be healed. Again he gives a clue to the experience. While reporting Martins's first interview with Anna, Calloway notes:

> Martins suddenly saw in that odd chamber of the mind that constructs such pictures, instantaneously, irrationally, a desert place, a body on the ground, a group of birds gathered. Perhaps it was a scene from one of his own books, not yet written, forming at the gate of consciousness.

Or perhaps it was a scene from Calloway's own book. Whatever. It is this associative capacity that allows Calloway to write his story and to affirm his compassion in the end: "Poor Crabbin. Poor all of us, when you come to think of it."

It's a good, tightly written story that must rank among the best of Greene's "entertainments" and novels, his disclaimer of the intent to publish it notwithstanding. But in its finished form, it retained the poignancy and depth of its themes—and became a film masterpiece.

WORKS CITED

Greene, Graham. 1977. *The Portable Graham Greene*. Edited by Philip Stratford. New York: Penguin Books.

INDIVIDUAL AND SOCIETAL ENCOUNTERS
WITH DARKNESS AND THE SHADOW
IN *THE THIRD MAN*

Paul W. Rea

Most film historians, having screened *The Third Man* once or twice, tend to see it as a *film noir*, a particular sort of psychological thriller made during and after World War II. As defined by Robert Sklar,

> the hallmark of *film noir* is its sense of people trapped—trapped in webs of paranoia and fear, unable to tell guilt from innocence, true identity from false. Its villains are attractive and sympathetic, masking greed, misanthropy, malevolence. Its heroes and heroines are weak, confused, susceptible to false impressions. The environment is murky and close, the settings vaguely oppressive. In the end, evil is exposed, though often just barely, and the survival of good remains troubled and ambiguous. (Sklar 1975, p. 253)

Unquestionably, *The Third Man* exhibits many of these characteristics: its trapped villain, Harry Lime, is played attractively by Orson Welles, and its ostensible hero, Holly Martins, is played by Joseph Cotten as "weak, confused," and "susceptible to false impressions." Its setting, postwar Vienna, is decidedly "murky and close," more than "vaguely oppressive." Its filmic style is indeed dark, with streetlights glaring on wet cobblestones and shafts of light penetrating the deep shadows.

The *film noir* is, however, essentially an American genre, and *The Third Man* is a very British film. Moving beyond the *film noir*, its stylistic influences are eclectic: its use of searchlighting and large shadows come from the German Expressionist cinema of the twenties, and its incessant use of camera angles tilted ten to twenty degrees off horizontal come from Orson Welles, who also used this technique in *Citizen Kane*. Most significantly, however, *The Third Man* incorporates the characteristic values of the British film at its best: highly literate and suggestive script; commitment to moral values such as order and decency, here embodied in the character of Maj. Calloway as played by Trevor Howard; and, in marked contrast to the *film noir*, concern with both psychological realism and political commentary.

Whereas Graham Green's fictional treatment is presented from the point of view of—and therefore is essentially about—Maj. Calloway, chief of the British Military Police, Green's shooting

script opens with Holly Martins as narrator. Holly's famous
opening voice-over narration—"I never knew the Old Vienna
before the War, with its Straus music, its glamour and easy
charm"—were added when the filmmakers became concerned that
audiences would not understand without them. Even without
them, however, *The Third Man* focuses clearly on the growth of
Holly Martins.

Viewed from one perspective, Holly is an American innocent
abroad who, in the course of the film, encounters evil in his
"shadow," or psychological double, as represented by his long-
time friend, Harry Lime. Although the script states that Holly
was a Canadian, the film suggests repeatedly that he was an
American—and an innocent. Immediately on his arrival at the
British command post, he is identified as the author of Westerns,
such as *The Lone Rider of Santa Fe.* Captain Crabbin, who runs
the Cultural Institute, initially refers to Holly as an American
author and later introduces him to an audience as "Mr. Martins,
from the other side." The American innocence theme appears
also when an American M.P. comments that he has never heard
of Harry Lime and expands further when Holly, speaking to the
Cultural Institute, reveals his utter ignorance about literature.

Although not essential either to the film or to this viewing that
Holly be an American, it is well to observe that *The Third Man*
was a British production directed by Carol Reed and that Graham
Greene created another misguided American idealist in *The Quiet
American.* In this novel, written five years later, Greene indicts
an ignorant, willfully innocent, but well-meaning CIA agent.
"Innocence," he writes, "is like a dumb leper who has lost his
bell, wandering the world, meaning no harm" (quoted in "Night
World" 1973, pp. 36-37). In the film, the two sides of the
American character are suggested by the punning on "ranch" and
"raunch."

The film offers ample verbal and visual evidence of parallels
between Holly and Harry. In the script, Holly links himself to
Harry when he remarks that "nobody reads Westerns nowadays,
Harry liked them though" (Greene 1968, p. 27). In the film,
Anna, Harry's former lover, repeatedly calls Holly "Harry," and
observes that "Harry never grew up," which also applies to
Holly. this doubling motif emerges also from dialogue between
Anna and Holly:

> Martins: "Come out and have a drink." Anna looks quickly up.
> Anna: "Why did you say that?"

Martins: "It seemed like a good idea."
Anna: "It was just what he (Harry) used to say."

Obliquely, Calloway, too, suggests parallels between the two men. He warns Holly that "you were born to be murdered," implying a parallel to Harry, whom they both believed to have been murdered. Finally, Holly himself suggests parallels. In a particularly telling slip, Holly, half drunk, remarks that "there's nobody who knew Harry Lime like he did...like I did." Ironically, neither knows Harry well at all.

Visually, too, *The Third Man* reinforces the Holly/Harry connection. Seeking the details of his friend's "death," Holly watches as "Baron" Kurtz shows him how Harry was supposedly run over as he stepped out to see a friend across the street. (Kurtz illustrates his explanation by saying that "you might have been Harry.") Later, Holly himself is almost run over as he steps out to see a friend—Harry. Visual parallels occur also as Holly attempts to play with a cat associated with Anna, and moments later, in a dark doorway, the same cat plays with Harry's shoestring and licks his shoe. (This cat, according to Anna, "only liked Harry," and thus parallels her loyalty to Harry and foreshadows her rejection of Holly in the end.) Moreover, Holly escapes from pursuers by running up a spiral staircase, and later Harry escapes from pursuers by darting down one, into the sewers. Finally, as Holly sits in a bar, attempting to lure Harry, the shop displays a sign on the glass reading "Döppel-Filter."

These parallels, then, suggest that Holly, the decent-seeming opposite of the morally degenerate Harry, is actually his psychological double. This potential becomes clear—especially in the script—as Holly hesitates before declining Harry's offer to cut him in on his racket. Harry thus represents Holly's "shadow," that side of his nature that he has only dimly understood. Holly's initiation into experience, into the evil represented by Harry Lime, becomes fully evident as Holly readies himself for his journey to the moral and literal underworld of the sewers.

In the script, Greene delineates Holly's moral growth: "A world is beginning to come to an end for Martins, a world of easy friendships, hero worship, and confidence that had begun twenty years before...but he will not admit it" (Greene 1968, p. 88). By the end of the film, Holly has, after considerable struggling, come to realize Harry's evil, has surmounted his loyalty to this "easy friendship," and has taken moral action to end it. (It is important that Holly kills his old chum, for to leave

it to Calloway and his men would be to endorse governments as a
means of combatting evil. Greene's sympathies ran toward
individuals; he liked to believe that his work made that of the
State more difficult.) Yet in helping Lime to avoid facing up to
his crimes, Holly may unconsciously avoid fully recognizing his
own shadowy side; by killing Harry Lime, he may be tempted to
imagine that he has extinguished his own darker tendencies.

From a Jungian perspective, Holly represents archetypal man—
the collective unconscious—in the process of individuation. The
first step in his journey toward psychic growth comes with his
encounter with the shadow, which occurs on the great wheel.
Harry's depravity both fascinates and shocks him. Once he
encounters this shadow, he follows it into the labryinthine
sewers, where he encounters the matriarchal consciousness—
suggested by his feminine name—that has kept him an
adolescent. Upon his return to the surface, having taken adult
moral action, he is free of his immature notions of woman as
creator/destroyer; he is ready to deal with his own "anima," and
can let Anna pass him by without giving pursuit. This is a
moment of growth; Holly begins to break with his tendency to
"chase girls," and ceases his attempts to replace Harry.

The Third Man is also a film about moral responsibility, or
the utter lack of it. Holly, Anna, and Major Calloway are each
tested by circumstances, by their willingness to run the risks
necessary to be responsible—i.e., to oppose evil for the common
good. Evil is especially embodied by Harry Lime and his cronies,
Kurtz, Winkel, and Popescu. With characteristic innocence and
bravado, Holly is willing to investigate the apparent death of his
friend, but pulls back, evading responsibility, when he is rightly
suspected of contributing to the death of his friend's porter.

Later, when his help seems necessary to Calloway's capturing
Harry, Holly plans to leave town and consents only grudgingly
to being Calloway's "dumb decoy duck." Only at the very end,
during the chase through the sewers, does Holly become fully
involved. This represents significant growth for Holly, who, after
all, had been writing escapist pulp fiction about people and
places he knew next to nothing about. Anna, by contrast, will
not betray her former lover, even though he has abandoned her,
to help Calloway halt his murderous racketeering. Calloway, the
professional in charge, is the moral hero of the film, not because
he has no flaws, but because he is unwavering in his
commitment to opposing evil. He musters all the help he can
find, hoping to make common cause for the common good.

Incorporating such moral considerations, *The Third Man* probes and comments upon Cold War politics in Europe. In her intelligent analysis, "'I Never Knew the Old Vienna': Cold War Politics and *The Third Man*," Lynette Carpenter places the film in its immediate historical context. She points out that when Sir Alexander Korda sent Greene to Vienna, he asked not for a murder mystery or a quoted romantic melodrama but for a treatment "about the four-power occupation" (in Phillips 1985, p. 41). Carpenter rightly points out that in the eighteen months or so before the filming, the Soviets had engineered a coup in Czechoslavakia and had blockaded Berlin, a city that, like Vienna, was divided among four powers. These cities are microcosms of Europe, itself divided into two camps.

The film satirizes petty provincialism and affirms internationalism. From Holly's initial nervousness at customs to the Viennese' complaints about too many foreigners to Anna's difficulties with her papers, *The Third Man* exposes the unnecessary bureaucratic difficulties created by an unnecessarily partitioned and divided world. Moreover, as a moral parable, it demonstrates that such divisiveness makes it more difficult to combat evil. Law enforcement personnel neither know one another nor speak a common language. Harry is able to slip from one occupied zone to another, evading capture.

Everything considered, *The Third Man* challenges Cold War orthodoxies. Although some viewers—then or now—might emphasize the fact that Harry ducks into the Soviet zone to evade capture, or that Anna faces deportation by the Soviets, to do so might be to indulge Cold War suspicions. On the contrary, the most significant fact, given the political climate of 1950, is that the Soviets are *not* part of Harry's deadly schemes—i.e., that evil is *not* caused simply by communism, and that Harry Lime, an American, is brought to bay *not* simply by *British* moral character, efficiency, and intelligence, though these traits are certainly affirmed in the Maj. Calloway and Sgt. Paine (Greene's script called for Popescu, who appears in the film as a Romanian, to be Tyler, an American. The change resulted largely from the strong objections of the American producer and distributor, David Selznick [Behlmer 1972, p. 386]). The script also makes it clear that the British do not capture Lime alone: Lime is tracked by an "International Patrol," which "includes Austrian, British, French, Russian, and American M.P.s" (Greene 1968, p. 103). Only through international cooperation, then, can evil be opposed.

Even more than most mysteries, *The Third Man* explodes assumptions, thereby inviting a reevaluation of Cold War assumptions. The central assumption—that Harry is dead— proves erroneous, as does Holly's naive belief that Harry does "publicity work for some kind of charity." Crabbin assumes that Holly is a serious writer, and Anna clings to her naive belief that Harry was simply a man "who never grew up." Most significantly, Holly presumes to play detective in a strange city where he hardly speaks a word of the language and persists in asking the wrong question, "who was the third man?" If all these assumptions prove false, why should one not also question that cluster of assumptions that comprises the Cold War mindset?

In this film, evil thrives not just as the result of individual depravity and greed, nor just as the result of bad governments, but as the result of an exhausted culture declining into moral decay. The faces of the Viennese bespeak moral shell shock and the stark futility that Ezra Pound voiced so memorably following the First World War:

> There died a myriad,
> And of the best, among them,
> For an old bitch, gone in the teeth,
> For a botched civilization.
>   ("Hugh Selwyn Mauberly")

Whereas Pound depicted cultural disintegration with images of the broken columns of a classic temple, Greene and Reed depict it with numerous shots of broken statues, bombed out buildings, and deserted squares.

Commenting on such images of cultural decay, David Denby observes that

> Reed and cinematographer Robert Krasker have framed the shots so that bits of rococo decoration appear in the corners of almost every composition, and Anton Daras's zither score is full of such care-repertory favorites as "unter dem Lindenbaum" and "Alter Lied," but these traces of imperial and gracious city are used in mocking contrast to its postwar dereliction. (Denby 1922 in Phillips 1985, p. 36)

The great culture of the Old Vienna—"the graves of Beethoven, Schubert, and Brahms" (Greene 1968, p. 101), the shots of buildings and statues from its glorious past—contast starkly with the physical and moral ruin. If all this art, architecture, and music ever ennobled, clearly they no longer do. Moreover, what remains of Old World charm has degenerated into *erzatz*: Kurtz is a fake baron who wears a toupee, and Winkel collects animal bones that pass for those of saints. His collection of religious art inspires neither belief nor morality. Culture has become antique, charm a crumbling facade.

Perhaps it is not coincidental that Old Vienna led Freud toward his first explorations of the repressed unconscious. Over-refined as it often was, traditional European culture contained demons that surfaced during the World Wars. At the end of the First World War, Carl Jung observed that "the shadow" had broken loose—that the "animal in us only becomes more beastlike" when it is repressed. Jung continues to state that this "is no doubt the reason why no religion is so defiled with the spilling of innocent blood as Christianity, and why the world has never seen a bloodier war than the war of the Christian nations" (Jung 1971, p. 22). European culture and Christian teachings repress the shadow.

But the film implies also that much of the evil in Vienna remains as a residue from the Second World War. The Wehrmacht uniforms and helmets worn by the Austrians, the bombed out buildings, the tilted camera angles, and the dark tones and deep shadows all suggest moral degeneration, often evoking the "there's a murderer amongst us" themes of the German Expressionist films. The legacy from the war is established early in the film when Kurtz informs Holly that "we all sell cigarettes and that sort of thing. Why, I have done things that would have seemed unthinkable before the war."

The Third Man stands at the crossroads of three powerful contemporary tendencies. The first is that of moral breakdown resulting from the failure of traditional culture and religion to speak to a world reverberating from the upheaval of World Wars I and II, from the shock waves of Auschwitz, Dresden,, and Hiroshima/Nagasaki. The second contemporary tendency is the temptation of guilt-free, long-range technological killing, posed so memorably by Lime looking down on "dots" from on high: "Victims? Don't be melodramatic. Look down there. Would you really feel any pity if one of those dots stopped moving forever?" Lime's corruption is contagious because it tempts Holly and others to avoid guilt as he does—by killing from a distance and abstracting individuals into numbers.

It is this third contemporary tendency toward abstraction and impersonality that Albert Camus exposes so graphically in *The Plague*, a novel about the Occupation on one level and about nuclear holocaust on another:

Ten thousand dead made about five times the audience in a biggish
cinema. Yes, that is how it should be done. You should collect the people at
the exits of five picture-houses, you should lead them to a city square and
make them die in heaps if you wanted to get a clear notion of what it means.
Then at least you could add some familiar faces to the anonymous mass.
(Camus 1948, pp. 25-26)

In attempting to justify his calloused perceptions of human
beings as "dots," Harry alludes to barbarities committed by
governments. They kill people all the time, he contends. Harry
identifies himself with dictatorships that treat people as a "mass"
to be manipulated; he succumbs to the amorality of a Hitler or a
Stalin. Though he may not recognize it consciously, Harry's
degeneration—and that of many others—may stem from experiences with governments, the war, and the holocaust. Harry has
swallowed a heavy dose of postwar cynicism.

In his "Thoughts for the Times on War and Death," Freud
points out that wars, with their official legitimation of mass
murder, "have repercussions on the morality of individuals":

When the community no longer raises objection, there is an end, too, to the
suppression of evil passions, and men perpetrate deeds of cruelty, fraud,
treachery and barbarity so incompatible with their level of civilization that
one would have though them impossible.
    Well may the citizen of the civilized world . . . stand helpless in a world that
has grown strange to him. (Freud 1984, p. 49)

Although Harry exhibits no restraints on his cynicism or greed,
Holly, "the citizen of the civilized world," at first continues his
adolescent innocence and willful ignorance, standing helpless in
a strange city.

Civilized societies always contain their Harrys and their Hollys,
just as the dark side of the unconscious may dominate or may
remain unacknowledged in individuals. Much as Jung lamented
that "civilized Germany disgorged its terrible primitivity" (Jung
1964, pp. 93-94), so Old Vienna, however civilized, refined,
cosmopolitan, enlightened, artistic, and progressive, collaborated
all too willingly with the Nazis. The Viennese, like Holly, have
tended to ignore the shadow, the sinister side of the unconscious.
Reed repeatedly films their city on a tilt, suggesting both a world
slipped morally askew and psychic imbalance. *The Third Man*
implies that, as Jung asserts eloquently,

Our times have demonstrated what it means for the gates of the underworld
to be opened. Things whose enormity nobody could have imagined in the
idyllic harmlessness of the first decade of our century have happened and
have turned our world upside down. Ever since, the world has remained in a
state of schizophrenia. (Jung 1964, p. 93)

Much as political realms are divided, so are individuals. Calloway and Harry Lime live in their heads, out of touch with feelings; Holly lives in his romantic sentimentalities, his mind stunted by platitudes.

When individuals or nations assume their own innocence, believing that evil is something that others once did, they ignore their own shadows and live schizophrenically, divided like the postwar world. Harry was "buried" once, but "rose" to do more evil. The demons that erupted in Germanic culture still haunt the bombed buildings, the darkened doorways, the empty squares, and the sewers. Evil still lurks within the dark recesses of the human mind. The moral statement of the film echoes Alain Resnais's excruciatingly powerful *Night and Fog*, another film on the legacy of World War II. Narrating this film as the camera inspects the ruins of a crematorium and a torture rack, Resnais comments first that "war nods, but keeps one eye open"; then he challenges the viewer to ask, "and who will warn us of our next executioners? Are their faces really that different from ours?"

Perhaps not. But we also resemble the Hollys and the Calloways, those incomplete mortals who take up arms against evil, doing what needs to be done. Despite its surface pessimism, *The Third Man* suggests that any one of us could choose to be one of those shafts of light that penetrate the darkness.

WORKS CITED

Behlmer, Ruby, ed. 1972. *Memo From David O. Selznick*. New York: Viking,

Camus, Albert. 1948. *The Plague*. New York: Random House.

Freud, Sigmund. 1984. *In a Dark Time*. Edited by Robert Jay Lifton and Nicholas Humphrey. Cambridge: Harvard University Press.

Greene, Graham. 1968. *The Third Man: A Film By Graham Greene and Carol Reed*. New York: Simon and Schuster.

Jung, C. G. 1971. *The Collected Works of C. G. Jung*. Vol X. Edited by Sir Herbert Read. Princeton: Princeton University Press.

———. 1964. *Man and His Symbols*. New York: Doubleday.

Mobile, Philip, ed. 1973. "Night World." In *Favorite Movies: A Critic's Guide*. New York: Macmillan.

Phillips, William D., ed. 1985. *Analyzing Films: A Practical Guide*. New York: Holt, Rinehart, and Winston.

Robert Sklar. 1975. *Movie-Made America: A Cultural History of American Movies*. New York: Random House.

DONA FLOR AND HER TWO HUSBANDS:
A TALE OF SENSUALITY, SUSTENANCE, AND SPIRITS

Enrique Grönlund and Moylan C. Mills

Jorge Amado's novel *Dona Flor and Her Two Husbands: A Moral and Amorous Tale* tells the story of Floripedes, a raven-haired Brazilian beauty "with eyes shining like oil and skin the color of tea" (Amado 1977, p. 77), and the two men she marries. This independent-minded woman of Bahia, who "had been born with the gift for seasoning" (Amado 1977, p. 61), a teacher of culinary arts who runs her own school, marries first the man of her youthful dreams—someone blond, dashing and poor—in the person of Vadinho who, in addition to being blond, dashing and poor, is a gambler, a randy rake, a mischievous, yet charming, fake, as well as a sensitive, loyal, generous human being. His lust for life takes him away from home practically every night, sometimes for days at a time; it returns him home often drunk; and it creates for him a perpetual state of insolvency, which, at times, causes him to beat Flor for the sole purpose of stealing a few cruzeiros from her to pay for his revelries. Vadinho's gambling, drinking, and womanizing carry him to an early grave; he dies at age thirty-one, while dancing the samba early one Sunday morning of *Carnaval*.

He is mourned by his friends, to whom he remains a hero, an example of manhood; his caring and loyalty are warmly remembered. To the majority of the people who have not been touched by his charm and genuine optimism, Vadinho's death provides an opportunity to malign his character with impunity. Flor, who for seven years had tolerated her husband's dissolute ways, is a kind, forgiving wife whose painful, heartfelt grief is not completely abated until his return from the netherworld some two and one-half years later.

Although the marriage of Vadinho and Flor may not have been made in heaven, their sex life was, for it is the poetic eroticism of their lovemaking that is destined to symbolize their relationship. Tender and animal-like, fiery and sweet, it is never obstructed by social or moral conventions. When the desire strikes, it is readily satiated. If there is no bed available, the floor offers a handy substitute. Clothes and bedsheets are minor impediments to be discarded on the road to concupiscent bliss. And, if the neighbors can hear the sighs of passion because the doors and windows have been left open, well, their jealousy be damned.

By the conclusion of the proper year of mourning, Flor's inner suffering, caused by the absence of a conjugal life, has become intolerable. She is urged to remarry, which she does. This time the fortunate man is the local pharmacist, an upstanding member of the community, a paragon of good-breeding, a man of means. All that and more is bassoon-playing Dr. Teodoro Madureira. This second marriage provides Flor with the economic security and social respect heretofore missing in her life. She travels in a new social world in which a regimented, straight-laced lifestyle is required in order to maintain superficial social airs. Yet, she is at peace with herself, happy with the new stable rhythms; she accepts the fact that there is a place for everything, and that everything is in its place. She seems content with the monotony of her new life. She learns to make love wearing nightclothes, always under the sheets, on "Wednesdays and Saturdays, at ten o'clock, . . . with an encore on Saturday, optional on Wednesday" (Amado 1977, p. 335), always modestly and quickly.

Flor has accomplished a marital Möbius loop by having shared her life with polar opposites. Everything that Vadinho was, Dr. Teodoro is not; everything that Dr. Teodoro has, Vadinho never possessed. In the end, although Flor respects and appreciates Dr. Teodoro for what he is and for what he provides, she, nevertheless, misses the spontaneity, the gaiety, the excitement of Vadinho.

Her heart, her burning womb, call out to Vadinho. And, so, he returns, naked and roguish as ever, more alive than dead, to wreak havoc upon Flor's libido. Flor, always the proper lady, does not succumb to her first husband's advances without a moral and spiritual struggle. But, when she eventually does, her life is fulfilled: the benefits of both matrimonies join together to form a most unusual union.

Such is the skeletal essence of the novel's storyline, through which Amado seriously examines the relationship between men and women, the flesh and the spirit. The muscle provided by Amado is comprised of quirky subplots, anecdotal asides, dream sequences, haunting *candômblé* spiritism, telling observations on people and life, and last, but certainly not least, the myriad of unforgettable characters representing all areas of Bahian society:

the good-natured gamblers and whores, the meddling gossips, and the stuffy upper crust, each a unique individual. The blood that brings to life Amado's creation is the language. It is at once humorous, touching, poignant, descriptive, and above all, lyrical. It weaves a tapestry rich in symbol, wit, sorcery, harmony, fragrance, poetic sexuality, and gastronomic delights. This eloquent amalgamation of language, theme, plot, and character is pure magic. Within this context, the sensuosity, the *candômblé* spiritism, and the gastronomic elements can be addressed as they are reflected in both the novel and in the 1977 translation of *Dona Flor and Her Two Husbands* to the film medium.

During the seventeenth century, West-Central African Yoruba culture with its spiritism was one of the numerous and diverse cultural groups imported into Brazil by Portuguese slave-traders. Subsequently, Sudan-rooted Yoruba culture became the dominant African one in Bahia, a Northeastern province in Brazil, whose capital, Salvador, is the setting of the novel.

Within the label *Yoruba*, one can also identify various ethnic sub-cultures called nations, each united by similar customs, beliefs, language, etc., among which the Ketu is "the major group in Bahia" (Bastide 1978, p. 207) and, as such, is predominant in the *candômbés* of that province (Bastide 1978, p. 106). Jorge Amado, the author, has become a lay protector (an *ogan*) as well as a minister (an *obá*) of the *candômbés* rituals as practiced by the Ketu nation in Bahia. Consequently, his presentation of Yoruba spiritism, Ketu in particular, is founded on personal knowledge and experience. Thus, the roles that various Yoruba spirits play throughout the course of *Dona Flor and Her Two Husbands* accurately reflect Ketu orthodoxy and lend credence to what may otherwise seem illogical goings-on during the course of the novel.

Although neither Dona Flor nor Vadinho worship non-Catholic dieties, they are, nevertheless, protected, unbeknownst to them, by Afro-Brazilian spirits. As a result, certain personality traits of Dona Flor and Vadinho, along with particular actions and beliefs of theirs, tend to reflect these spirits more so than any Christian omnipresence.

For example, Vadinho's protector is Exú (Amado 1977, p. 410), god "of doors, paths, and openings" (Bastide 1978, p. 193). Although among most Afro-Brazilian cultures, including the Yoruba, Exú is identified "with the devil" (Bastide 1978, p. 251), the Ketu nation has "faithfully preserved the African image (of a) god of orientation, a young boy, mischievous rather than spiteful" (Bastide 1978, p. 253). In addition, he "loves pranks and likes to play tricks" (Bastide 1978, p. 252), yet "he has a good heart in spite of all his nonsense" (Bastide 1978, p. 252). Above all, Exú "presides over the sexual act" (Bastide 1978, p. 252), and "eats anything in the way of food" (Amado 1977, p. 409).

And mischievous Vadinho is. He met Flor after having gate-crashed an exclusive gala affair, pretending to be a government official rather than the penniless, indolent gambler he in fact was. His so-called gift of gab (Amado 1977, p. 16) sustains his avocation, enabling him to sweet-talk people with money out of countless loans, most of which will go unpaid, and also rescues him from equally countless situations when creditors come calling. On the other hand, whenever the number *17* comes up, lining his pockets with money, Vadinho spends lavishly on his friends and Flor. Moreover, upon his return to the world of the living, Vadinho delights his friends and cronies by having their bets win continuously, thus bringing the treasuries of the very same gambling establishments that so often emptied his own pockets perilously close to financial ruin. Not one to plan for the future, Vadinho views each day as a new life whose pleasures of gambling, whoring, eating, drinking, and loving Dona Flor must be enjoyed to the fullest. Thus the correlation between the monicker "Vadinho" and the Portuguese verb "vadiar"—to wander about, also to loaf—becomes evident. Amado's symbolic intent is clear in the original Portuguese.

Yet, Vadinho's failures on the gaming tables rarely interfere with his love for Flor. It is undeniable that, on rare occasions, he physically abuses his beloved wife in order to obtain money she has saved from her cooking school. But somehow his sexual prowess is so pleasing and satisfying that it overcomes all else. When it comes to making love, Vadinho has no peer. Neither clothes, nor clocks, nor furniture, nor social convention interfere with his sexual appetite. Bluntly stated, the man loves to screw and teaches Dona Flor to love screwing on an equal basis. As he, himself, states, "Screwing is a blessed thing. It was invented by God in Paradise" (Amado 1977, p. 12). The language in Harriet de Onis's translation is considerably less to the point than its Portuguese counterpart, where, again, the verb "vadiar"— euphemistically, to fornicate—is ever present on Vadinho's lips, not as a negative epithet, but as an earthy natural desire. Once again, Amado's correlation between the Portuguese verb and the alliterative monicker cannot be ignored.

Although Vadinho expresses his masculinity and manhood by seducing women whenever possible, his favorite partner is Flor, who is protected by the goddess Oxun (Amado 1977, p. 252). Oxun is associated with water, especially sweet, "fresh water" (Bastide 1978, pp. 206, 377). Also, Oxun is the "goddess of sensual love" (Bastide 1978, p. 263), "the image of the eternal feminine" (Bastide 1978, p. 256), who practices "erotic magic" (Bastide 1978, p. 238). Hence, sex and water are integral elements that join forces at some of the critical moments in Flor's life. For example, Flor and Vadinho's premarital consummation of their love occurs in a cottage by the sea, with the sea howling "a hallelujah" (Amado 1977, p. 117) of approval at the point of orgasm. Later, after her marriage to the straight-laced Dr. Teodoro, who makes love according to the calendar, Flor's honeymoon night is spent in a small hotel near the very same sea where she and Vadinho made love for the first time. Furthermore, Vadinho's return from the hereafter (answering Dona Flor's call) inevitably leads to his second seduction of Flor. On a "Saturday" (Amado, 1977, p. 486) night, which is, incidentally, Oxun's feast day (Bastide 1978, p. 208), with "the rain pattering on the roof" (Amado 1977, p. 486), Flor does not deny Vadinho "water to drink" (Amado 1977, p. 487).

It is also important to consider Oxun's demeanor. To the unknowing, she is "gentleness itself . . . outwardly still water" (Amado 1977, p. 252). Nevertheless, upon closer inspection, it is revealed that the goddess is "over proud" (Amado 1977, p. 252), a woman unafraid to become concubine and wife to another god (Bastide 1978, pp. 226, 256), rejecting her first husband. Oxun's exterior calmness, thus, is betrayed by her libidinous desires, which foment "inwardly, a squall" (Amado 1977, p. 252).

Dona Flor, like Oxun, the "two-timer" (Amado 1977, p. 252), has been married twice. Unlike Oxun, Flor's relationships are a result of death, not adultery. Now, after her first husband's death, Flor follows the requisite mourning code expected of her. The young, vibrant, sensual widow develops a "roaring blaze" (Amado 1977, p. 255) inside her womb, which can be extinguished only by a man. Her demeanor becomes affected, for she is "outwardly, modesty personified. . . . meekness itself; inwardly, a raging fire" (Amado 1977, p. 255). Dr. Teodoro, fortunately, extinguishes the conflagration. On the other hand, unfortunately, the doctor's systematic, controlled, and inhibited style of lovemaking provides, at best, temporary relief—very temporary. Consequently, although Flor is in love with her second husband, the lack of passion, spontaneity, and reckless abandon that defined her first marriage causes her to call out to Vadinho. His return from the hereafter is sponsored by his protector Exú, god of the crossroads. Vadinho's explanation that he has come in order "to prevent [Flor] from taking a lover and dragging [her] name and honor through the mud" (Amado 1977, p. 506), confounds the "decent, respectable woman [who is] not going to betray [her] husband" (Amado 1977, p. 487). After all, Flor understands fully why Vadinho has returned. As has been posited, like Oxun, whose "favorite meat" (Amado 1977, p. 409) is "goat" (Amado 1977, p. 409), Flor realizes that she might well be unfaithful. Yet, is it truly a case of adultery? After all, Flor does not fornicate out of wedlock. Besides, the horns of cuckoldry never manifest themselves upon the brow of the good doctor. In the end, both the outer and inner selves of Flor are satisfied: she has achieved complete fulfillment, she is one. Love has conquered all.

On a somewhat different level, Oxun's importance as a deity of the waters also evinces itself, provided that the generally accepted symbolism between water and life is agreed upon, in Dona Flor's prowess as an expert cook. As the name of her cooking school indicates, "Savor and Art" (Amado 1977, p. 3) reflect the concern, care, and creativity with which she lends her expertise to provide sustenance for living. She gives of herself to the fruits of the earth and the sea with the same ardor and willingness with which she gives herself to Vadinho. Unabashedly, she flavors her recipes and lovemaking with the spices of life. And, in Vadinho, than whom "nobody had a more delicate palate" (Amado 1977, p. 42), she has a man who relishes all of her offerings, and, also, like Exú, a man who eats anything.

So, it is not surprising when water and food join hands in the novel. *Moqueca de siri mole* (Amado 1973, p. 55), braised marinated soft-shell crabs, is Vadinho's "favorite dish" (Amado 1977, p. 42), never to be made again by Flor after his death. *Siri*, Bahian for crab, occupies a different, yet no less important, place in Vadinho's frolicsome life. Expert dancer that he is, when the mood strikes him to burst the hypocritical balloon of social convention, Vadinho "with perfection and grace'" (Amado 1977, p. 112) performs the steps of the smuttily licentious *siri-boceta*. By imitating a crab's undulating and grinding movements as it attempts to dig itself into the sand, the dance becomes a racy representation of sexual intercourse. Interestingly enough, the word *boceta* is a Portuguese vulgarism for vagina. Thus, with *siri* and *boceta*, Vadinho's favorite foods are clearly designated, and Flor's are no doubt the best.

Oxun, water, and Flor intertwine once again during Flor's period of mourning. Again, the catalyst is a recipe, in this case *cágado guisado* (Amado 1973, p. 221), stewed fresh water turtle. In preparation of this dish, the animal is killed and carved up in a rather gruesome manner. This brutal procedure symbolizes Flor's current state of existence. Flor's spirit is encased in a moral shell furnished by social conventions and restrictions. If the shell were removed, an inner self mutilated by the violent struggle between Flor's desire to break free and her need to adhere to conventional morality would be revealed. Her thoughts are expressed thus:

> But if your guest wants even finer and more unusual game, if he is looking for the *ne plus ultra*, . . . the pleasure of the gods, then why not serve him up a young and pretty widow, cooked in her tears of suffering and loneliness, in the sauce of her modesty and mourning, in the moans of her deprivation, in the fire of her forbidden desire, which gives her the flavor of guilt and sin?
>
> Ah, I know of such a widow, of chile and honey, cooking over a slow fire every night, just ready to be served (Amado 1977, p. 209).

Like that of Oxun, Flor's calm demeanor projected externally is belied by her consuming inner passion. Fortunately, Dr. Teodoro will serve himself a sizable portion, even a second helping at times, of Flor's delectable ingredients.

Caviar, another product of the waters, is used to define Flor's sexual relationships with both husbands. At a reception following a concert in which Dr. Teodoro has played on the bassoon a composition honoring his wife, Flor and her best friend, Dona Norma, discuss the merits of caviar in the following exchange:

> Dona Norma: "This stuff has a rancid taste. I don't know how to describe it."
>
> Dona Flor (quoting Vadinho): "It tastes like tail . . . and it's very good" (Amado 1977, p. 390).

In the original Portuguese, the word that has been translated as "tail" is *boceta* (Amado 1973, p. 403). This curiosity is not lost on Dona Norma, who acknowledges that Vadinho "understood those tastes" (Amado 1973, p. 391).

Later that evening, Dona Norma, who has drunk a bit too much champagne, teasingly asks Dr. Teodoro: "'Did you like the caviar?'"

He responds: "'I know that it is a delicacy for the gods,...
[but] I did not find it altogether to my liking.'"
Dona Norma persists: "'And what did it taste like to you?'"
Dr. Teodoro answers: "'To tell you the truth, I can't recall
anything that tastes like it....I thought it tasted awful.'"
And, Dona Norma finishes the discussion thus: "But there are
those who like it, aren't there, Flor?'" (Amado 1977, p. 393).

This charmingly witty scene not only underlines the basic
attitudinal differences toward sex between the two husbands, but
also serves to return the presence of Vadinho to the forefront of
the narrative. He has not been forgotten; he is spoken of openly
once again. His return is foreshadowed. Dona Flor's life will
finally be complete, thanks in part to Exú, god of the crossroads,
who had aided Vadinho's transmutation. And it is through
Amado's creative genius that water, food, and sex become one as
a result of eating imported caviar.

This same sensuous amalgam of sex, food, music, and *carnaval*
is used by Bruno Barreto to flavor his 1977 adaptation of the
novel into a film, a film that has become the most successful film
in the history of Brazilian cinema. *Dona Flor and Her Two
Husbands* is, however, only one of the Brazilian films to have
exploded on the international cinema scene in recent years with
great impact. It might be in order, therefore, to point out briefly
some of the attributes of Brazilian cinema that have contributed
to this success, and also to place the film *Dona Flor* in context.

From the early part of the twentieth century through the 1960s,
Brazilian films were very heavily influenced by Hollywood, and
American films dominated Brazilian screens. It was during the
late 1950s and early 1960s that the so-called Cinema Novo
movement began in Brazil—with such films as *Black Orpheus, O
Pagador de Promessas (The Given Word), Antonio das Mortes,*
and others. These films explored in graphic terms the social
conflicts and violence in Brazilian society, the cultural cost of
progress, and the influence of Indian and African traditions on
the European colonial cultures.

Typically, the Cinema Novo and subsequent films of the 1970s
and 1980s employed:

—a very colorful *mise en scene*, taking great care in portraying
the true Brazilian urban and rural landscapes;
—brilliant use of color to explore the rich *mise en scene* and to
define the emotional concerns of the protagonists;

—effective utilization of the various techniques of international cinema, most notably those of the Italian Neo-Realists, the French New Wave auteurs, and individual filmmakers such as Welles, Losey, and Jansco;

—inventive use of lively and sensuous Brazilian music, especially that of Antonio Carlos Jobim and Luis Bonfa;

—very frank language; very candid depictions of nudity and sex;

—extensive utilization of Indian and African fables and rituals; and

—a focus on the social conditions of the country, often in a highly critical way.

Brazilian films are often flamboyant and extravagant in style. Indeed, this combination of social critique and stylistic vivacity is highly appropriate for expressing the lives of people perpetually in crisis and *carnaval*.

The film *Dona Flor* is, of course, an excellent exemplar of these attributes, all of which blend together to create a delightful and colorful romantic comedy that upon closer examination yields a meaning at once ironic and socially explosive: that to be totally happy one must have erotic freedom and fulfillment, as well as all of the more practical middle-class virtues and values.

Vadinho tells Flor in the novel: "[Teodoro] gives you: your own house, conjugal fidelity, respect, order, consideration, and security. . . his love is made up of these noble (and tiresome) things, and you need all of them to be happy" (Amado 1977, p. 505). But Flor needs more, as she learns in the novel and film, and by a supreme act of will, she provides her own happiness by bringing Vadinho back from the dead to give her, as Vadinho points out, "impure, wrong, crooked love, dissolute and fiery, . . . to bring you joy, suffering, and pleasure" (Amado 1977, p. 505).

In the film, director Bruno Barreto and the screenwriters Eduardo Coutinho and Leopoldo Serran deftly cut away most of the subplots that embellish the novel's narrative to concentrate on Flor and her involvement with the two men in her life. To achieve this intense concentration, Barreto excises certain extended episodes that appear in the novel, such as the pharmaceutical debate, the movie theatre excursion, the concert, and the buying of the house by Flor and Teodoro. This condensation is clearly related to Andre Bazin's chandelier/usher's flashlight comparison wherein the novel is equated with the multiplicity of rays emanating from a chandelier, and the film adaptation is equated with the strong single beam of an usher's flashlight.

One of the film director's most noticeable cinematic techniques is his use of close and medium-close shots to bring the audience into an intimate relationship with Flor and her dilemma. Barreto is adroit in his use of the theory of proxemic distance, thus creating audience empathy with Flor and her confusions, dissatisfactions, and ultimate fulfillment. This theory suggests that the closer the camera gets to its subject, the more involved the audience becomes with that same subject. Barreto's camera lingers incessantly on the luminous copper-colored flesh of Flor and also on the golden blond body of Vadinho. Interestingly, Vadinho, who appears naked throughout the final third of the film, does not have a beautifully muscled athletic body. Instead he has the slight paunch of the sensualist, the man who loves food almost as much as he loves women and gambling.

Barreto uses the *mise en scene* very creatively. The film opens with a long shot of an empty square in Bahia, Dona Flor's house on one side, the local church on the other. The audience waits for the square to be populated, to be filled up, for the story to begin. The *mise en scene* itself suggests the need for action to lead to fulfillment. The film ends appropriately with the same square in long shot, now filled with people, but also filled with the joy and satisfaction of Dona Flor, who has resolved the conflict between the giddy needs of the senses and the quotidian demands of the practical world. Barreto also uses the film's *mise en scene* to indicate the joyous but messy disorder of Flor's life with Vadinho and her ordered but dull existence with Teodoro. In the scenes with Vadinho, Flor and her friends stand in overlapping configurations. With Teodoro, Flor and her friends sit in ordered rows, each in her or his particular place. Barreto also contrasts the blonde Vadinho, naked and free, with Teodoro soberly clothed in his dark suit.

To understand the full command that Barreto has over his cinematic medium, one has only to recall a key scene near the beginning of the film. From close-ups of Flor's memory of her wedding night. Barreto gives his audience ecstatic close-ups of the glowing flesh of Flor and Vadinho, actually bathing the joyous couple in a golden light; then he films the love scene in a series of overlapping dissolves that prolong the ecstasy, emphasizing the delirium of the love-making, enforcing the fact that Flor will lose this ecstasy with the death of Vadinho. This erotic sequence establishes Flor's longing for this sensual joy, a longing that haunts her during the rest of the film, until her need, so strong, so insistent, brings Vadinho back, enabling Flor to complete her existence. The scene culminates in a close-up of Flor's face, her satisfaction mainfest in her expression of postcoital fulfillment. Later she turns to Vadinho, to find him gone. The scamp has left his wedding bed for a night of gambling and whoring. Thus, the sequence epitomizes the various elements that lead to the story's subsequent conflicts and resolution.

Because Barreto has made his necessary deletions, certain moments that may be overlooked in the lengthy, episodic literary narrative stand out in the film. For instance, near the beginning of the film, Vadinho goes to the church to ask the priest for gambling money. While there, he comments on the lascivious look that a male angel is giving to a statue of Saint Clare. Later Flor looks at the same statue, notes the same flirtatious look on the angel's face and realizes the full impact of her longing for Vadinho. In the novel, Flor thinks to herself:

> Poor Saint [Clare]: her sanctity, however strong and fortified, however great in virtue, could not hold out against the lascivious eyes of that [angel] devil, the poor blessed creature succumbing to him, handing over to him her decency and her life, risking for him her salvation already gained, trading heaven for hell, for without him, what was heaven or life worth? (Amado 1977, p. 397)

The film sacrifices Flor's interior monologue, but because the two scenes are now closer together, the audience recognition of their linkage is that much greater.

Another moment that adds to the characterization of Flor and underscores dramatically her desperate desire for Vadinho is the mad cry she emits after the *candômbé* that she has initiated to get rid of the reincarnated Vadinho begins to work, causing Vadinho to begin to fade away. The scream, mentioned only obliquely in the novel, erupts with full force on the screen followed by an extreme close-up. It is unequivocally clear that Flor's overwhelming need, made manifest in sound and image, keeps Vadinho in her life. This moment in particular underlines the strength of the film adaptation, indicating how faithfully Barreto cleaves to the essential narrative line, emphasizing always the madding dilemma of a human being attempting to resolve the disparate longings of all human beings for both security—economic and social—and sensual excitation and delirium. Incidentally, this scream repeats Flor's anguished outburst at the beginning of the film when she sees Vadinho's lifeless body spread out on the cobblestones of the square, and she realizes with horror that her adored husband is dead. Barreto designs a kind of visual parentheses with these screams. The difference, of course, is that after the first outcry, Flor loses Vadinho; after the second, she regains him for good.

The novel's unique intermingling of eroticism and gastronomy is manifested in the film through Barreto's tantalizing close-ups of food, especially the braised soft-shell crabs, and through his obsessive focus on the radiant face and succulent torso of Brazilian film star Sonia Braga. Thus, Barreto, following the dictates of Amado, interweaves in a very graphic way those two tempations, food and sex. There is, for instance, the director's unabashed realization of the moment in the nightclub when Flor asks Vadinho if he likes caviar, and he replies, "Of course, because it tastes just like your *boceta*," Flor's "little box." And again, Barreto, by means of an artfully arranged, slow, reverse zoom shot of the supine and incandescently naked Sonia Braga, suggests visually the young widow simmering in her own tears, about to explode, so she says, if she does not soon find a man to give her sexual ecstasy and release.

The one element of the novel that is minimized in the film is Amado's emphasis on spiritism, relegated by Barreto to an atmospheric background element—for instance, in the opening carnaval sequence—and a plot device by which Flor tries to exorcise Vadinho after his sudden return to her life. Barreto, perhaps because of the influence of the Cinema Novo movement, underscores much more obviously the conflicts that Flor has with bourgeois social attitudes, even with the prevailing moral views of the Catholic Church. Barreto designs a striking visual juxtaposition by placing the imposing and very grand Catholic Church edifice on one side of the square in which much of the film's action takes place and by setting Flor and Vadinho's love nest on the other side of that same area, with the local prostitute's abode somewhere in between, creating a marvelous holy/unholy trinity. In fact, when Flor finally makes her decision to have her cake and eat it too, appearing in public, subsequently, arm-in-arm with her Sunday-suited second husband and her stark naked first husband, she boldly and happily flaunts her outrageous behavior on the steps of the very same sacred citadel. And to make his point even more visually explicit, Barreto, unlike Amado, places a large crucifix conspicuously over the bed blasphemously occupied by Flor and her two husbands.

Another component that adds to the unique flavor of the film is the expressive, sensual beat of the Brazilian samba, used by Barreto and his composer Francis Hime as a constant reminder of the sexual tides that control and confound Flor in her quest for fulfillment. Appropriately, the musical track becomes less native and more classical as Teodoro becomes the dominant element in Flor's life.

Because of his rich, poetic style and discursive structure—emphasizing anecdote, incident, digression, and a great number of colorful characters—Amado can be compared to the great English novelists of the eighteenth and nineteenth centuries. In fact, whether Amado would agree or not, he might be termed the Brazilian Dickens. Barreto, on the other hand, crafts a much more direct interpretation of Dona Flor's plight, never forgetting, of course, Amado's central and comical thematic concerns, which he brings to cinematic life by means of his own lushly evocative images.

If the film misses some of the subtlety and color of the novel, it provides enough *carnaval*, *candômbé*, and feverishness to give filmgoers the flavor of Amado's romance. If the film sacrifices the episodic, leisurely pace of the novel, the larger canvas, the seemingly endless roster of eccentric Bahians, it gains a certain intrinsic force because of its seamless narrative drive and because Barreto has cut to the essential spine of the novel, creating a film at once amusing, provocative, and enormously satisfying. Thus, Barreto's creation, which can be understood and enjoyed by a vast audience, has become the most popular and successful film in Brazilian cinema, grossing close to $40 million dollars at last count and having been seen by about 30 million people worldwide.

Although the film has great mass appeal, the more discerning filmgoer will discover and savor the underlying themes—discreetly placed within the more overtly sensational *ménage à trois* plot contrivances—which lead to the recognition that Flor's goal is the ultimate desire that many of us have: to possess outward and inner fulfillment, the yes and no of our beings, the completion of ourselves. The film ends with this triumphal image: the threesome—Flor and her two husbands—one naked and glowing, caressing his lover's buttocks; the other, soberly suited, dignified, supporting his wife with his strong, conservative arm. No words need accompany this last shot, no explanation. On every level of recognition, this image is all that is needed.

The final irony of the film and the novel, of course, is that this kind of paradise on earth occurs rarely and that these rare occurrences most often take place on the printed page or on the silver screen. It is unusual for a truly fine novel to be translated into a film of equal caliber; for example, one need only consider the films of *War and Peace, Crime and Punishment, The Stranger, The Great Gatsby, The Sun Also Rises*, even *Sophie's Choice*. Jorge Amado's sublimely sensual and sensible fable, *Dona Flor and Her Two Husbands*—beautifully and sensitively and carefully adapted to the screen by Bruno Barreto—may be one of the unique exceptions.

WORKS CITED

Amado, Jorge. 1977. *Dona Flor and Her Two Husbands: A Moral and Amorous Tale.* Translated by Harriet de Onis. New York: Avon Books.
———. 1973. *Dona Flor e Seus Dois Maridos: Historia Moral e de Amor.* 21 edicao. Sao Paolo: Martins.
Barreto, Bruno (director). 1977. *Dona Flor and Her Two Husbands.* With Sonia Braga, José Wilker, Mauro Mendonca, *et. al.* Film Distributors Limited.
Bastide, Roger. 1978. *The African Religions of Brazil: Toward a Sociology of the Interpenetration of Civilizations.* Translated by Helen Sebba. Baltimore: The Johns Hopkins University Press.

MYTHICAL PATTERNS IN JORGE AMADO'S NOVEL *GABRIELA—CLOVE AND CINNAMON* AND BRUNO BARRETO'S FILM *GABRIELA*

John Martin and Donna L. Van Bodegraven

A weaving of classical Greek and Roman mythical patterns highlights the Brazilian novel *Gabriela—Clove and Cinnamon* by Jorge Amado and the cinematic treatment of that novel by Bruno Barreto. The presence of these mythical elements serves to underscore the apparent conflict of hopes and desires of the two principal characters, Gabriela and Nacib, and contributes to the eventual failure of the latter character to sustain his self-appointed role as a Brazilian Pygmalion.

In Greek mythology, Pygmalion is a woman-hating sculptor who takes a vow of celibacy. Then he makes a striking statue of ivory, embodying his ideal of feminine beauty, which looks so real that he falls in love with it. He names the statue Galatea and begins treating it like a real woman, giving it presents of shells, stone, beads, birds, jewels, earrings and a dress. Finally, he asks Aphrodite to give him a woman exactly like his ivory virgin. The flame on the goddess' altar shoots up twice in affirmation, and she brings Galatea to life.

In modern times, George Bernard Shaw's play, *Pygmalion*, in which Professor Higgins trains a Cockney street hawker, Eliza Doolittle, to speak like a lady, introduces into the myth the theme of rigid class barriers, maintained by superficial differences in manners and speech patterns. More recently, the Brazilian writer Jorge Amado has recast the legend in his novel *Gabriela, cravo e canela*, which was subsequently made into the movie *Gabriela* (1982), directed by Bruno Barreto.[1]

In discussing cinematic adaptation, André Bazin, borrowing a metaphor from Baudelaire, has likened the literary source to a dazzling chandelier, while comparing the film version to the beam of a movie usher's flashlight (Bazin 1967, p. 107). In these terms, the film adaptation represents not only a simplification—the usher's flashlight leaves most of the theater in the dark—but also a narrowing and sharpening of focus.

Barreto's film reduces the complex political and economic conflicts so prominent in the novel to rapidly, even sketchily

presented subplots, often difficult to follow if one is unfamiliar
with the book. The movie concentrates on the relationships
between men and women in Ilhéus in 1925, specifically on the
love of Nacib and Gabriela, a union that moves full circle from
love affair to marriage, to annulment and back to love affair.

In his recent book, *Concepts in Film Theory*, Dudley Andrew
points out that "the broader notion of the process of adaptation
has much in common with interpretation theory, for in a strong
sense adaptation is the appropriation of a meaning from a prior
text" (Andrew 1984, p. 97). It could be argued that, in the case of
Gabriela, the specific meaning appropriated is the reworking of a
variety of classical myths, including that of Pygmalion as
embodied in the relationship between Nacib and Gabriela, which
becomes the film's governing motif.

The marriage of Nacib and Gabriela turns sour because Nacib
tries to transform his wife from the free-spirited backlands waif
with whom he is smitten into a typical, repressed, bourgeois
spouse. Known to his fellow townsmen by the generic label of
"Turk," Nacib is of Syrian and Sicilian heritage and has rigidly
orthodox ideas about marriage. As he puts it, "one marries a
good girl, from a good family, educated, with a dowry and,
above all, a virgin."

Needless to say, Gabriela hardly fits this quaint Victorian
cameo. She has come to Ilhéus from the drought-striken interior,
traveling with a motley band that appears as a freeze-frame
background to the opening credits, springing to life to frolic in
some mud puddles in the road. She is still covered by a dusting of
clay when Nacib hires her as a cook at the slave market. She has
no family history, no identification papers, and does not even
know how old she is. And, as played by Sonia Braga, the sensual
gleam in her eye and the voluptuous abandon with which she
moves make it evident she is no virgin.

She is immediately attracted to Nacib, played with a certain
diffidence by Marcello Mastroianni. It is apparent that she thinks
she is being taken on as mistress as well as cook and seems
puzzled that Nacib doesn't immediately take her to bed. But when
they do become lovers, this unexpected delay makes their
lovemaking all the more passionate.

Gabriela is perfectly content with her new position, sleeping
with Nacib, cooking for him, washing his clothes. Dona
Arminha, an older black woman, chides her that she ought to be
thinking about marriage, because she won't be young and

beautiful forever. But Gabriela has no interest in marriage or even in bettering her situation. When one of the rich colonels offers to set her up in her own flat with a maid and charge account, she turns him down without hesitation, saying "I have everything I need."

Nacib, is not content, however, for he has fallen deeply in love with her and becomes jealous when the patrons of his bar, the Vesuvio, ogle and paw her. He points out that, in the Near East, women do not show themselves, particularly their breasts, the way they do in Brazil. Before long, he tells Gabriela not to come to the Vesuvio anymore (lest it erupt), giving her a present of a caged bird to alleviate her disappointment.

Tonico Bastos, the son of the most powerful of the colonels, tells Nacib that he should marry Gabriela and, after some thought, he accepts the idea. The way he proposes to her is significant. He makes a special trip home from the bar to announce to her, "I have decided to marry you." Gabriela doesn't understand the need for marriage, but agrees, because that is what he wants. Oblivious to her lack of enthusiasm, he proclaims plans for a "vida nova." They will hire servants, paint the house, and buy new furniture. Until the ceremony Gabriela will sleep at Dona Arminha's house, because, if they sleep under one roof now that they are engaged, people will talk.

Perhaps his most important plans for change involve Gabriela herself. After the wedding, Nacib takes upon himself a role similar to that of Henry Higgins, setting out to transform Gabriela into a pallid copy of the wives of the town's elite. But if Professor Higgins succeeded brilliantly in transforming Eliza Doolittle into a dazzling pseudo-aristocrat, Nacib fails miserably at his self-appointed task. Perhaps his failure is owing to laziness; he seems content for the most part simply to issue commands rather than to teach his pupil the fine points of being a lady, including such a simple skill as the ability to read the titles for the silent films shown in the Ilhéus movie house. But perhaps his attempts to transform Gabriela into "a lady" were doomed from the start by other mythical undercurrents in both the novel and the film that identify Gabriela as something other than the simple backwoods waif she appears to be.

In her classic study of Greek and Roman mythology, Edith Hamilton tells us that Mother Earth was given the name Gaea by the ancients, but that "she was not really a divinity. She was never separated from the actual earth and personified" (Hamilton

1942, p. 402). It is apparent that in creating the character of Gabriela, Jorge Amado attempted to do what the Greeks and Romans never did. Amado, in his novel, and Bruno Barreto, in his screen adaptation of the novel, present a woman/child who embodies all the physical and spiritual attributes that might be associated with the personification of a classical earth goddess, a deity rather than a simple backlands waif who is a potential candidate for an Eliza Doolittle type of transformation.

The personification of an earth goddess would clearly require a strong tie to each of the four Aristotelian elements of earthly life— water, air, fire, and earth. Both the novel and film make frequent references to the proximity of the town of Ilhéus to the sea, and, indeed, a subplot of both consists of the attempt to dredge the city's port to allow access by large ships. In addition to the physical contacts with water, mythological contacts occur in a voodoo ceremony described at the end of the novel but absent from the film. In this episode, Gabriela appeals to the goddess of the sea, Yemanja, and in exchange for gifts, asks that the goddess help her to rekindle her early relationship with Nacib. The relationship between Gabriela and water is underscored periodi- cally in the film by the fact that the intensity of Nacib's longing for the missing Gabriela increases while he is drenching his hair under an outdoor spigot.

The relationship between Gabriela and air is suggested by the association of Nacib's thoughts of Gabriela with the gentle sea breezes that caress his mustache at various moments in the novel. In the film, Nacib's house, which Gabriela later shares, has numerous open windows that allow those gentle sea breezes to flow freely through the house. Also, their first love-making scene in the film emphasizes the relationship between Gabriela and air or wind by having her lean halfway out an open window.

Another link to the classic elements of life is apparent in reference to fire, be it celestial, emotional, or terrestrial. When Nacib first encounters Gabriela, the glaring sunlight of celestial fire cannot penetrate the caked-on clay that conceals her true appearance. Later that evening, when he returns to the house after work, he discerns her beauty through the gentle glow of moonlight. References to the fire of Gabriela's passion appear frequently in the novel, and on a particular night of love- making, the narrator describes her as "a raging bonfire, an inextinguishable flame, an ashless fire of sighs and moans. Her skin burned into his" (Amado 1962, p. 332). Gabriela's use of terrestrial fire to prepare the culinary masterpieces that delight Nacib and his customers in the bar is another tie between this earth goddess and the element of fire.

The preparation of those perfectly seasoned dishes demonstrates Gabriela's link to the vegetable world of the final element, earth. She uses all types of vegetables and fruits, as well as meats and fish to prepare the meals, the pastries, and the appetizers for which she becomes famous in Ilhéus. The title of the novel makes clear the association between two elements of the vegetable world and Gabriela. One is the cinnamon color of her skin tone, described vividly in the novel and a characteristic of Sonia Braga as well. The other, a dominant feature of the novel only, is the scent of clove that permeates Gabriela's hair, clothing, and the rose that she leaves for Nacib every day, and that lingers in the mattress and sheets of the bed she shared with Nacib before dishonor forced her to leave. The plant world also serves as a rich scenario: in the film, the back yard of Nacib's house is a veritable jungle of tropical plants. This concept is reiterated in the surname provided for Gabriela in the falsified documents necessary for her to marry Nacib. That name, da silva, is closely related to *de selva*, which in Portuguese means "from the jungle."

In addition to providing vegetables for consumption, the earth provides plants from which are derived the natural fabrics of clothing. In the film, while Gabriela is still Gabriela and not Mrs. Saad, she wears light, cotton dresses, in white or pastel colors or floral prints. In the film, the first dress that Nacib buys for her is a green floral print, and the novel tells us that it is cotton. In the film, on her wedding day, Gabriela's wardrobe changes, and she begins to dress in filmy fabrics that appear to be synthetics; however, she never abandons the floral prints characteristic of her status as a single woman. After the annulment of her marriage, when she becomes Gabriela again, she returns to the simple cotton dresses of the first part of the film.

Gabriela makes direct physical contact with the earth not only through her clothing but also through the earth on which she walks. Throughout the novel and the film, we see that she prefers to go barefoot or to wear slippers rather than shoes. When Nacib buys her shoes, she either refuses to wear them or removes them as soon as possible. In the movies, she kicks off her shoes to watch the film in comfort, and when the circus parade arrives in

town, Gabriela, barefoot, joins in the joyous dance of the circus
performers. This action is viewed with horror by members of
proper society, including Nacib himself; however, going barefoot
puts Gabriela in constant direct contact with the earth she seems
to represent.

Gabriela also has a unique relationship with the creatures that
roam the earth. In the novel, her friendship with an unwanted
stray cat is noted as unusual, because the cat apparently never
trusted anyone else:

> How, then, had Gabriela made friends with it? Why did it follow her about,
> mewing, and come to lie in her lap? . . . Gradually it came to trust her, to feel
> safe with her. Now it spent most of the day in Nacib's back yard, sleeping in
> the shade of the guava tree. It was no longer so thin and dirty, although it
> remained as dissolute as ever and continued to prowl the hillside and roofs at
> night. (Amado 1962, p. 203)

Gabriela also demonstrates a special communication with a bird
that Nacib presented to her as a gift. We are told that she
"laughed in tune with the bird's trill" (Amado 1962, p. 233), and
that Nacib had described her as "the rays of the sun, the light of
the moon, the song of birds" (Amado 1962, p. 233). The sofre
(from the Portuguese word meaning "to suffer") remained in a
cage for a short time until Gabriela could no longer tolerate its
lack of freedom and set it free.

Gabriela's unusually close relationship with the four classic
elements of life is particularly evident in a lingering shot from
the film of Sonia Braga, dressed in a loose, white cotton dress,
squatting on a sunlit beach, her feet almost covered by sand as
the water laps gently at her feet and the breeze blows through her
loose hair. This relationship to nature is not the only aspect that
sets the character of Gabriela apart from the rest of human
society. Her first appearance in both the novel and the film
underscores her unique ageless quality. Her playful behavior is
childlike, yet her figure is that of a fully developed young
woman. The clay caked on her face and in her hair obliterates her
features and makes it impossible for the viewer of the film or for
Nacib in the novel to guess her age. This first appearance is
symbolic of the mystery surrounding Gabriela. No one knows
anything about her, and she does not act like any of the other
women in town. For the men of Ilhéus she is "a mystery, and a
mystery is by definition inexplicable" (Amado 1962, p. 372). In
the novel, in a discussion by some of the men about love,
Gabriela is alluded to again:

"It's like Gabriela. It exists, and that is enough. The fact that you can't understand or explain something doesn't do away with it. I know nothing about the stars, but I see them in the heavens; and my ignorance in no way affects either their existence or their beauty." (Amado 1962, p. 376)

The uniqueness of Gabriela in relation to the other women of Ilhéus is also important to note. Many of the women who appear in the film are prostitutes or entertainers who dress in exotic fabrics, brilliant colors, and garish styles, and who use extremes in make-up and hair-do. Others are proper society women who dress in rigid clothing designs rendered in synthetic fabric. Gabriela, when she is Gabriela and not assuming the imposed identity of Mrs. Saad, selects loose-fitting or contour-revealing clothing without the restraints of undergarments. For the men of Ilhéus, living in a town struggling to remove the restrictions of an out-of-date moral code, Gabriela represents a strong contrast to the other women they know. Gabriela, for them, is "a fragrant rose in a bouquet of artificial flowers" (Amado 1962, p. 361).

Gabriela's free-spirited fashion is a reflection of a similarly unrestricted morality that is also unique in the society in which she lives. For her, marrying Nacib was not necessary. She loved him, as she had loved almost all the men with whom she had slept. She also liked to go to the bar and receive all the compliments from the male patrons, but she would never accept any of their offers to be kept by them. She wanted the love of Nacib plus the freedom to enjoy the attention of the others. But "it was awful being married, she didn't like it at all" (Amado 1962, 339), because she was forced to give up all the activities that she had enjoyed so much. "Everything that Mrs. Saad should do was something Gabriela hated" (Amado 1962, p. 340). Mrs. Saad was forced to go to a lecture; Gabriela wanted to go to the circus (and did so in secret, taking her shoes and stockings off when she got there). Mrs. Saad wore her hair pinned up; Gabriela preferred to feel the wind through her loose, flowing hair. Mrs. Saad was required to stay home and direct the activities of the household help; Gabriela preferred to play leapfrog in the street with the children. Mrs. Saad was to remain faithful; Gabriela had an affair.

In the Greek myth, Pygmalion, gave shape to his ideal woman *before* falling in love with her. The ivory he worked on could not talk back, it had no choice but to assume the form into which he molded it. He then fell in love with Galatea because he had made her exactly the way he wanted her. In Shaw's play, love does not complicate, to any noticeable degree, the relationship between the professor and his pupil, or impede the efficacy of instruction. In *Gabriela*, Nacib's problem is that he falls in love with a beautiful woman who has an uncultivated yet distinct mind of her own. His efforts to change her are complicated further by the underlying mythical content that seems to indicate that Gabriela is something other than a normal woman. Ironically for Nacib, his efforts to "civilize" her bear fruit in the one area where, no doubt, he least desired it, and their love life, so torrid before marriage, slips into the routine and boredom of wedlock. Neither seems to understand why, but since in other areas, Nacib has been trying his best to suppress Gabriela's spontaneous enthusiasm for life, his complaint that she is now but "a gentle breeze" rather than "a furious wind" smacks of blaming the victim. Gabriela, for her part, seems to realize, if only subconsciously, that someone who wants so badly to change her doesn't appreciate her all that much. She responds by taking a lover, Tonico Bastos, an action that results in the removal of the abhorred rubric of Mrs. Saad and allows her to resume her former, and preferred, identity of simply Gabriela.

Nacib failed in his efforts to transform Gabriela into Mrs. Saad, to make her into a woman that she was not, to cage her as he had done the sofre. Her behavior defied the norms for a married woman in Ilhéus. Throughout the novel and the film, Gabriela appears as a free spirit, unfettered by and alien to the demands of Ilhéus society and unique as a human being. In assigning to her mysterious origins; strong ties to earth, air, fire and water; a love of freedom; a childlike innocence; and a strikingly sensuous physical presence, Jorge Amado and Bruno Barreto have appropriated and blended a variety of mythical elements to create a singular character who does not and cannot respond to normal rules of behavior.

In a recent review article on the criterion of fidelity to the source in adaptation criticism, Christopher Orr argues that this concept is, in the end, meaningless. Basing his stand in part on Barthes's theory of intertextuality, Orr contends that "by placing the notion of adaptation within the theory of intertextuality, we can describe the literary source as one of a series of pre-texts which share some of the same narrative conventions as the film adaptation" (Orr 1984, p. 72). Barreto's *Gabriela* would seem to be an apt illustration of this point of view. Amado's novel is the immediate, the essential source. Yet, behind it stand other pre-texts (classical Greek, Roman, African, and others), which have themselves helped to shape the novel and which continue to resonate within the film. It is the Pygmalion motif that provides perhaps the clearest example of this interplay. According to Sir James Frazer, the Greek myth is itself an adaptation of an earlier Phoenician legend, which makes Nacib's Syrian heritage uncannily appropriate from the mythic as well as the sociological standpoint.

Similarly, Shaw's *Pygmalion*, as well as his ideological preoccupations reverberate through the novel and the film. This is not surprising. Shaw was a socialist, opposed to the inanity of war and interested in women's issues. Amado is a Marxist and a passivist who often expresses the need for sweeping social change from a feminist perspective. In the novel, he is clearly against the violence and the exploitation perpetrated by the colonels' oligarchy, and the rigid class structure it maintains, illustrated in the film by Nacib's extreme obsequiousness when he serves them brandy. Amado's heroine, a woman of the people, rejects the opportunity to move up in social rank, preferring to remain true to her proletarian roots. Thus, it is fitting that, in the ultimate resolution of the Nacib-Gabriela love affair, she reestablishes her identity as the free-spirited, backlands earth goddess and he, renouncing any Pygmalionesque desire to change her, loves her once again simply as she is.

NOTES

1. Several other novels by Amado have been made into movies, notably Barreto's *Dona Flor e seus dois maridos* (1975). Nelson Pereira do Santos filmed *Tenda dos milagros* (1976) and, much earlier, Eddie Bernoudy and Paulo Machado made a film version of *Terra violenta* which was called *Terras do sem fim* (1948). See Mahieu, José H., "La literatura en cine brasileño," *Cuadernos Hispanoamericanos*, 369 (March 1981), 570-87.

WORKS CITED

Amado, Jorge. 1962. *Gabriela—Clove and Cinnamon*. Translated by James L. Taylor and William Grossman. New York: Albert A. Knopf, Inc.
Andrew, Dudley. 1984. *Concepts in Film Theory*. New York: Oxford University Press.
Bazin, André. 1967. *What is Cinema?* Berkeley: University of California Press.
Barreto, Bruno (director). 1983. *Gabriela*. MGM/UA Classics Release.
Chamberlain, Bobby J. 1981. "Escape from the Tower: Women's Liberation in Amado's *Gabriela, Cravo e Canela*." *Prismal/Cabral*. 6:84.
Frazer, Sir James. 1927. *The Golden Bough*. New York: MacMillan.
Frye, Northrop. 1957. *Anatomy of Criticism*. Princeton: Princeton University Press.

Hamilton, Edith. 1942. *Mythology.* New York: The New American Library.
Lottman, Herbert R. 1982. *The Left Bank: Writers, Artists and Politics from the Popular Front to the Cold War.* Boston: Houghton Mifflin.
Mahieu, José H. 1981. "La literatura en cine brasileño." *Cuadernos Hispanoamericanos.* 369:570-87.
Orr, Christopher, 1984. "The Discourse on Adaptation." *Wide Angle.* 6:72-76.
Pasini, Roberto. 1978. "Il tema del circo nei romanzi de Jorge Amado." *La letteratura latino americana e la sua problemica europea.* Edited by Elena Clementetti and Vittorio Minardi. Rome: First Italian-Latin American.

NOTES ON THE AUTHORS

Robert Murray Davis is Professor of English and Director of Graduate Programs at the University of Oklahoma. He is author of *Evelyn Waugh, Writer*; compiler of *A Catalogue of the Evelyn Waugh Collection at the Humanities Research Center* and (with others) of *A Bibliography of Evelyn Waugh* and *Donald Barthelme: A Bibliography*; and editor of *The Novel: Modern Essays in Criticism, Evelyn Waugh* (in the Christian Critic series), *John Steinbeck* (Twentieth Century Views), *Modern British Short Novels*, and *Evelyn Waugh, Apprentice*. He has published more than eighty critical and bibliographical essays on modern English and American fiction. He has served as visiting professor at Eotvos University (Budapest), the University of Brunswick-Saint John, and Dalhousie University, and he has lectured at other universities in France, Yugoslavia, Hungary, and Germany.

Horton Foote ranks among the world's finest screenwriters. His contributions to cinema include such notable achievements as the screenplay for *To Kill a Mockingbird*, which won an Academy Award for Best Screenplay; *The Displaced Person*, which is regarded as one of the best of the American Short Story Film Series; *1918; Tender Mercies*; and *The Trip to Bountiful*. Geraldine Page publically acknowledged Foote's contributions during the ceremony when she was awarded Best Actress Academy Award for her role in *The Trip to Bountiful*.

Ghislaine Géloin is currently teaching French Studies at Scripps College. She received the Ph.D. at the University of Illinois and has held appointments as lecturer and Associate at the Universities of Minnesota, Washington, and Monterey Institute of International Studies. She has been involved in developing international programs for studying abroad and has participated in international conferences. Her publications and research interests are in modern French culture, and literature and film.

Richard J. Golsan is Assistant Professor of French at Texas A&M University. He has taught previously at Case Western Reserve University in Cleveland, Ohio. He earned the Ph.D. at the University of North Carolina at Chapel Hill. He has published on André Malraux, Henry de Montherland, René Girard, and others in *Romance Quarterly*, *MLN*, *Essays in French Literature*, *Helios*, and elsewhere. His book, *Service*

Inutile: A Study of the Tragic in the Theatre of Henry de Montherlant, is forthcoming in the Romance Language Monographs series. His current interests include the relationship between French politics and literature in the 1930s and Poetic Realist Cinema.

GARY L. GREEN is an Assistant Professor in the Department of English at Youngstown State University in Ohio, where he teaches film and American literature. He is currently at work (with Joanna Rapf) on *Buster Keaton: A Bio-Bibliography*, which is scheduled to be published by Greenwood Press. He also has in progress a book on American Gothic fiction and its relationship to Colonial and Nationalist literature. The author of numerous conference papers on film, Green earned the Ph.D. from the University of Oklahoma.

ENRIQUE A. GRÖNLUND, a native of Buenos Aires, has degrees in both English and Spanish literature from the Pennsylvania State University. At the Ogontz Campus, he teaches courses in language, Spanish and Latin American culture, as well as contemporary Latin American fiction. He has presented papers and given lectures at professional meetings, various institutes, and community organizations on Spanish and Latin American culture, Brazilian film, Latin American music, and modern Latin American fiction.

LYNN HOGGARD teaches French at Midwestern State University. She received the M.A. from the University of Michigan as a Woodrow Wilson Fellow and taught at the Faculté de Lettres in Pau, France, for two years before completing the Ph.D. in Comparative Literature at the University of Southern California. She has published several dozen items, including scholarly articles (*Studies in Scottish Literature*), translations (*The Pawn Review*), book reviews (*The Dallas Times Herald*), and poetry (*Descant, Travois*). At the 1985 SCMLA Meeting she presented a paper on Jean Cocteau entitled "The Cocteau in Breton's Surrealism."

EDWARD A. KEARNS is an Associate Professor of English at the University of Northern Colorado. He has published articles on Melville, Wright, and English composition in professional journals; "T.V. Sex Taboos" appears in *The Television Book*. His writing interests also include fiction, and he is currently working on a novel. In addition to teaching composition, creative writing, and courses in American literature, he teaches in the Humanities program at UNC and focuses his Twentieth-Century course on the art of film.

PEGGY KIDNEY teaches in the French and Italian Department of the University of California, Davis. She was previously a lecturer in Italian at UCLA, where her work was focused on Svevo's *The Confessions of Zeno*. She has been an editor and contributor to *Carte Italiane*, the graduate student journal of the Department of Italian at UCLA.

HARRIET MARGOLIS is Assistant Professor in the Department of Communication at Florida Atlanta University. She received the Ph.D. in Comparative Literature from Indiana University, where she specialized in the study of film and worked with the collection of film scripts and press kits at the Lilly Library. She has published articles in *Poetics Today, Semiotica*, and *Magill's Survey of Cinema: Foreign Language Films*. Her conference presentations range from nineteenth-century German literature to the politics of subcultural signifiers, and from feminist critical theory to the importance of Victor Turner for film studies.

JOHN MARTIN is a Lecturer in French at West Virginia University. He is author of *The Golden Age of French Cinema, 1929-1939*. He has also published articles on *Sir Gawain and the Green Knight*, Camus, Carpentier, García Márquez, Mandiargues, Wenders, Carné, and Antonioni. He is presently working on a critical anthology on the diffusion of Italian neorealism and its influence on the cinemas of other nations.

SAMUEL MARX has been involved with writers and writing in Hollywood since the 1930s as story editor, film producer, and author. He suggests that perhaps his greatest claim to fame was his discovery of nine-year-old Elizabeth Taylor for his film *Lassie Come Home*. He also discovered and arranged for the publication of Graham Green's *The Tenth Man*, when it was a forty-year old manuscript buried in the MGM Studio archives. Among his own published books are biographies of Louis B. Mayer and Irving Thalberg, Richard Rodgers and Lorenz Hart, and a colorful American lady who became queen of the Hotel Ritz in Paris.

MOYLAN C. MILLS is Acting Director of Academic Affairs and Associate Professor of English, Humanities, and the Arts at the Ogontz Campus of the Pennsylvania State University. He has presented many papers on film and literature, including the National Conference on Literature and Film, the Mid-Hudson MLA Conference, the University of West Virginia Colloquium, and the International Conference on Educational Technology in London. He discussed the work of Brazilian novelist Jorge Amado at the 1984 Modern Language Association Convention. He has published on film, literature, and theater and is currently a special lecturer on film and television for the Pennsylvania Humanities Council. In addition, he is the recipient of both the Lindback and Amoco Awards for outstanding teaching.

JOANNA E. RAPF is Associate Professor and Coordinator of Film Studies in the English Department at the University of Oklahoma. She received the M.A. from Columbia University and the Ph.D. from Brown University. She has taught film at Dartmouth College and the New School for Social Research in New York City. Her articles on film have appeared in *Studies in American Humor, Literature/Film Quarterly, Post Script, Western Humanities Review*, and *The Texas Review*.

PAUL W. REA is Associate Professor of English at the University of Northern Colorado. He earned degrees from Eastern Michigan, Wayne State, and Ohio State Universities. His primary research interest is the international cinema. He writes on film, politics, and nature, and regularly reviews books for *The Bloomsbury Review*.

THOMAS J. SLATER teaches in the English Department of Illinois State University. He is writer and producer of *Need a Little Shelter*, a half-hour video documentary about battered women, and author of a two-part interview with Milos Forman that appeared in *Post Script*. He has also published several biographical essays in reference works and taught in the English Department at Northwest Missouri State University.

DONNA VAN BODEGRAVEN is Assistant Professor in the Department of Modern Foreign Languages at Alright College in Reading, Pennsylvania, where she teaches Spanish, Latin American and Peninsular literature, foreign language pedagogy, and comparative culture. She has presented papers on various aspects of film studies in Latin American Studies, the Kentucky Foreign Language Conference, and the Modern Language Association. She earned the M.A. and Ph.D. from Temple University.